Fashion, Design and Events

The importance of fashion and design in an events context remains under-researched, despite their ubiquity and significance from a societal and economic perspective. Fashion-themed events, for example, appeal to broad audiences and may tour the globe. Staging these events might help to brand destinations, boost visitor numbers and trigger popular debates about the contributions that fashion and design can make to identity. They may also tell us something about our culture and wider society.

This edited volume, for the first time, examines fashion and design events from a social perspective, including the meanings they bestow and their potential economic, cultural and personal impacts. It explores the reasons for their popularity and influence, and provides a critique of their growth in different markets. Events examined include fashion weeks, fashion or design themed exhibitions, historical reenactments, extreme/alternative fashion and design events, and large-scale public events such as royal weddings and horse races. International examples and case studies are drawn from countries as diverse as the USA, the UK, Germany, Bhutan, New Zealand and Australia. These are used to develop and critique various thematic concepts linked to fashion and design events, such as identity, gender, aspirations and self-image, commodification, authenticity, destination development and marketing, business strategy and protection/infringement of intellectual property. *Fashion, Design and Events* also sets out a future research agenda.

This book has a unique focus on events associated with fashion and design and features a swathe of disciplinary backgrounds. It will appeal to a broad academic audience, such as students of art and design, cultural studies, tourism, events studies, sociology and marketing.

Kim M. Williams is Lecturer in Hospitality and Tourism in the Department of Marketing, Tourism and Hospitality at La Trobe University, Australia.

Jennifer Laing is Senior Lecturer in Tourism and Events in the Department of Marketing, Tourism and Hospitality at La Trobe University, Australia.

Warwick Frost is Associate Professor in Tourism and Events in the Department of Marketing, Tourism and Hospitality at La Trobe University, Australia.

Routledge Advances in Event Research Series
Edited by Warwick Frost and Jennifer Laing
Department of Marketing, Tourism and Hospitality, La Trobe University,
  Australia

Events, Society and Sustainability
Edited by Tomas Pernecky and Michae Lück

Exploring the Social Impacts of Events
Edited by Greg Richards, Marisa deBrito and Linda Wilks

Commemorative Events
Warwick Frost and Jennifer Laing

Power, Politics and International Events
Edited by Udo Merkel

Event Audiences and Expectations
Jo Mackellar

Event Portfolio Planning and Management
A holistic approach
Vassilios Ziakas

Conferences and Conventions
A research perspective
Judith Mair

Fashion, Design and Events
Edited by Kim M. Williams, Warwick Frost and Jennifer Laing

Forthcoming:

Food and Wine Events in Europe
Edited by Alessio Cavicchi and Cristina Santini

Event Volunteering
Edited by Karen Smith, Leonie Lockstone-Binney, Kirsten Holmes and
  Tom Baum

The Future of Events & Festivals
Edited by Ian Yeoman, Martin Robertson, Una McMahon- Beattie, Elisa
  Backer and Karen Smith

Sports Events, Society and Culture
Edited by Katherine Dashper, Thomas Fletcher and Nicola McCullough

The Arts and Events
Hilary Du Cros and Lee Jolliffe

Event Design
Edited by Greg Richards, Lénia Marques and Karen Mein

Rituals and Traditional Events in the Modern World
Edited by Warwick Frost and Jennifer Laing

Fashion, Design and Events

Edited by
**Kim M. Williams, Jennifer Laing and
Warwick Frost**

Routledge
Taylor & Francis Group

LONDON AND NEW YORK

First published 2014
by Routledge
2 Park Square, Milton Park, Abingdon, Oxon OX14 4RN

and by Routledge
711 Third Avenue, New York, NY 10017

First issued in paperback 2017

Routledge is an imprint of the Taylor & Francis Group, an informa business

British Library Cataloguing in Publication Data
A catalogue record for this book is available from the British Library

Library of Congress Cataloging in Publication Data
Fashion, design and events / edited by Kim Williams, Jennifer Laing and Warwick Frost.
    pages   cm. – (Routledge advances in event research)
Includes bibliographical references and index.
1. Fashion design.   2. Fashion shows.   3. Special events.   I. Williams, Kim.
TT507.F347 2013
746.9′2–dc23
2013021503

ISBN 13: 978-1-138-08204-5 (pbk)
ISBN 13: 978-0-415-62720-7 (hbk)

Typeset in Times New Roman
by Out of House Publishing

In memory: this book is dedicated to Paris Kyne (1966–2013), who kindly consented to be interviewed for Chapter 9 of this book.

Contents

Figures

Tables

Contributors

Gary Best lectures in cultural tourism, festival and event management, and gastronomy at La Trobe University, Australia. His research interests are diverse but tend to focus on tourism and the media; travel writing; automotive history and heritage; and the means by which all of the above operate in popular culture. He has published on the media/Sydney Mardi Gras/tourism dynamic; on Australian film landscapes; on film-induced tourism; on writing the American road; and on forms of dark tourism. He has also discussed cultural tourism on both Australian and US radio.

Judith C. Everett is Professor Emeritus of Merchandising at Northern Arizona University. She taught a wide range of merchandising and fashion related courses. Her research interests include fashion promotion and tourism retailing. Professor Everett has co-authored, with Professor Kris Swanson, three books, including *Promotion in the Merchandising Environment* (second edn, Fairchild, 2007), *Writing for the Fashion Business* (Fairchild, 2008) and *Guide to Producing a Fashion Show* (third edn, Fairchild, 2013). She was named one of the ten Fashion Icons by the Arizona Chapter of Fashion Group International for 'Teaching the Future of Fashion'.

Warwick Frost is Associate Professor in the Department of Marketing, Tourism and Hospitality and Research Associate in the Tourism and Hospitality Research Unit (THRU) at La Trobe University, Australia. His research interests include heritage, events, nature-based attractions and the interaction between media, popular culture and tourism. He has co-written two books – *Books and Travel: Inspiration, Quests and Transformation* (Channel View, 2012) and *Commemorative Events: Memory, Identities, Conflict* (Routledge, 2013). Warwick is the editor of *Tourism and Zoos: Conservation, Education, Entertainment?* (Channel View, 2011) and a co-editor of *National Parks and Tourism: International Perspectives on Development, Histories and Change* (Routledge, 2009) and the Routledge *Advances in Events Research* series.

Alison L. Goodrum is Professor in the Department of Apparel at Manchester Metropolitan University and has held posts at the University of Auckland

and Nottingham Trent University. Having trained initially as a cultural geographer she earned her PhD on fashion and 'Britishness' in 2001. Latterly, Alison has undertaken archival work on rural dress focusing on the interwar period and equestrian wear. She is author of *The National Fabric* (Berg, 2005), editor of the *Understanding Fashion* series and sits on the board of a number of academic journals.

Jennifer Laing is Senior Lecturer in the Department of Marketing, Tourism and Hospitality and Research Associate in the Tourism and Hospitality Research Unit (THRU) at La Trobe University, Australia. Her research interests include travel narratives, the role of events in society, heritage tourism and adventure travel. Together with Dr Warwick Frost, Jennifer is a foundation co-editor of the Routledge *Advances in Events Research* series. They have co-written two books – *Books and Travel: Inspiration, Quests and Transformation* (Channel View, 2012) and *Commemorative Events: Memory, Identities, Conflict* (Routledge, 2013) – and are currently working on a new book on explorer travellers for Channel View (2014).

Min-Young Lee is Associate Professor at the University of Kentucky. She received her PhD in Retail and Consumer Sciences at the University of Tennessee. Her research has been published in refereed journals including *Journal of Retailing and Consumer Services*, *Journal of Product and Brand Management*, *Managing Service Quality* and *Journal of Customer Behaviour*.

Kimberly Miller-Spillman is Associate Professor at the University of Kentucky. She received her PhD in Textiles and Design at the University of Wisconsin-Madison. Dr Spillman is the lead co-editor of the third edition of *The Meanings of Dress* (Fairchild, 2012). Her research has focused on reenactors and the public, private and secret self model.

Peter Shand is currently Associate Professor of Fine Arts at the University of Auckland. He holds a PhD in Art History from the University of Auckland and an LLM specializing in intellectual and cultural property from King's College, London. As a writer and curator, his research interests are concentrated on contemporary art, fashion and the inter-relation of creativity and law. In New Zealand he is well known for curating major retrospective exhibitions of the fashion houses WORLD and Zambesi at Auckland War Memorial Museum and writing the comprehensive historical introduction to *New Zealand Fashion Design* (Te Papa Press, 2010).

Paul Strickland is Lecturer at La Trobe University, Australia, specialising in Hospitality Management subjects. Paul has a vast background of job titles including hotel and restaurant management roles in many countries. His research interests include food, wine, ethnic restaurants, Bhutanese studies and space tourism. Paul has published in a variety of journals and contributed to book chapters. He also teaches in a Hospitality Management programme in Bhutan. Paul is currently enrolled in a PhD that focuses on wine events, social media and entrepreneurial behaviour.

Paul Sugden is a member of the Business Law and Taxation Department at Monash University, Australia. He completed a BA in 1981, LLB (Qld) in 1984 and Master of Laws at Queen Mary College, University of London in 1988. Upon graduation, he worked as a Judge's Associate before admission to the bar and practice in government and private capacities. His interest in fashion began as a childhood desire to be a fashion designer but he became a lawyer passionate about the legal protection of creativity. This manifests in being the honorary solicitor and legal columnist for the Australian Forum for Textile Arts Ltd for the past sixteen years. He has written articles for refereed and professional journals.

Kristen K. Swanson is Professor of Merchandising in the School of Communication at Northern Arizona University. She has taught a wide range of merchandising and fashion related courses. Professor Swanson has co-authored, with Professor Judy Everett, three books, including *Promotion in the Merchandising Environment* (second edn, Fairchild, 2007), *Writing for the Fashion Business* (Fairchild, 2008) and *Guide to Producing a Fashion Show* (third edn, Fairchild, 2013). Her research interests relate to tourism retailing and the American Southwest. She has published articles and chapters on souvenirs phenomena, culturally sustainable entrepreneurship and themed retailing.

Karen Webster is Associate Professor and Deputy Head of Fashion and Textiles at RMIT University, Australia, where she has held senior positions for over twenty years. From 2005 to 2010, through an industry secondment, Karen was appointed Director of the L'Oréal Melbourne Fashion Festival. Karen has held numerous board positions across government, corporate and creative sectors. She currently sits on the boards for Council of the Textile and Fashion Industries of Australia, Australian Design Alliance, Balletlab, Federal Government's Positive Body Image Advisory Panel and is Chair of the Australian Fashion Council. Karen worked as a fashion designer prior to going into academia. She is a sought-after strategic and design consultant within the fashion industry.

Kim M. Williams is Lecturer in the Department of Marketing, Tourism and Hospitality and Research Associate in the Tourism and Hospitality Research Unit (THRU) at La Trobe University, Australia. Her research background is concerned with human resources issues, with a prime focus on professional development and training. She is also interested in fashion, heritage and wine tourism. Kim has published in journals such as the *Australian Journal of Career Development*, the *Journal of Vocational Education & Training* and the *Australian Journal of Teacher Education*. On a personal note, she has recently spent two and a half years studying for her certification in Millinery.

1 Social conformity or radical chic? Fashion, design and events

Kim M. Williams, Jennifer Laing and Warwick Frost

Fashion and design provide ideal vehicles for investigating the links between events and society. Hugely popular right around the globe and across various cultures, fashion and design are arguably two of the strongest cultural forces at play in the modern world. While fashion is sometimes marginalised as a frivolous or lightweight pursuit, there is a 'secret need for it' (König 1971: 33). An alternative discourse is to see fashion as a 'semiotic language through which cultural meanings are constructed' (Troy 2003: 11, following Barthes 1967; see also König 1971 and Thompson and Haytko 1997). For both individuals and groups, it defines *identity*. Many of us see our fashion style as making a statement as to who we are, whether that be conservative or radical, classical or avant-garde, stylish or quirky. This can be termed *self-representation*, where fashion is used or even manipulated to alter the way others see us (Argyle 1988; Goffman 1956). It is a means of expressing *status* or social class (Argyle 1988; Wolfe 1973). Fashion allows us to either fit into a group or sub-culture, or to break away and assert our individuality. It thus acts simultaneously as a 'barrier and connection' (Moseley 2005: 7) to others. We can be *fashionistas*, *dedicated followers of fashion* or *slaves to fashion*. We can proudly be *in fashion* or *out of fashion*. Though our tastes may vary widely, an interest in fashion transcends generations and social classes. As lecturers and researchers, we are interested in fashion and we know our students also share that interest.

These messages can be radical. As Quinn (2002: 442) notes, fashion is 'a realm heavily freighted with contradictions, dualities, defiance and subversive ideas'. The ability of fashion to enchant as well as shock us may be a prelude to or a reflection of societal change. The outfit of visiting English model Jean Shrimpton caused a scandal at Melbourne's Derby Day races in 1965 (Figure 1.1). Invited as a judge for the *Fashions in the Field* competition, not only was her hemline high, but her lack of hat, stockings and gloves symbolised a new era of female liberation and sexual freedom (Harrison 2005). Punk, with its body piercings, ripped clothing, heavy boots and mohawk hairstyles, came to prominence in the 1970s as an anti-establishment movement in a period marked by social unrest, unemployment and strikes.

Figure 1.1 Model Jean Shrimpton shocks conservative 1960s Melbourne with her racing attire.
Source: News Ltd

Fashion and design can form important elements of an event, or constitute its overall theme. We cover both examples in this book. The following is a basic typology of *fashion or design themed events*:

Exhibitions in galleries or museums

These display retrospectives or the latest examples of fashion or design. The Victoria and Albert Museum in London has a permanent fashion collection, the largest in the world, with many items on display in its Fashion Gallery. It also stages popular temporary exhibitions such as *The Golden Age of Couture: Paris and London 1947–57* (2007/2008), and the recent *Ballgowns: British Glamour since 1950* (2012/2013). Other outstanding fashion collections

Figure 1.2 Admiring the elegance of drapery at the Madame Grès Exhibition, Musée Bourdelle, Paris, in 2011.
Source: J. Laing

include the Bath Fashion Museum, the Philadelphia Museum of Art, the Metropolitan Museum of Art in New York, the MoMu Fashion Museum in Antwerp and the Musée Galliera in Paris. In 2011, the latter staged an exhibition of Madame Grès' creations in the Musée Bourdelle (Figure 1.2), where the marble sculptures made a stunning backdrop for her Grecian-style draped gowns.

The Maryhill Museum of Art in Goldendale, Washington State, is home to the *Théâtre de la Mode* – a group of fashion dolls, one-third human size, that were created at the end of the Second World War and toured European and North American cities 'to prove that [French] couture had survived in full force' (Dorner 1975: 27). The couture houses that took part, including Balmain, Nina Ricci and Schiaparelli, could save on the cost (and risk) of live mannequins travelling the world. There were no

Figure 1.3 Exhibits of Nudie Cohn creations at the Lone Pine Museum of Western Film History, California.

Source: W. Frost

cutting corners however on the workmanship. These dolls are miniature works of art (Peers 2004), with the clothes exhibiting perfect tailoring and delicate trimmings, sumptuous fabrics and exquisitely rendered accessories. Sets were created as a backdrop, by artists like Jean Cocteau (Steele 1997). Profits collected on attendance at the exhibition (nearly 100,000 saw it in Paris alone) went to charity – the French war relief (Steele 1997). This philanthropic underpinning perhaps stymied criticism of couture as self-indulgent and whitewashed concerns that the French fashion industry was tainted by allegations of collaboration with the Nazis during the occupation (Peers 2004; Walford 2008). The dolls were argued to be both a *labour of love* and a form of *resistance* (Steele 1988: 270). The *Théâtre de la Mode* collection was acquired by the museum in the late 1950s and toured the world for a second time in the 1990s.

Museums of design can be found around the world, including London, Ghent, Helsinki and New York City. Examples of exhibitions showcasing design include *Art Deco: 1910–1939* at the National Gallery of Victoria in Melbourne (2008) and *Bauhaus: Art as Life* at the London Barbican Art Gallery (2012). Fashion and design exhibitions are also found in a range of cultural heritage museums. California's Lone Pine Museum of Western Film History, for example, features the elaborate *singing cowboy* and rodeo costumes of Nudie Cohn (Figure 1.3).

Industry events

These act as a showcase for new collections, such as the prestigious and aspirational couture line (Quinn 2002), and more accessible *prêt-à-porter* (ready to wear) clothing (Reinach 2005). Individual designers stage their own fashion events, as well as participating in those organised by their industry or their destination. Some of these industry events are global, such as *Vogue*'s Fashion's Night Out (http://fashionsnightout.com), where attendees have the opportunity to shop after hours at parties hosted by labels such as Coach, Dior and Mulberry, sometimes alongside an A-list crowd. They may also attract extensive international media coverage, particularly where the collection is provocative or heralds a change in fashion.

Fashion and theatre have long been intertwined concepts (Steele 1988), with the 'dramatic potential of fashion shows' self-evident (Troy 2003: 81). Fashion shows were staged from the early years of the twentieth century, with the idea often accredited to Lady Duff Gordon, a couturier known as Lucile and later to become famous as a *Titanic* survivor. The aim of the show was to counteract the 'crassness associated with obvious merchandise promotions' (Troy 2003: 91). It was also recognised that live mannequins display clothes to their best advantage, as a form of spectacle (Evans 2011). The resulting show can be highly entertaining, as well as aspirational (Troy 2003). Oderberg (2012: 25) describes the appeal of a modern fashion show for onlookers: 'The room is buzzing. There's palpable anticipation. The pumping music comes up. The lights come on, bright and furious.' Such theatricality is now a key theme in popular culture reflections on fashion, such as in the film *Zoolander*.

Large capital cities associated with fashion such as London, Paris, Milan or New York have traditionally staged *fashion weeks*, which might play a part in shaping the image of a destination (Skov 2006), as well as providing a focus for innovation. Designer Kirrily Johnston labels Australian Fashion Week 'the creative pinnacle of the year for us' (Breen Burns 2012a: 5). Attracting an order from a buyer, particularly the new e-tailers like Net-a-Porter, with their international reach, can 'anoint a brand with global credibility, marketing and potential sales to all points of the planet' (Breen Burns 2012b: 6). These shows also generate revenue for professional event organisers. The global corporation IMG Fashion has a portfolio of fashion weeks, including Sydney, Tokyo, Zurich, New York, Berlin and Miami, and observe that their audiences 'are in the millions and will keep increasing' (Breen Burns 2012a: 5). The centrepiece of these industry events is often a *parade*, which is commonly choreographed to surprise audiences, aside from showcasing the fashions themselves. Australian Fashion Week has seen everything as accessories, from pythons to rats (Breen Burns 2012a). Models stride down a catwalk in front of an audience composed of the media, VIPs, buyers and other industry players and fashion leaders. Celebrities often get to sit in the front row, and are there to see and be seen, as much as for the clothes (Blanchard 2012; Entwistle and Rocamora 2006). American *Vogue*'s creative director, Grace Coddington, is scathing about the trend towards 'celebrities walking in and being filmed and having their moment … Every season when it comes to collection time, you have to take a deep breath and try to ignore all that crazy stuff' (Blanchard 2012: 24). The concept of a fashion week has spread to many parts of the world eager to promote their fashion industries and brand themselves as linked to fashion and design. Reinach (2005: 48) observes that the Shanghai Fashion Festival aims to make Shanghai the 'sixth most important center of world fashion'.

Other destinations, such as Hong Kong and Düsseldorf, stage fashion events such as *trade fairs or shows*, more for their commercial benefits than to brand the destination as associated with fashion and design (Skov 2006). Trade shows have a long history, particularly the bridal fair. In 1881, the Grand Wedding Exhibition at the Royal Aquarium in London was acknowledged to be the first bridal fair in Britain. It displayed wares and samples by various wedding-related businesses, including 'dressmakers, jewellers, caterers, florists, stationers, photographers and furniture makers' (Ehrman 2011: 85).

Product or brand launches

These are events that accompany the launch of a new fashion line or label or the opening of a new store. They aim to maximise media exposure and create a buzz around a new brand, which might attract buyers (Skov 2006). The centrepiece of the highly anticipated openings of the Zara stores in central Sydney and Melbourne in 2011 involved invitation-only parties, attended by VIPs and the social set.

Reenactments

These attempt to recreate the past, by the playing out of roles, and can be argued to form a subset of living history (Frost and Laing 2013). They usually involve participants donning appropriate costumes, either authentic (vintage) garb or clothes that have been styled to resemble the original. For those involved, these events allow immersion in a social world where authenticity, research and design are all highly regarded (Belk and Costa 1998; Frost and Laing 2013).

Fan events

These are organised by sub-cultures, with clothes acting as markers of membership of a group or fan club (Kozinets 2001). Steampunk, manga, gothic and anime devotees sport distinctive clothing, which is often shown off at events. The bustle, corset, top hat and lace-up Victorian boots for women and the airmen's goggles, bowler hat, fez or pith helmet for men, are steampunk staples, while goths are often identified by their dark garb, crucifixes and skull motifs, dead white foundation and black-rimmed eyes. The event might be approached as a liminal space, allowing people to either feel free to adopt different personas or instead be what they regard as their true selves (Sharpe 2008). This might then encourage greater self- expression with respect to clothing and the taking of risks that perhaps would be seen as more difficult in their everyday lives. Others dislike that the emphasis on clothing sets them apart and makes them potentially a figure of fun. As one disgruntled *Star Trek* fan remarked:

> Can someone please tell me why whenever there is a media story on *Star Trek* fans, the first person they grab is someone with cheap Spock ears and a bad fitting costume, a total geek ...? A *Star Trek* fan in a suit and tie or jeans and a T-shirt doesn't make 'good television' but one in full uniform and makeup does ...
>
> (quoted in Kozinets 2001: 74)

Fashion auctions

These are a small but high-profile example of a fashion event. Australian fashion designer Lisa Ho recently auctioned her collection of vintage clothes at Fox Studios in Sydney. She chose an auction to divest herself of these items, to attract the 'right' kind of buyer: 'It is not the kind of thing you can just dump ... If you own it, you have to take care of it. These old fabrics – some are more than 100 years old – have to be properly stored in acid-free tissue, and catalogued' (Overington 2012). The event met with huge excitement, yet unexpectedly low prices, given no reserve was set for the items. This was contrary to recent trends in fashion auctions (Tulloch 2012), with a number making high profits. The exhibition of 79 dresses belonging to Princess Diana at Christie's in London attracted huge crowds, and the subsequent auction in New York resulted in a charitable donation of almost £2 million, together with £1.5 million raised on the sale of the commemorative catalogue (Graham and Blanchard 1998). The highest sum raised for any individual dress was for the midnight blue velvet ballgown worn by the Princess when waltzing with John Travolta at the White House. Some of the dresses subsequently toured the globe in a travelling exhibition, while others found their way into private and public collections (Graham and Blanchard 1998). Actress Debbie Reynolds recently auctioned her collection of Hollywood clothing that she had built up over the years, including the black and white *Ascot* dress worn by Audrey Hepburn in *My Fair Lady* for US$3.7 million, and the blue gingham pinafore dress and red sparkly shoes worn by Judy Garland as Dorothy in *The Wizard of Oz*, which raised US$910,000 and US$510,000 respectively. The auction room was packed, with many present to catch a glimpse of some of cinema's most iconic costumes, as well as other movie memorabilia such as props and scripts hailing from Hollywood's Golden Age. Tulloch (2012: 20) speculates on the reasons why private collectors are keen to snap up a souvenir from fashion auctions: 'Is it about nostalgia for another era? A unique means of self-expression? Ownership of something that no one else can possess? A harmless hobby or private insanity? For some dedicated collectors, it's all of the above.'

Three events

A comprehensive understanding of Events Studies requires us to go far further than just operational issues like staging and logistics (important though they are). It is vital that we explore what organisers are trying to achieve, how society interprets what is staged and how that might even change society. Events are often a vehicle for showcasing fashion and design innovations and bursts of creativity. Such issues demand a normative rather than a positivist approach to research; we can only subjectively evaluate these motivations and impacts and it is important to realise that there are many possible interpretations of the same phenomena. In line with the general aims of the Routledge *Advances in Events Research* Series, we seek to explore these sociological aspects of fashion and design events, hopefully provoking further research and debate.

We have chosen three short case studies to introduce the book, as they illustrate the complex interplay between fashion and design events, society, culture and the economy. These relationships are central to this work and these introductory cases allow us to begin to draw out some interesting themes, dualities and contradictions.

Art Deco style

Gazing back over the ages, it is apparent there are certain fashion and design events that are turning points, inspiring dramatic change within society. The 1925 *Exposition Internationale des Arts Décoratifs et Industriels Modernes*, held in Paris, is a cogent example. It stunned visitors with its exhibits, which showcased the most vibrant, dynamic and ultra alternative thinking and demonstrated inspiration and originality in design (Bayer 1992; Weber 1989). This event encouraged a revolution in design, fashion and architecture across the globe, especially in the western world, later to be dubbed *Art Deco*. Many inspiring and long lasting fashion and design concepts evolved and developed from this exhibition, a number of which are still popular in the present day.

The Art Deco Exposition ran from April to October and was located in the centre of Paris, on both sides of the River Seine. It was intended to be a revolution against the design norms of the previous eras. While it has been argued that many of the exhibits did not fully embrace modernism, the Exposition was promoted and perhaps perceived as having done so; the 'combined result of wishful thinking, artful labels and political spin' (Gura 2000: 195). It is now acquainted with the style known as *Art Deco*, taking this title in the mid 1960s from the original 'Art Decoratifs'. Greenhalgh (1988: 165) observes that 'it would be reasonable to suggest this as a unique instance, where an exhibition gave birth to and then publicised a style'. Originally, it was called *Art Moderne* (Bayer 1992; Greenhalgh 1988; Van de Lemme 1986). Art Moderne and the later *Streamline Moderne* were movements which ran counter to the austere Victorian era that preceded them. There was an introduction of straight lines, minimalism, geometrics and attention to symmetry and the use of metal, ivory, exotic wood and glass, producing a modern appearance which had not been witnessed before. Most of the pavilions were constructed in the new architectural style (Greenhalgh 1988).

It is only now, with some hindsight, that the extent of the contribution of this exhibition can really be appreciated. It took place against a backdrop of a world which was coming out of the bleak austerity of the First World War and the rigid structure and configurations of the Victorian era. The early part of the twentieth century signalled the introduction of industrial design and mass-produced products that were available to all sections of society, and notably embraced the Art Deco style. Even the average person had an opportunity to purchase or experience something modern and up-to-date, depicting a new direction towards beauty, modernity and speed; especially in regard to transportation (McCourt 2012; Van de Lemme 1986). The Exposition was tremendously popular, attracting more than 16 million visitors, and was also a financial success (Gura 2000). Media exposure was global, and mostly positive, although one editor labelled it 'the most serious and sustained exhibition of bad taste the world has ever seen' (Gura 2000: 201). Dramatic transformations of design occurred after this exhibition and are still revered and replicated into the current era. These include fashion, architecture and even objects of everyday use, like cutlery, crockery, automobiles and public transportation (Cerwinske 1981).

Art Deco developed under the influence of the incredible archaeological discoveries of the period. In Egypt, the discovery of the astounding and remarkable tomb of the Pharaoh Tutankhamun in 1922 led to a mania for all things Egyptian. The designs from this ancient epoch had a fundamental influence on the Art Moderne designs of the 1920s (Cerwinske 1981; McCourt 2012). There was a fascination about the exotic and relatively unknown rulers of the Egyptian empire. Simple lines and the symbols and colours of ancient Egypt – gold, silver, sapphire, turquoise and red – came to the fore. Similarly, the Aztec Empire gave design direction to this new movement, particularly the sunburst motif (Cerwinske 1981; Greenhalgh 1988).

Figure 1.4 Art Deco architecture in Miami Beach.
Source: K. Williams

The 1920s and 30s also saw a rise in the phenomenon of mass travel at high speeds, particularly by sea. The middle class now had the opportunity to vacation on magnificent ocean liners, especially between Europe and the Americas. This travel also included those that were going to start a new life in the New World. The *Normandie*, an ocean liner of the era, was synonymous with speed, grace and luxury and it was expounded as one of the most magnificent forms of transportation, incorporating the style and fashions of the Art Moderne of the 1920s. These included designs from René Lalique, Jean Dunand and Louis Sile.

Ocean liners replicated aspects of land dwellings and, in turn, designs from ocean liners were subsequently incorporated into the features of residential

Figure 1.5 Chrysler Building – architect: William Van Allen, 1930.
Source: K. Williams

and commercial architecture. Exceptional examples of this can still be seen in places like Miami Beach (Figure 1.4) and Napier in New Zealand. The Chrysler Building (William Van Allen) (Figure 1.5), constructed in New York in 1930, is another classic example of Art Deco architecture that took its inspiration from the Paris Exposition. Some of this influence might have been the result of a spin-off exhibition, which travelled to New York's Metropolitan Museum of Art a few years after the 1925 Exposition. It was organised by the American Association of Museums, in the hope that it would spawn a 'parallel movement' in the United States (Gura 2000: 201). Bayer (1992) describes the Chrysler Building as covered with bold, jazzy ornamentation;

including the chromium nickel-steel *Moderne* eagle gargoyles projecting from the 59th floor. It is a Manhattan landmark, with unsurpassed beauty more than 80 years later.

In addition to these design initiatives stemming from the Exposition, an entire new and dynamic artistic direction expanded and flourished in Paris in the period between 1920 and 1930, which can be partly attributed to the creative atmosphere linked to the Exposition, as well as a desire to escape the horrific memories of the First World War. The city was notorious for its bohemian past, yet symbolised a shiny modern future. A new and provocative genre of artist was attracted to Paris, including the painters Matisse and Pablo Picasso, the entertainer Josephine Baker, the composer and songwriter Cole Porter and the writers Gertrude Stein, Ernest Hemingway and F. Scott Fitzgerald (Watson 2000). Known as the Lost Generation, and recently immortalised by film-maker Woody Allen in *Midnight in Paris* (2011), they formed a movement which has become part of Parisian mythology (Field 2006) and led to one of the great creative outpourings of the twentieth century.

Dior and the New Look

Paris was again the focus of controversy in 1947, with the first couture collection launched by Christian Dior, known as the *New Look*. The volume of material used in the skirts was a revelation to those who had become used to wartime austerity and rationing, and attracted admiration as well as criticism for its extravagance and focus on the feminine shape. The hips and breasts were emphasised, waists were cinched with corsets and shoulders were soft, 'the antithesis of militaristic wartime fashions' (Palmer 2009: 27). Special corsets or *hipettes* were required (Dorner 1975). The launch of the New Look re-established Paris as the centre of the fashion world and Dior as its saviour or the devil incarnate, depending on your point of view. While *Harper's Bazaar* journalist Carmel Snow coined the phrase 'New Look', there was a gradual evolution in style over several years by various Paris couturiers, who pushed hemlines lower and made clothing more feminine (Steele 1997). Dior took the credit, much of which is due to the attention-grabbing style of the event to launch his collection. Dorner (1975: 28) notes that it is rare 'in fashion history when a change in style can be precisely dated'.

Many of his Parisian rivals had salons which were faded and tawdry after the war years. Dior, by contrast, enjoyed generous financial backing, and was able to create an elegant setting for his collection viewings, using his trademark grey, with luxurious soft furnishings, neo-Louis XVI decor and a chandelier (Palmer 2009). The debut of the New Look was met with lavish praise, not just for the startling nature of the clothes, but also the theatricality of the presentation (Walford 2008). The audience were entranced by the spectacle:

> The first girl came out, stepping fast, switching with a provocative swinging movement, whirling in the close-packed room, knocking over ashtrays

with the strong flare of her pleated skirt, and bringing everyone to the edges of their seats in a desire not to miss a thread of this momentous occasion ... We were given a polished theatrical performance such as we had never seen in a couture house before. We were witness to a revolution in fashion and to a revolution in showing fashion as well.

(Ballard, 1960: 237)

The reporter who wrote this was apparently unaware of the shows produced by couturiers like Lucile, Paul Poiret and Jeanne Paquin in the period before the Great War. It was said that 'people went to a fashion parade as their fathers had gone to a play or to a private view of pictures' (Laver 1937: 91). Gardens as well as lavish interior settings with stages were used to show off the latest designs (Troy 2003). Paul Poiret had designed for the theatre and threw lavish parties or *fêtes*, with Oriental themes like *The Arabian Nights*, possibly inspired by the Ballet Russes' production of *Schéhérazade* (Troy 2003). His fashion shows incorporated 'stagecraft and showmanship', with models appearing from hidden entrances, like a play (Evans 2011: 115). Nevertheless, Christian Dior was a master of showmanship of his time. Like Poiret, he was comfortable with a theatrical approach, having designed clothes for the French cinema during the Second World War (de Marly 1990), and reasserted and revitalised French couture's reputation for setting worldwide trends (Palmer 2009). His influence can be seen on his heir at the House of Dior, Yves Saint Laurent, whose shows of the 1970s, particularly his Opéra collection, evoked a hysterical response: 'Yves was pulling Paris and fashion into a rip tide of wealth and theatre, colour and voluptuous indulgence' (Drake 2006: 210).

Women who embraced the New Look, such as Nancy Mitford and Princess Margaret, loved the exaggerated femininity after the austerity of the war years (Guinness 1984; Palmer 2009). One young American woman described the collection as a life-saver, now that 'becoming clothes are back' (Steele 1988: 270–271). Even Princess Elizabeth wore a version, albeit less exaggerated than the Paris original (Walford 2008). It immediately made the old styles look passé, with their short skirts and mannish shoulder pads. Textile manufacturers were also pleased at the generous amounts of fabric the Dior collection required (Drake 2006). While it was argued that this was a style only available to the very rich, women of lesser means, faced with fabric shortages and rationing, were ingenious in employing patchwork on skirts, using blackout material or combining several dresses into one (de Marly 1990).

Other women, however, were incensed that a designer was effectively holding them to ransom, forcing them to adopt the longer, more voluminous length or look hopelessly behind the times. For English women, still undergoing clothes rationing, the look was frustratingly unobtainable and seen as unpatriotic (de Marly 1990). It mocked the wartime sacrifices made to comply with austerity measures. Some felt that the restrictive style, with its 'undercurrent of eroticism', treating women as either sexy sophisticates or girlish ingénues, was anti-feminist (Palmer 2009: 32) and a return to the

past (Walford 2008). This led to petitions and organised protests with plac-
ards featuring slogans like 'Women! Join the Fight for Freedom in Manner
of Dress' and 'Burn Monsieur Dior' (de Marly 1990; Dorner 1975; Palmer
2009). The mood turned ugly in some instances, with women attacking a
New Look model being photographed on the streets of Paris and tearing
her dress off (Dorner 1975; Palmer 2009). Nevertheless, the die was cast. As
Palmer (2009: 30) notes: 'Regardless of controversy ... the New Look dominated postwar fashion design at all prices'. This influence lasted for a decade
(Ehrman 2011) and was particularly long-lasting in cinema, although less
as a marker of radical chic and more for its spectacular silhouette and as an
expression of traditional femininity (Bruzzi 2011).

A minute's warning: fashion and dark commemorative events

2012 saw the 70th anniversary of the Bombing of Darwin, Australia. For
the first time, the anniversary was declared a National Day of Observance.
There was a memorial service, a reunion of survivors, a reenactment and the
opening of a new museum; standard features of such commemorative events
(Frost and Laing 2013). There was a 'Black-Tie Ball', hosted by the Mayor of
Darwin. And there was a fashion show.

For the 70th Anniversary, the City of Darwin organised a programme of
creative and artistic projects that would remember and reflect upon the attack.
Remembering is a key component of commemorations and many cultural
events are specifically staged to encourage modern communities to look back
upon their past (Frost and Laing 2013). One of these artistic projects was a
fashion show – *A Minute's Warning*. This was designed by Matilda Alegria,
a 22-year-old Charles Darwin University fashion degree graduate. Fashion
shows are occasionally included in commemorative event programmes, though
usually focussing on recreations of historic costumes. For example, the town
of Tombstone in Arizona holds an annual *Helldorado Days*, an event commemorating the Gunfight at the OK Corral. Many attendees are in costume
and one event is a parade of women's fashions from the 1880s (Figure 1.6).
What was different at the Darwin Anniversary was that the parade was of
modern fashions.

Alegria's designs were described in great detail in an article in *The Age*
newspaper:

> Its pale silk bodice grips ... tightly around the ribs and rises in four jag-
> ged shards cut to jut sharply away from her body. 'That's the ship, the
> USS Peary', Alegria explains seriously. 'It took several direct hits in the
> air raids, so it's breaking up, it's disappearing beneath the waves ... The
> historic detail was very important to me', she says. 'I wanted to empha-
> sise that.' Somewhere under the billowing skirts of her USS Peary gown,
> for example, a tiny '266, the number originally painted on the vessel that
> sank after five direct hits, is secreted between layers of silk. The collection

Figure 1.6 Retrospective fashion parade held during the 2012 Helldorado Days Festival, Tombstone, Arizona.
Source: W. Frost

also includes a mini frocklet with stiffened pink and grey silk 'flames' leaping from its bodice and shoulders. Another features an exaggerated bell skirt and circular bodice sculpted with boning and red silk to resemble a hybrid of the Japanese flag and a bomber's propeller.

(Breen Burns 2012c: 3)

Such an approach at a commemorative event has the strong potential to upset some stakeholders. In this case, sections of the media certainly tried to beat up a controversy, suggesting it was disrespectful. However, intriguingly, this approach to a fashion show had the support of key players in the anniversary. In particular, the main veterans group – the Returned Services League (RSL) – endorsed it. According to RSL spokesperson John Lusk, the Darwin veterans were at first surprised by the proposal. However, as they thought about it, Lusk argues they began to see the merit of this different approach aimed at engaging a younger generation:

Here is a young person with a completely new idea to show what happened in Darwin. There was no suggestion of her trying to make a mockery and I'm glad that negativity came and went … Some of us oldies could never imagine anything like it. But, we thought, she's showing that terrible time in a different light and a way that will attract a younger person – what the hell, we'll give her a go.

(quoted in Breen Burns 2012c: 3)

Some dualities

Considering these three introductory case studies highlights that fashion and design events are marked by some dualities, even contradictions. These illustrate the complexities and dynamic nature of the relationships between events and society. Five are worth examining in detail.

1. Fashion events, or events utilising fashion?

Fashion events conjure up images of catwalk shows, fashion weeks and product launches. However, the range of events to be considered is wider than that. In addition to events directly themed around fashion and design, there are events that will include aspects of fashion. For example, the Academy Awards (as with many award ceremonies) includes the ritual of the *red carpet* (Cosgrave 2007). Prospective winners and other celebrities parade before the crowd and media. The links between fashion and celebrity culture, including the marketing opportunities they present, have been noted by Church Gibson (2012). Many celebrities at the Academy Awards are wearing the works of major designers, who see this film industry event as a way to promote their creations. Creating a gown for a Best Actress nominee is particularly coveted. The red carpet has been dubbed 'the new catwalk for the twenty-first century' (Church Gibson 2012: 54).

However, interest in the fashions worn at the Academy Awards has a long history, even if it was not perhaps as intense as today. The first winner of the statuette for Best Actress, Mary Pickford, wore haute couture (Cosgrave 2007). While many actresses in later years wore gowns created by the studio designers, notably Grace Kelly in 1955 in an Edith Head design, the biggest splash was made by those who gave famous designers free rein. Marlene Dietrich, a presenter in 1951, turned heads by wearing a black satin Dior cocktail dress, which made a dramatic contrast to the rest of the women in the room clad in pale colours. Nothing was left to chance. The angle at which Dietrich would cross the stage was considered before Dior decided where to place the slit on her skirt. The newspaper headlines proclaimed Dietrich's triumph, as much as the six Oscars won by *All About Eve* (Cosgrave 2007).

Gender stereotypes are often reinforced, with actresses expected to look feminine and sexy in haute couture, with a well-toned and lithe body to match. Female attendees are torn to shreds by critics and scrutinised within an inch of their Manolo Blahniks. Male actors, by contrast, barely rate a mention in their standard tuxes and suits, and might even be labelled 'anti-fashion icons' for their workaday attire on screen, exemplified by Gregory Peck (Bruzzi 2005). Some actresses use this spotlight to their advantage. In 1936, Bette Davis was castigated by a magazine editor for choosing a dress she wore in the movie *Housewife* to accept her award for *Dangerous* – 'You don't look like a Hollywood star! ... [yet] your photograph is going around the world' (quoted in Cosgrave 2007: 31). Davis was making a statement through her choice of clothes to her employer, Jack Warner, for his refusal to give her better roles. She was tired of the fluff she was given, and regarded *Housewife* as a turkey. She didn't pull a stunt like that again. In 1955, as a presenter, Davis could hardly be overlooked; resplendent in gold lamé and black velvet, with a gold turban to match (Cosgrave 2007).

Attempts to wear cutting-edge fashion at the Oscars mostly end in disaster. No Cher-like disasters, with feathers and cut-outs, are tolerated these days. Neither is too much skin. A gothic effort by Gwyneth Paltrow at the 2002 Oscars, complete with Heidi braids, was soundly ridiculed, notably for her temerity in wearing a transparently sheer top without a bra. In 2012, she learnt her lesson, appearing in fashion-forward but elegant Tom Ford, complete with a Jackie Kennedy style cape. Quirkiness is also criticised. A case in point is Icelandic singer Bjork's infamous swan dress in 2001, complete with a large egg, which missed its mark: 'They didn't get it', said Bjork of the Hollywood press corps' missing the humour of her swan stunt. 'They actually thought I was trying to look like Jennifer Aniston and got it wrong' (Cosgrave 2007: 255).

Royal weddings similarly generate a great deal of interest regarding the design of the bride's dress. Queen Victoria is credited with making the white wedding dress *de rigueur* (Ehrman 2011). Princess Diana's dress in 1981 was the inspiration for romantic full-skirted confections in taffeta and lace that appear over-the-top to modern sensibilities (Ehrman 2011). Sarah Burton of Alexander McQueen made world headlines when it was announced that she was to design the gown of Kate Middleton when she married Prince William of Wales in 2011. The choice of designer, not revealed until the day of the wedding, was greeted with cheers by the fashion crowd, who in the past had generally found Kate's sartorial style too conservative. Burton did not create anything too edgy, but found the perfect balance of high fashion and tradition. Resembling the iconic wedding dress of Princess Grace, with its lace bodice and sleeves, it spawned numerous copies.

Exhibitions at galleries and museums often include examples of fashion and design as historical or cultural artefacts. The *Napoleon: Revolution to Empire* exhibition at the National Gallery of Victoria in 2012 was not a fashion event, but included an exquisite original court dress worn at the crowning of Napoleon as Emperor. It was extremely popular with visitors, fascinated with its diminutive size and pristine condition (generally historic clothing is not well preserved). The *Art Deco 1910–1939* exhibition at the same gallery in 2008 also presented a number of Roaring Twenties gowns by designers like Chanel and Charles James, as well as a 1937 Cord 812 Westchester sedan.

Exhibitions or expos can act as a vehicle for displaying the latest design innovations in products such as motor cars, jewellery, furniture, computers and mobile phones. The Great Exhibition of 1851 in London showcased cutting-edge industrial design and manufacturing techniques, including textiles like lace (Ehrman 2011). Fashion was often a feature of these exhibitions, given its importance as an industry and reflection of cultural vigour or resurgence, and they are subsequently argued to have influenced department store displays (Steele 1988). All the Parisian international exhibitions between 1855 and 1932, for example, highlighted their leadership in fashion (Steele 1988). The couturier Jeanne Paquin was responsible for the fashion section of the Paris Exposition Universelle in 1900, which included historical fashions, as well as the most up-to-date creations and a towering statue of *La Parisienne*, clothed in a Paquin creation (Steele 1988; Troy 2003). In 1911, Paquin created her own pavilion to display her creations at the International Exposition in Turin, the only French couture house to do so, as well as being represented in a pavilion of French fashion, which publicly celebrated their collective achievements (Troy 2003). Hardie Amies, couturier to the Queen, however bemoaned the lack of fashion displayed at the 1951 Festival of Britain (Amies 1976), amidst the showcasing of the nation as open for business and culturally flourishing after the Second World War.

2. Cultural or economic objectives and meanings

As with many other events, organisers may be aiming for economic aims, or cultural objectives, or both. As opposed to these strategic goals, the meanings of an event may be interpreted by society, the media or particular groups in quite different ways (Frost and Laing 2011). For example, the launch of the New Look had a major economic objective. Christian Dior had only recently established his fashion house and wanted to make his mark and grow his business. It was also important for the future of France's couture industry that the reputation of Paris as the fashion capital of the world be reasserted (de Marly 1990; Palmer 2009). Dior was aware of his burden: 'I would be risking the livelihood of 1,200 people if I made an unbalanced collection' (Palmer 2009: 6). However, the launch of the New Look had a greater impact than this, for it was widely seen as a significant cultural change, particularly signalling an end to wartime austerity. Matilda Alegria staged her fashion show commemorating the Bombing of Darwin with objectives of gaining a foothold in the fashion industry. It was supported by the RSL, not so much because they wanted to find her a job, but rather as a new way of engaging with younger people. This balancing of competing objectives and meanings between different stakeholders is common to many events. It may be problematic, increasing the potential for confusion and failure, but it may also add drama, excitement and uncertainty, which may aid its success.

3. Innovation

All three of our introductory case studies involve innovation. Indeed, this is a major feature of the fashion and design industries, with a constant search for new trends. As Robinson (1958: 127) observes: 'Fashion, defined in its most general sense, is the pursuit of novelty for its own sake.' Innovation, highlighted through events, may cause controversy and debate. Indeed, this may be a key hope of the organisers and events may be staged to be deliberately provocative and shocking. It is also important to understand that innovation is not only creative, but destructive. As new fashion and design trends emerge through events, old ones quickly fall *out of fashion* and techniques, materials and styles become redundant.

4. Co-creation by audiences

While event organisers have their objectives, these may be adapted by the audience. In certain cases, the audience may even subvert or reject what the organisers intended. These processes of *co-creation* are becoming increasingly recognised as important in the staging of events in general (Frost and Laing 2011). Many fashion and design events rely heavily on the involvement and reactions of the audience. The audience is no longer seen as passive and with high levels of fashion literacy there may be ongoing reflection and comment. The rise of fashion blogs is a good example of this phenomenon. For event organisers, this raises new challenges as they must plan to integrate audience responses into staging the event. Bloggers are now invited guests at many fashion shows, and are given front-row seats, a mark of their status and importance *vis-à-vis* the success of the event.

5. Social worlds

Enthusiasts who share a common approach to or perspective on fashion might be regarded as engaging in the same *social world* (Unruh 1979, 1980). Members share the same values, norms and behaviours, which often put them in conflict with those of the broader populace (Green and Jones 2005). This element of deviance gives them something in common with the idea of a *sub-culture*, but the social world is a broader concept, encompassing 'imagery, processes, interaction and relationships' (Unruh 1980: 272). Access to social worlds might be difficult, especially for casual participants (Green and Jones 2005; Unruh 1979). Clothing might be a symbol of identity or credibility within a social world, such as the shorts/tracksuit bottoms and cap or T-shirt advertising a past race worn by long-distance runners, even when not competing (Shipway and Jones 2007).

Social worlds can be constructed in a variety of ways. Some are based on a common interest in history or a historical event. The Mountain Men Rendezvous, where participants dress as pioneers from the early nineteenth century, is a 'fantastic consumption enclave ... in which a "subworld" is jointly enacted using special time, place and clothing' (Belk and Costa 1998: 219). Those taking part use clothing as a way of reinforcing and building mythology, but also to denote membership of a community 'set apart from the outside world', and affirming their common identity.

For steampunk enthusiasts, their social world has developed around a common *philosophy* – a reaction against ugliness and a sense of alienation from technology. Fashion is important as a way of turning modern sensibilities on their head – Victoriana with a twist.

A third kind of social world is constructed around a shared social space. The club culture studied by Thornton (1996: 3) relies on a disco, dance club or rave as a 'symbolic axis and working social hub'. Rituals such as girls dancing around a pile of their handbags, or the donning of sexualised items of clothing, like short skirts and high heels, identify those who are part of the group.

Overview of this book

Events examined in this book include fashion weeks, fashion or design themed exhibitions, historical reenactments, extreme/alternative fashion and design events, and large-scale public events such as royal weddings and horse races. International examples and case studies are drawn from countries as diverse as the USA, UK, Germany, Bhutan, New Zealand and Australia, by academics from multiple countries and a swathe of disciplinary backgrounds, working in the areas of events, tourism, art and design, creative arts and industries, apparel and textiles, trademark law, architecture, and communications. We believe that this multidisciplinary approach is important, to bring different theoretical and practical perspectives to the field of study and therefore provide a richer and more nuanced analysis of the pertinent issues.

The book is divided into three sections – Glamour and Spectacle, Industry and Destination Perspectives, and Emerging Trends and a View of the Future. Individual chapters develop and critique various thematic concepts linked to fashion and design events, such as identity, gender, aspirations and self-image, commodification, authenticity, destination development and marketing, business strategy and protection/infringement of intellectual property. We conclude with a suggested research agenda.

References

Amies, H. (1976) 'No clothes ... no fashion', in M. Banham and B. Hillier (eds), *A Tonic to the Nation: The Festival of Britain 1951*, London: Thames & Hudson (pp. 40–55).

Argyle, M. (1988) *Bodily Communication*, 2nd edn, London; New York: Methuen.

Ballard, B. (1960) *In My Fashion*, David McKay: New York.

Barthes, R. (1967) *The Fashion System*, 1985 reprint, London: Cape.

Bayer, P. (1992) *Art Deco Architecture: Design, decoration and detail from the Twenties and Thirties*, London: Thames & Hudson.

Belk, R. and Costa, J. A. (1998) 'The Mountain Man Myth: A contemporary consuming fantasy', *The Journal of Consumer Research*, 25(3): 218–240.

Blanchard, T. (2012) 'Divine Grace', *The Saturday Age Good Weekend magazine*, 1 December: 24–27.

Breen Burns, J. (2012a) '"Sicilian gypsy thing" with a dash of the Flying Nun', *The Saturday Age*, 28 April: 5.

Breen Burns, J. (2012b) 'Tailors tinker with silky smooth moves to woo the online world', *The Age*, 3 May: 6.

Breen Burns, J. (2012c) 'Darwin bombings inspire a woven lesson in history', *The Age*, 18 February: 3.

Bruzzi, S. (2005) 'Gregory Peck: Anti-fashion icon', in R. Moseley (ed.), *Fashioning Film Stars: Dress, culture, identity*, London: British Film Institute.

Bruzzi, S. (2011) '"It will be a magnificent obsession": Femininity, desire, and the New Look in 1950s melodrama', in A. Munich (ed.), *Fashion in Film*, Bloomington: Indiana University Press.

Cerwinske, L. (1981) *Tropical Deco: The architecture and design of Old Miami Beach*, New York: Rizzoli.

Church Gibson, P. (2012) *Fashion and Celebrity Culture*, London; New York: Berg.

Cosgrave, B. (2007) *Made for Each Other: Fashion and the Academy Awards*, London: Bloomsbury.

de Marly, D. (1990) *Christian Dior*, London: B. T. Batsford.

Dorner, J. (1975) *Fashion in the Forties & Fifties*, Shepperton, UK: Ian Allen.

Drake, A. (2006) *The Beautiful Fall: Fashion, genius and glorious excess in 1970s Paris*, New York: Bay Back Books.

Ehrman, E. (2011) *The White Wedding Dress*, London: V & A Publishing.

Entwistle, J. and Rocamora, A. (2006) 'The field of fashion materialized: A study of London Fashion Week', *Sociology*, 40(4): 735–751.

Evans, C. (2011) 'The walkies: Early French fashion shows as a cinema of attractions', in A. Munich (ed.), *Fashion in Film*, Bloomington: Indiana University Press.

Field, A. N. (2006) 'Expatriate lifestyle as tourist destination: *The Sun Also Rises* and experiential travelogues of the Twenties', *The Hemingway Review*, 25(2): 29–43.

Frost, W. and Laing, J. (2011) *Strategic Management of Festivals and Events*, Melbourne: Cengage.

Frost, W. and Laing, J. (2013) *Commemorative Events: Memory, identities, conflict*, London: Routledge.

Goffman, E. (1956) *The Presentation of Self in Everyday Life*, 1990 reprint, New York: Doubleday.

Graham, T. and Blanchard, T. (1998) *Dressing Diana*, Princeton, NJ: Benford Books.

Green, B. C. and Jones, I. (2005) 'Serious leisure, social identity and sport tourism', *Sport in Society*, 8(2): 164–181.

Greenhalgh, P. (1988) *Ephemeral Vistas: The Expositions Universelles, Great Exhibitions and World's Fairs, 1851–1939*, Manchester: Manchester University Press.

Guinness, J. with Guinness, C. (1984) *The House of Mitford*, 1987 reprint, Glasgow: Fontana.

Gura, J. B. (2000) 'Modernism and the 1925 Paris Exposition', *Antiques*, 158(2): 194–203.

Harrison, S. (2005) 'Jean Shrimpton, the "four inch furore" and perceptions of Melbourne identity in the 1960s', in S. O'Hanlon and T. Luckins (eds), *Go! Melbourne in the Sixties*, Beaconsfield: Circa.

König, R. (1971) *The Restless Image: A sociology of fashion*, 1973 transl. F. Bradley, London: George Allen & Unwin.

Kozinets, R. V. (2001) 'Utopian enterprise: Articulating the meanings of Star Trek's culture of consumption', *Journal of Consumer Research*, 28: 67–88.

Laver, J. (1937) *Taste and Fashion: From the French Revolution to the present day*, 1945 reprint, London: George G. Harrap.

McCourt, M. J. (2012) 'Art Deco and the automobile', *Hemmings Classic Cars*, December: 21–29.

Moseley, R. (2005) 'Introduction', in R. Moseley (ed.), *Fashioning Film Stars: Dress, culture, identity*, London: British Film Institute.

Oderberg, I. (2012) 'Drama that's on parade makes night', *Herald Sun*, 12 March: 25.

Overington, C. (2012) 'The lifetime collection', *Weekend Australian* magazine, 11–12 August.

Palmer, A. (2009) *Dior*, London: V & A.

Peers, J. (2004) *The Fashion Doll: From Bébé Jumeau to Barbie*, New York: Berg.

Quinn, B. (2002) 'Exhibition review: "Radical" fashion? A critique of the radical fashion exhibition, Victoria and Albert Museum, London', *Fashion Theory*, 6(4): 441–446.

Reinach, S. S. (2005) 'China and Italy: Fast fashion versus prêt à porter. Towards a new culture of fashion', *Fashion Theory*, 9(1): 43–56.

Robinson, D. D. (1958) 'Fashion theory and product design', *Harvard Business Review*, 36: 126–138.

Sharpe, E. K. (2008) 'Festivals and social change: Intersections of pleasure and politics at a community music festival', *Leisure Sciences*, 30: 217–234.

Shipway, R. and Jones, I. (2007) 'Running away from home: Understanding visitor experiences and behaviour at sport tourism events', *International Journal of Tourism Research*, 9: 373–383.

Skov, L. (2006) 'The role of trade fairs in the global fashion business', *Current Sociology*, 54(5): 764–783.

Steele, V. (1988) *Paris Fashion: A cultural history*, 1999 reprint, Oxford; New York: Berg.

Steele, V. (1997) *Fifty Years of Fashion: New Look to now*, New Haven; London: Yale University Press.

Thompson, C. J. and Haytko, D. L. (1997) 'Speaking of fashion: Consumers' uses of fashion discourses and the appropriation of countervailing cultural meanings', *Journal of Consumer Research*, 24(1): 15–42.

Thornton, S. (1996) *Club Cultures: music, media and subculture capital*, Hanover; London: University Press of New England.

Troy, N. J. (2003) *Couture Culture: A study in modern art and fashion*, Cambridge, MA; London: MIT Press.

Tulloch, L. (2012) 'Magnificent obsession', *The Saturday Age Good Weekend magazine*, 8 December: 20–23.

Unruh, D. R. (1979) 'Characteristics and types of participation in social worlds', *Symbolic Interaction*, 2(2): 115–130.

Unruh, D. R. (1980) 'The nature of social worlds', *The Pacific Sociological Review*, 23(3): 271–296.

Van de Lemme, A. (1986) *A Guide to Art Deco Style*, New Burlington Books: Chartwell House.

Walford, J. (2008) *Forties Fashion: From Siren Suits to the New Look*, London: Thames & Hudson.

Watson, S. (2000) *Prepare for Saints: Gertrude Stein, Virgil Thomson, and the mainstreaming of American modernism*, Berkeley: University of California Press.

Weber, E. (1989) *Art Deco*, London: Bison.

Wolfe, T. (1973) 'Introduction', in R. König, (1971) *The Restless Image: A sociology of fashion*, 1973 transl. F. Bradley, London: George Allen & Unwin.

Part I
Glamour and spectacle

2 A dashing, positively smashing, spectacle...

Female spectators and dress at equestrian events in the United States during the 1930s

Alison L. Goodrum

Introduction

Little is known of the life of Miss Boopie Jenkins (see Figures 2.1 and 2.2) other than that she was part of an elite social set of wealthy, white, American men and women who enjoyed fulsome participation in a leisured lifestyle during the interwar years. Jenkins features in just a handful of black and white photographs held within the *Gerald B. Webb Jr. Album Collection*, a photographic archive of the life and work of the equestrian journalist and founder of the specialist newspaper (established 17 September 1937) *The Chronicle of the Horse*. These few glimpses of Jenkins captured in 1938 as a young woman of twenty-one years are instructive. They offer a visual entrée into the nuances of dress and dressing in – and for – a contemporary high class lifestyle, one punctuated by equestrian occasions both sporting and social.

Amateur snapshots and family albums are endorsed by Taylor as being an 'immensely useful ... source of clothing detail' (2002: 169–170) offering 'significant tools in the dress historian's search for the coded cultural meanings that lie within clothing'. The two photographs of Boopie Jenkins included in this chapter are indeed richly encoded clothing texts. Both images are taken in the geographical setting of her home locale – Warrenton, Virginia – itself an area synonymous with equestrian activity of all kinds but particularly fox-hunting and horse trialling. In Figure 2.1, Jenkins is positioned centre, following the action at the Warrenton Hunter Trials from a makeshift vantage point: the back of a horse-drawn wagon. Hunter trials are a form of cross-country equestrian event, usually taking place in open parkland. The course is laid out over several kilometres and comprises both permanent and temporary obstacles designed to simulate the jumps and tests typically found in the hunting field (such as logs, rails, gates and water features). The competition is scored against the clock with time and fault penalties. In Figure 2.2, from the same photograph album, Jenkins is shown riding out with the Warrenton Hunt. Viewed in juxtaposition, these two images capture the remarkable contrast in dress and the associated *techniques* (Mauss 1973) of dressing and appearance management engaged in by Jenkins (and, indeed, many of her social peers).

Figure 2.1 Boopie Jenkins (centre) at Warrenton Hunter Trials, 1938. A handwritten caption identifies 'Mrs Carhart' (sitting) on the left of the frame.

Source: Webb Archive, National Sporting Library and Museum, Virginia

The contrast in hairstyles between each image is noteworthy: hanging loose and curling naturally under a jaunty peaked cap in the group shot, the appearance presented in this first photograph is one of informality. Rugged up in a knee-length fur topcoat, Jenkins is shown wearing what was a staple item among the equestrian set of the day. Fur is a material, writes Bolton (2004: 43), charged 'potently and profoundly with symbolic meaning', and its meaning becomes far heightened in this particular context of hunt-related sport. Made of animal pelt, the coat signals a deferred engagement with the quarry itself, a transposed symbol of the hunt. Also connoting luxury, wealth, status – and even, perhaps, sexualised, animalistic connotations – the fur coat is imbued with symbolism *but also* fulfils important serviceable requirements,

Figure 2.2 Boopie Jenkins in side-saddle habit dress, Warrenton, 1938.
Source: Webb Archive, National Sporting Library and Museum, Virginia

offering warmth and cosiness against prolonged periods spent outdoors in the wintery Virginian elements.

The second portrait of Jenkins, mounted side-saddle with both rider and horse groomed to perfection, demonstrates an alternative dress code, one based around formal sanctions and the cultivation of a highly maintained and disciplined body. Jenkins appears as the embodiment of the interwar equestrienne, a persona governed by its 'fervour of sobriety' (Matthews David 2002: 182) and 'severity of plainness' (Goodrum 2012: 87). In this photograph, her hair is tamed, being scraped smoothly and tidily under her formal hunting topper as dictated in foxhunting etiquette and policed by the officiating Hunt Club Master and Secretary. Writing in their treatise on equitation of 1932, Lady Diana Shedden and Lady Viola Apsley forged a determined campaign against what they condemned as the disorderly and undesirable trait of 'wispiness'. Lady Shedden and Lady Aspley were members of the Anglo-British nobility and their volume on hunting and riding is presented, essentially, from an Anglo-British perspective. However, their written observations and advisories on equestrian pursuits transposed readily to a North American context, which looked to, and admired, Anglo-European traditions for authentication of practice (see Goodrum 2012 for further discussion).

In their words, 'a tidy head is one of the two hall-marks [the other was the stock tie] of a good woman to hounds' (Shedden and Apsley 1932: 136). This in turn suggests that, in the hunting field, appearance management was guided as much by socio-cultural codes of respectability than by purely functional concerns. Keeping up appearances was a matter of great import, reflective of individual self-worth and Hunt Club honour.

The case of Boopie Jenkins foreshadows some of the overarching themes to be presented in this chapter: the identity politics surrounding wearers and the wearing of both sporting and spectator dress during the 1930s; the centrality of the practice of dressing to equestrian events; the commodity, commercial and design cultures surrounding spectatorship at them; as well as an exploration of the broader socio-economic conditions – related to the American national project and Depression era – that contemporary sportswear mobilised, reflected and reproduced. Dant (1999: 107) suggests that 'there is a system of relationships between ideas and values, material things (clothes) and people'. This chapter seeks to unpack and understand these sartorial and social relationships, using equestrian events in the historical context of 1930s America as a richly textured field of enquiry through which to do so. 'America' may be qualified here as an abbreviation of the United States of America (USA). Equestrian activity differed in form and popularity across the USA. Western riding emerged as part of Frontier life, and had a Hispanic heritage whereas steeplechasing and hunting developed from an Anglo-European tradition and was practiced in the Mid-Atlantic and Southeast. First, however, some notes on previous studies pertinent to the historical relationship between dress, female spectators and equestrian events.

Dress and equestrian events: reviewing fashion history and theory

Foremost, perhaps, the case of Boopie Jenkins complicates definitions and understandings of contemporary female spectatorship and, indeed, contemporary sporting females. Arnold (2009) suggests that the 1930s saw a rise in women's interest in, and engagement with, sports as part of a modern, fashionable lifestyle. Similarly, Campbell Warner (2005: 82) argues that 'by the 1930s, playing sports suggested leisure, money, and success in the larger sense of living well'. Allied practices around personal hygiene, diet and a growing consumer culture promoting female cosmetics, beauty rituals and health salons also flourished. Indeed, an almost disproportionate amount of column inches was given over to the promotion of female beauty products in the contemporary specialist equestrian press. Marketers, perhaps, realised the commercial potential in forcing a link between consumer culture and the cultivation of athletic appearance. Monthly periodicals such as *Spur* and *Polo* carried regular full page advertisements for cosmetic brands such as Helena Rubenstein and Elizabeth Arden. The copy used to sell these products fully exploited fashionable anxieties about the maintenance of youth and beauty. For example, advertising for Dorothy Gray cosmetics read: 'A droopy chinline has a way of suggesting stodginess and middle age, in the unkind sense of the word' (Spur 1931: 77).

Wealthy, white, athletic, young and fashionable American women – such as Jenkins – were multi-dimensional and accomplished characters, and thereby able to inhabit a variety of identities in equestrian culture as both knowledgeable onlookers *and* as active participants. Furthermore, they were able to move between these varied roles with relative ease and frequency, and in some instances were able to inhabit authoritative and influential positions such as owners, trainers and/or hunt masters. Dress assumed an important part of this process, being part of Goffman's (1961) *identity toolkit*, and enabling the material construction and bodily enactment of each social and sporting role. Women required an encyclopaedic knowledge of specialist dress codes since each equestrian discipline (be it dressage, showing, point-to-point racing, fox hunting, coaching and driving or even hacking) was regulated by esoteric rules concerning appearance, dress and bodily presentation known as *appointments*. As a spectator in the grandstand, terrace or the assembled ranks of the crowd, dress was equally prescribed, surveilled and regulated. Particularly in the more structured setting of the man-made race track (rather than, perhaps, the natural environs of the field event), both men and women were held to status-related edicts whereby entry to certain areas of the concourse required sumptuary compliance, with a debarring if one was deemed in breach of protocol. More subtly, however, the sanctioning of spectator dress was also guided by acquired, tacit skills of taste and discernment: a precariously balanced combination of peer-group consensus, media commentary, social convention and Bourdieuian *cultural capital*. Dressing appropriately as a spectator was an art form and was steeped in social skill and fashion sensibility as well as economic privilege.

MacAloon's (1984) work, albeit related to the Olympics rather than regional scale equestrian sports of yesteryear, offers theoretical insight here. Drawing on Goffmanian concepts of *social framing*, the sporting event is understood as a culturally and spatially ordered experience, organised around three concentric frames of *game-festival-spectacle*. At the core is the field of action (the game), surrounded by a literal and metaphorical frame comprising spectators, track, ring and/or stadium (namely, the festival) that is, in turn, encompassed by a discursive structure of mass-media representations, narratives and imagery (the spectacle) stretching well beyond the geo-temporal limits of the game-play itself. This sporting frame model is useful in identifying and considering the social order constructed within, and through, equestrian events and the spaces and behaviours of the race ground in particular (for a populist account of the various social *tribes* at present day racetracks in Britain, see Fox 2005; the thesis forwarded is consistent with that of this chapter: that the racing crowd is far from amorphous and comprised, instead, of its own distinctive customs, rituals and sub-cultural groupings).

MacAloon (1984: 250) reminds us that 'frames have histories', and the history of 1930s sport and spectators considered here makes a case for the agency of dress in the construction and maintenance of social ordering. In the framing process, the performative qualities of dress along with the ability to dress *the part* (or, indeed, to subvert and/or transgress it), assume a powerful visual and material signifying device: of belonging, status and role. Dressing appropriately for a day at the races – and for one's chosen or acquired role(s) while there – was a highly mediated practice. The spaces of the stable block, paddock, open air bleachers, covered pavilions and winner's enclosure were each framed by particular codes of dress. As Crane (2000: 1) explains:

> One of the most visible markers of social status and gender and therefore useful in maintaining or subverting symbolic boundaries, clothing is an indication of how people in different eras have perceived their positions in social structures and negotiated status boundaries.

Far from being consigned to the literal and metaphorical sidelines of the 'cheering section' (Spur 1930: 19), the female spectator has long been a key agent in the pageantry of equestrian sport. Referring to the example of the Longchamp Racetrack in Paris, the importance of the crowd and, specifically, the stylish modes of dress of the females within it, are noted by Brevik-Zender (2009). Although both the historical and geographical setting of this example (late nineteenth century France) fall outside of the direct focus of this chapter, it nonetheless offers insight as to the root (and, indeed, route) of the abiding connection between high fashion, its display and the site of the horse-racing track. Horse-racing in the English national context also has firm, and historic, connections to fashionable dress, assisted by courtly patronage of the sport. The Ascot festival of racing (Berkshire, England) has a reputation as a fashion spectacle. Sherwood (2011: 17) traces its history from Queen Anne in 1711 to the present day, stating that:

> In those three hundred years, the world's most influential, fashionable and, perhaps, hedonistic ladies and gentlemen have gathered annually for Royal Ascot in the Royal Enclosure as guests of the monarch to observe superlative flat racing and, of course, each other.

This is a connection which remained pertinent during the 1930s and still endures today. At least once a year, the Hippodrome de Longchamp became:

> … an incomparable site of fashionable pageantry … The Grand Prix de Paris, held every Spring starting in 1863, was a daylong affair that attracted thousands of spectators, as much for the chance to observe the

well-dressed attendees and to witness the new clothing styles that inevitably made their debut as for the high-stakes horse race.

(Brevik-Zender 2009: 19)

The legendary Parisian-based designer, Charles Frederick Worth (1825–1895) and, later, Madeleine Vionnet (1876–1975) and Paul Poiret (1879–1944) identified and exploited the potential of these race meets as high-profile showcases for their most fashionable, and newest, creations. Using (in) famous female muses, including members of Royalty, actresses and courtesans, to model fashionable designs on race day, Longchamp served various interrelated purposes. It engaged a suitably elite physical and cultural backdrop; provided a ready supply of wealthy patrons; and was a favoured site with illustrators and photographers (such as the Seeberger Brothers during the early 1900s), which ensured the wide dissemination of designs via the burgeoning fashion press (see Aubenas and Demange 2007, Rocamora 2009). The fashionable crowds at Longchamp have also formed the subject of fine art – notably Manet's *Races at Longchamp*, 1864 – and of literary texts. Émile Zola's novel *Nana* (1880) offers a compelling and much vaunted account of the eponymous heroine's emboldened sartorial display at the Grand Prix de Paris. As Nana makes her entrance, all attention turns from the actual race (the *game*, in MacAloon's terminology) to the courtesan, who is dressed in a daring, provocative, outfit with an added 'touch of jockey … a jaunty little blue toque with a white feather above her curly blonde hair, which was gathered in the nape of her neck and then allowed to stream down her back like an enormous red horse-tail' (Zola 1880: 311). Zola's characteristic layering of sartorial and social metaphor here suggests an understanding of the racecourse as a site of display – wherein the fashion *festival* and *spectacle* (to invoke, again, the language of sporting frames) may become blurred (Hardy *et al.* 2009).

From Second Empire Paris onwards, the racecourse as a spectacular site of *and because of* fashion is undisputed. However, curiously, few *sustained* academic studies have been made on the many connections between equestrian sport and its fashionably dressed (female) attendees. This chapter begins to redress this oversight and, in so doing, extends the existing discussion to an alternative place and time: that of the United States during the 1930s.

Framing the field of 1930s sportswear: New York versus Paris

Dress historians Mendes and de la Haye (1999: 76) note that the Wall Street Crash of 1929 and the ensuing Depression signalled an 'inauspicious' start to the Thirties. However, the contemporary equestrian and sporting press made only few, and somewhat oblique, references to the wider travails that beset the contemporary American economy. Nor, towards the end of the decade, was any suggestion made of the impending World War. Writing under the *nom de plume* of 'Amory', the female fashion correspondent for *The Sportsman* opened her July 1933 column with the observation that:

> One has only to walk down Fifth Avenue this June to realize that, in spite of gloomy prediction, grass is not growing in our city streets. It is a pleasure to report that I did not see a single lawn mower anywhere this month between Thirty-fourth and Fifty-seventh Streets.
>
> (Amory 1933: 44)

Amory's passage here is, however, an exception. Largely, it appeared that a 'fiction of stability' (Arnold 2002: 46) prevailed in the rarefied circles of equestrian society and its hobbyist press, which omitted discussions of Depression era political-economy from its esoteric concerns. American socialites, so Madgison (2008: 108) suggests, were often 'cushioned' from the financial strife of the 1930s due to factors such as marriage or personal wealth. Certainly the readership (both male and female) of monthly specialist periodicals such as *Spur* and *Polo* magazines was addressed as athletes and sports fans *but also* as consumers with a significant expendable income with which to purchase high-end luxuries and status-bestowing items. Alongside advertisements for technical equipment, sports kit and associated paraphernalia were those for European sailings of the Red and White Star lines, Oldsmobiles and Cadillacs, luxury hotels and apartments in fashionable metropolitan centres.

Importantly for the purposes of this chapter, fashionable female (and, on occasion, male) dress was also featured heavily and extensively across the pages of these sporting titles, and several different media devices (mobilising the frame of spectacle) were employed to accomplish this: the advertisement, the fashion-columnist-cum-style-commentator and the photo montage. Yet, given the recurrence of (spectator) fashion coverage in these sporting titles the paucity of scholarship on its significance is remarkable. Dress historians specialising in 1930s fashion have mined the archives of well-known style publications – for example Arnold's body of work (2002, 2009) on New York fashion in the 1930s and 1940s concentrates on representations in *Vogue* and *Harper's Bazaar* – but have yet to harness the rich and fulsome promise of sports, and especially equestrian, journalism as conduit, mediator and repository of contemporary fashion.

According to Reynolds Milbank (1989: 98) 'the 1930s was the only decade in which a new look was immediately perceptible'. With the abandonment of the vogue for girlish pertness, as personified in the Twenties by the chemise-clad Flapper, the 1930s heralded a decade synonymous with a sleeker, leaner, female body adorned in athletic-inspired clothing known as *sportswear* (see Figure 2.3). This was a novel mode of dress based on smart, yet casual, clothing (separates, dresses and coats) aimed at active, modern, young women.

It is useful to provide a note of explication regarding terminology here as sportswear is an ambiguous term, with several applications. *Active* sportswear,

Figure 2.3 Female spectators in contemporary sportswear at the (Middleburg or Warrenton) Races, Virginia, 1937. Captioned 'Mrs. Wm. Miller – Jim Blackwell – Judy Molton – and etc'.
Source: Webb Archive, National Sporting Library and Museum, Virginia

for example, referred to the very specific outfits required for, and worn during, sporting activities (such as riding habit dress, golfing costume and tennis attire). Sportswear in its permutation as one of the defining fashion statements of the 1930s, on the other hand, drew design influence from the field of often traditional Anglo-British rural pursuits, but met the needs of a contemporary American (sub)urban lifestyle rather than the requirements of actual sporting play. These garments 'emerged directly from the radically simple clothing that was free of linings, understructures, confining fit and unnecessary decoration that sport and athletic activity demanded' (Campbell Warner 2005: 80). Also referred to as 'passive sportswear', 'semi-sports' and 'spectator sports' dress, they (and the wearing of them) engaged desirable, nationalised, discourses of dynamism, vitality, functionalism and adaptability so enabled by their athletic invocations (Arnold 2009: 24). Sportswear, explains Campbell Warner (2005: 95) 'answered the needs of a casual American way of life, of lean athletic bodies and their loose-jointed mannerisms. Sportswear was about practicality and comfort; mass-manufacture and mix-and-match, and menswear was transformed into a feminine form'. Martin (1985: 10), too, underscores the informal essence of sportswear, writing that contemporary American style 'was fundamentally one of recreation'.

The belted cardigan or pullover, worn over a tweedy skirt was widely adopted as a fashionable look (refer to the female dress in Figure 2.3 for illustration). Tweed was, indeed, a popular material in the making of fashionable sportswear and Reynolds Milbank (1989: 83) argues that it was 'all the rage' in spectator dress on both sides of the Atlantic during the 1930s. Durable and practical, it also mobilised aspirational connections to British royalty, being favoured (along with tartans and checks) by the stylish, and increasingly notorious, Duke of Windsor (married in 1937 to American divorcée, Wallis Simpson, herself one of the most influential fashion mannequins of the era). This ensemble not only emphasised the natural trim waist (a departure from the dropped waist of 1920s fashions) but was a versatile design solution, enabling women to adjust the fit of their clothing. Versatility was, indeed, a watchword of 1930s sportswear, not least because of its 'syntax of separates' (Martin 1985: 20). This bestowed American women with a wider range of choice and freedom within their wardrobes as they combined individual garments into an almost limitless array of fashionable outfits.

Modern and progressive, sportswear mobilised the American national character and an inherent sense of American-ness in numerous ways. For example, sportswear was often constructed from technologically innovative synthetic materials such as rayon, artificial silk and a newly invented elastic substance called Lastex, which was woven into wool and other knits. It was also promoted for its easy-care properties and washable fabrics, assisted by the process of Sanforization, an anti-shrinking measure patented in 1930 – all of which were value-adding factors in the busy lifestyle of the contemporary female fashion consumer. These advances placed American sportswear at the leading edge of mass manufacturing. Its simplicity of design called for minimal pattern pieces which followed Taylor-ist principles, producing cheaper garments that made fashion accessible to greater numbers – a fact in itself that was viewed as symptomatic of the American democratic character. Sportswear was, then, a particularly *American Look*, a phrase coined in 1945 by Dorothy Shaver, Vice President of the New York department store Lord and Taylor and prominent member of the Fashion Group, a trade association founded in 1931 (Arnold 2009; Rantisi 2006; Webber-Hanchett 2003).

Crucially, it was a look that was developed, through careful curation by key cultural intermediaries such as Shaver, in marked opposition to the perceived snobberies and stuffiness of its high class rival – the French couture fashion system centred on the city of Paris. Doubtless, throughout the 1930s, Parisian high fashion continued to be acclaimed and reified: 'to be sure' writes Rantisi (2006: 118) 'Paris still had the cachet of world fashion capital'. But the domestic American fashion industry – clustered around sportswear designers such as Claire McCardell, Clare Potter, Jo Copeland, Dorothy Cox, Tina Leser, Vera Maxwell and Elizabeth Hawes – underwent an exceptional period of strategic growth and development. New York emerged as a force in the manufacturing and retailing of domestic design talents so that, by 1930, the wholesale garment trade was the country's fourth major industry and the city's largest (Mendes and de la Haye 1999: 78). Shaver was an instrumental figure, using the merchandising platform of Lord and Taylor on Fifth Avenue to develop a seminal in-store campaign of April 1932 titled *American Fashion for American Women*. Perhaps somewhat surprisingly, then, it was against a backdrop of Depression-era austerity that fashionable sportswear flourished. Parisian originals became expensive to import and to purchase, and therefore the American fashion industry was forced to become more self-reliant, de-coupling both trade and creative dependency from the long held influence of France. As Scheips (2007: 37) observes 'the grim economic truths of 1930s America ... afforded designers an unexpected benefit – a great demand for domestic clothing'.

The style stakes: spectacular sportswear on show

The shirt-dress was one such item of sportswear that became recognised as a symbol of the transformation in American women's dress during the 1930s. 'As a straightforward dress, simple in line and design, it became a basic of American women's wardrobes' (Campbell Warner 2005: 95; for an extended discussion of the design provenance, gender politics and social history of the shirt-dress see Campbell Warner 2005). Equestrian events offered an ideal venue for the wearing and display of the latest seasonal fashions. Analysis of the Gerald B. Webb Jr. scrapbook collection – and a notable clutch of photographs within it – shows *Society* at the National Cup Steeplechase (Fair Hill, Maryland). These images, attributed to 1938 or 1939, confirm that the sporty yet stylish shirt-dress prevailed among the smart set in attendance (see Figures 2.4 and 2.5). Allowing ease of movement around the rambling precinct of the racetrack, it was well suited to the outdoorsy setting and offered its wearer comfort, practicality *and* fashion credence. The shirt-dress combined function with fashion, making it an ideal garment for a day at the races. Functionality was indeed an important property in equestrian spectator dress. Foxhunting, for example, was part of the winter sporting calendar and took place in the bitter cold, and even snow, with little regard for the comfort of onlookers (indeed, hunting may not be regarded as a spectator sport *per se*). The demands of the physical environment required spectators to take care in clothing selection, and functional adaptations were made, or conceded, to accommodate the landscape (such as slip-on overshoes and steamer rugs to guard against the mud and chill respectively). It was, it seems, necessary for the spectator to anticipate all manner of climatic and physical conditions and to adapt their dress accordingly. A *Boston Evening Transcript* (13 June 1933) report of racing from Brookline, Massachusetts, offers the following vignette:

> ... even a sudden heavy shower couldn't drive them [the spectators] away. They merely raised their umbrellas, as Mrs Winthrop Pyemont did, shielding her brown straw with the red feather or donned raincoats like Mrs George S West who also changed her brimmed hat matching a pink wool suit, to a more serviceable brown ... Mrs Bird was costumed for any weather. Her high boots were perfect for the wet grass: she wore a brimmed white pique hat, a beige sweater, which kept the rain off and

Figure 2.4 'Society at the National Cup Steeplechase', dated as 1938 or 1939. Mrs Morris H. Dixon (centre) pictured with Mrs William Griscom Coxe (left) and Mrs William du Pont Jr. (right) wears fashionable Thirties attire from head to toe. This comprises distinctive hat, shirt-dress and two-tone 'spectator' shoes (known as co-respondents in the UK), a vogue in footwear 'undoubtedly boosted by their association with Fred Astaire' (Mendes and de la Haye 1999: 90).

Source: Webb Archive, National Sporting Library and Museum, Virginia

could easily be removed, leaving a brown gingham dress in case the sun came out. She brought her 'sit-stick', prepared for a long stay.

No discussion of female race-goers would be complete without mention of headgear, hats and millinery. In the 1930s, of course, it remained customary for women to don a hat for outdoor wear (in the multiple interests of propriety, protection and aesthetics). However, the racecourse offered a heightened opportunity for the exhibition of high fashion styles and statement pieces. Headgear for women was diverse during the era and by the mid-1930s, surrealist affectations, pioneered in the artistic design work of couturier Elsa Schiaparelli (1890–1973), blazed a trail. Referring, again, to Figure 2.4, Mrs Dixon's distinctive cap is at the apex of contemporary spectator fashion (a number of photographs lodged in the Webb archive show female spectators at the same event in Fair Hill, and also at the Rolling Rock races of 1938/9 in Ligonier, Pennsylvania, sporting almost identical styles). Although the actual provenance of Dixon's cap is unknown, its impish styling is reminiscent of

Figure 2.5 Miss Wilhemine S. Kirby as she attended the National Cup Steeplechase, Fair Hill, MD, c. 1938/9. Miss Kirby wears shirt-dress and a platter-type beret.

Source: Webb Archive, National Sporting Library and Museum, Virginia

Schiaparelli's Mad Cap concept and her customarily witty designs such as the *Napoleon* tri-corn (Evans 1998). The *Robin Hood* style of the hat does, however, lend itself readily to another, filmic, interpretation and channels the dashing figure of Errol Flynn in his swashbuckling performance as the hero in the 1938 hit *The Adventures of Robin Hood*. There is a suggestion, then, of Hollywood's impact on trends and micro-trends in fashionable accessories of the period, as evidenced in the spectacular spaces of the steeplechase event.

As Schieps puts it (2007: 41) the 'silver screen' and its glamorous movie celebrities 'could sell clothes'. And the dramaturgical metaphor may be extended here with the race course posited as a stage in the life-as-theatre performance of identity and dress.

In Figure 2.5, Wilhemine Kirby is snapped wearing an equally popular 1930s style of hat: a round, saucer-like beret, perched at a rakish, and fashionably asymmetrical, angle. Although widely adopted by 1930s spectators as a modish flourish, these angled caps were neither always well-executed nor well-received. Reporting in *Polo* from the Paris races during the Grande Semaine of 1931, 'Parasite' (the pseudonym used by American sportswear designer and sometime journalist/author, Elizabeth Hawes) forwarded the following pithy critique:

> Most people want to be dignified, or impressive in some way, and one can't possibly be impressive with a small, round felt platter held to the side of one's head by a velvet ribbon. These hats, which are doubtless in America by now, are a fad, but surely not a fashion. Women really have to enjoy wearing anything which becomes a fashion, and women can't enjoy having their usually-not-too-beautiful faces openly exposed to the public gaze.
>
> (Parasite 1931: 61)

Parasite's acerbic observations invoke, once more, the notion of the sporting frame and offer an historical case of the journalistic influence in constructing the spectacle. What was worn, and who wore it, was scrutinised by other attendees but also by a burgeoning fashion press that stood in (often harsh) judgement on the winners and losers of the style stakes at a particular event. This process of looking and being looked at was also harnessed for commercial effect and used to sell consumer products in the pages of equestrian periodicals. In some knowing advertising copy for (none other than) Elizabeth Hawes' made-to-measure dresses in *Polo* (1931: 39) the marketing play on peer surveillance was fully apparent. 'Who goes to a horse race to see horses?' went the strapline, '... the majority of women who attend horse races are really smart. Ninety-nine percent of the time spent at any race is consumed looking at them.' Fashionable female spectators were ambiguously positioned at, and within, equestrian activity, as both subject and object of the gaze: complicit in this sense with Melchior-Bonnet's (2002: 145) 'self dialogue with itself' and simultaneously 'confirmation of the gaze of others'.

Contemporary advances in print media also played a significant role in recruiting the gaze. Grundberg (1989: 17) explains that the 1930s were a time of 'increasing ease, economy and sophistication in printing, and the development of better halftone reproduction technology fuelled the demand for images of all sorts'. The increasing portability of handheld cameras enabled photographers (both professional and amateur) to capture fleeting moments and action shots with greater ease and effect (Arnold 2009). Equestrian publications certainly made extensive use of photo montage as part of these emerging documentary techniques, using this as a vehicle through which to record horse-related events and, importantly, the people at them (as seen, for example, in *Polo*, *Spur* and *The Sportsman*, throughout the 1930s). This point, to do with the mediation of spectator dress by multiple authors and audiences, is made particularly manifest in the chinagraph pencil markings – imposed by a contemporary professional editor, perhaps Gerald B. Webb Jr. himself – that are inflected across the image of Wilhemine Kirby at Fair Hill (Figure 2.5). The *marking up* of this photograph for publication betrays both substantive and conceptual processes of image construction and of social framing. Style arbiters and/or those with cultural and social capital were sanctioned and appointed in the stroke of a pencil, their mediated images disseminated to a critical readership as 'part of a wider revolution in visual consciousness' (Grundberg 1989: 117).

Conclusion

The foregoing discussion makes a case for the potency of the relationship between fashion, females and equestrian sporting events in the United States during the 1930s. The outfits worn at horse trials and race meets by such fashionable characters as Boopie Jenkins, Mrs Morris Dixon and Miss Wilhemine Kirby provide rich narratives on the lifestyle and mores of contemporary American Society. Theirs was a changing wardrobe, fit for a modern existence, and one in which taste, dress and behaviour were agents in a socially charged sporting frame. Required to maintain a balance between the sometimes conflicting needs of decorum, decoration, practicality and fashionability, these women were skilled in the art of dressing for spectatorship. The management of the female body – how it was dressed, groomed and appeared – when displayed in these public spaces came under intense scrutiny, instruction and framing. The power of press surveillance, be it through words or pictures, made its own particular new demands, as did the growing consumer culture of the period that played, and preyed, on fashions for svelte, toned, youthful and athletic bodies on which to display the most current trends in sportswear. If, as Entwistle (2000: 73) puts it, 'the modern individual is one who is aware of being read by his or her appearance', the contemporary female spectator, adorned in her modish mix-and-match separates, was subject and object of that reading: a multi-dimensional character inhabiting a mix of social identities and athletic roles. The equestrian field of sport as a site of 1930s fashionable sportswear offers ripe opportunities as a scholarly repository for the dress historian. But, importantly, the study of sportswear as worn, performed and consumed at, and for, these equestrian events also mobilises a broader history of American industry, politics and economy – a history charged with stories of trans-Atlantic rivalry, of national austerity and Depression, of a Made-in-America patriotic project and of a design revolution that crystallised the American Look.

Acknowledgements

The Gerald B. Webb Jr. archive (accession number: MC 0010) is held at the National Sporting Library and Museum (NSLM), Middleburg, Virginia and comprises some sixteen scrapbooks of photographs, many published in Webb's journal *The Chronicle of the Horse*. Dating from between 1935 and 1961 (post-dating Webb's death in 1947), the bulk of photographs are from 1937 to 1941. Subjects are mainly, but not exclusively, confined to the Virginian countryside around Middleburg and include hunts, horse shows, steeplechase and point-to-point races as well as individual portraits of owners, trainers, jockeys and spectators. Much of the research for this chapter was undertaken at the NSLM under the auspices of its annual John H. Daniels Fellowship programme (January–April 2011). I extend my thanks and appreciation here to the fellowship committee and NSLM staff for their enthusiastic and generous support of my work.

References

Amory (1933) 'The Sportswoman observes', *The Sportsman*, July: 44.

Arnold, R. (2002) 'Looking American: Louise Dahl-Wolfe's fashion photographs of the 1930s and 1940s', *Fashion Theory: The Journal of Dress, Body and Culture*, 6(1): 45–60.

Arnold, R. (2009) *The American Look: Fashion, Sportswear and the Image of Women in 1930s and 1940s New York*, London: IB Tauris.

Aubenas, S. and X. Demange (2007) *Elegance: The Seeberger Brothers and the Birth of Fashion Photography*, San Francisco: Chronicle Books.

Bolton, A. (2004) 'The lion's share', in A. Bolton (ed.), *Wild: Fashion Untamed*, New York: Metropolitan Museum of Art, (pp.42–79).

Boston Evening Transcript (1933) 'Society goes country club', 13 June.

Brevik-Zender, H. (2009) 'Tracking fashions: risking it all at the Hippodrome de Longchamp', in J. Potvin (ed.), *The Places and Spaces of Fashion, 1800–2007*, London: Routledge, (pp.19–33).

Campbell Warner, P. (2005) 'The Americanization of fashion: sportswear, the movies and the 1930s', in L. Welters and P. Cunningham (eds), *Twentieth-Century American Fashion*, Oxford: Berg, (pp. 79–98).

Crane, D. (2000) *Fashion and Its Social Agendas: Class, Gender and Identity in Clothing*, Chicago: Chicago University Press.

Dant, T. (1999) *Material Culture in the Social World*, Buckingham: Open University Press.

Entwistle, J. (2000) *The Fashioned Body: Fashion, Dress and Modern Social Theory*, Cambridge: Polity.

Evans, E. (1998) 'Schiaparelli – humour and surrealism', in N. Cawthorne, E. Evans, M. Kitchen-Smith, K. Mulvey and M. Richards, *Key Moments in Fashion: The Evolution of Style*, London: Hamlyn, (pp. 74–83).

Fox, K. (2005) *The Racing Tribe: Portrait of a British Subculture*, New Jersey: Transaction Publishers.

Goffman, E. (1961) *Asylums*, New York: Anchor.

Goodrum, A. (2012) 'A severity of plainness: the culture of female riding dress in America during the 1920s and 1930s', *Annals of Leisure Research*, 15(1): 87–105.

Grundberg, A. (1989) *Brodovitch: Master of American Design*, New York: Harry Abrams.

Hardy, S., J. Loy and D. Booth (2009) 'The material culture of sport: toward a typology', *Journal of Sport History*, 36(1): 129–152.

MacAloon, J. (1984) 'Olympic Games and the theory of spectacle in modern societies', in J. MacAloon (ed.), *Rite, Drama, Festival, Spectacle: Rehearsals Toward a Theory of Cultural Performance*, Philadelphia, PA: Institute for the Study of Human Issues, (pp. 241–280).

Magidson, P. (2008) 'Fashion showdown: New York versus Paris 1914–1941', in D. Albrecht (ed.), *Paris/New York: Design/Fashion/Culture/1925–1940*, New York: Monacelli Press, (pp. 102–127).

Martin, R. (1985) *All-American: A Sportswear Tradition*, New York: Fashion Institute of Technology.

Matthews David, A. (2002) 'Elegant amazons: Victorian riding habits and the fashionable horsewoman', *Victorian Literature and Culture*, 30(1): 179–210.

Mauss, M. (1973) 'Techniques of the body', *Economy and Society*, 2(1): 179–210.

Melchior-Bonnet, S. (2002) *The Mirror: A History*, London: Routledge.

Mendes, V. and A. de la Haye (1999) *20th Century Fashion*, London: Thames & Hudson.

Parasite (1931) 'Horses and hats: A few notes gathered in Paris during the Grande Semaine', *Polo*, September: 61.

Polo (1931) 'Who goes to a horse race to see horses?' Elizabeth Hawes advertisement, July: 39.

Rantisi, N. (2006) 'How New York stole modern fashion', in C. Breward and D. Gilbert (eds), *Fashion's Worlds Cities*, Oxford: Berg (pp. 109–122).

Reynolds Milbank, C. (1989) *New York Fashion: The Evolution of American Style*, New York: Harry N. Abrams.

Rocamora, A. (2009) *Fashioning the City: Paris, Fashion and the Media*, London: IB Tauris.

Scheips, C. (2007) '1929/1938 dramatic beginnings: Hollywood and New York designers bring luxury and sport to Depression-era America', in *Council of Fashion Designers of America American Fashion*, New York: Assouline, (pp. 34–63).

Shedden, D. and V. Apsley (1932) *To Whom the Goddess: Hunting and Riding for Women*, London: Hutchison.

Sherwood, J. (2011) *Fashion at Royal Ascot: Three Centuries of Thoroughbred Style*, London: Thames & Hudson.

Spur (1930) 'Altman fur and sportswear', advertisement, September: 19.

Spur (1931) 'A double chin marks the surrender of youth', Dorothy Gray advertisement. February: 77.

Taylor, L. (2002) *The Study of Dress History*, Manchester: Manchester University Press.

Webber-Hanchett, T. (2003) 'Dorothy Shaver: promoter of the American Look', *Dress*, 30: 83–87.

Zola, E. (1880) *Nana*, Oxford: Oxford World's Classics, 2009 edn.

3 Glamorous intersection

Ralph Lauren's classic cars at the Musée, and the fashioning of automotive style

Gary Best

Style is very personal. It has nothing to do with fashion. Fashion is over very
quickly. Style is forever.

Ralph Lauren
(http://global.ralphlauren.com/worldofralphlauren/au#/history/about)

Fashion, style, art, and cars – exemplars of each have earned iconic status, and
endure as the ultimate expressions of chic. Ralph Lauren's observation above,
however, proposes a critical distinction between fashion and style. While
there is, and has always been, a symbiosis between the two phenomena, style
transcends the frequent changes that both inform and characterize fashion.
Style, however, began as fashion but has endured, outlasting fads and annual
changes because of elements that struck an aesthetic chord and still resonate
across the seasons and the decades. Style in the wider automotive domain,
however, may endure, but, like fashion, may also be celebrated only for a
year or three, then relegated, ignominiously, to the used-car lot or junkyard.
Fashion, according to Robinson, is merely 'the pursuit of novelty for its
own sake' (1958: 127), a view many fashionistas would argue; style, as a
counterpoint, is timeless, and occupies an eternal, elegant pantheon.

Museums and motoring

In 2011, the Musée des Arts Décoratifs, Paris – just such a pantheon – bought
fashion, style, and cars together in one event. *The Art of the Automobile:
Masterpieces from the Ralph Lauren Collection* displayed seventeen of his
classic cars (from his collection of sixty) in a gallery with soaring ceilings
where cars on plinths became art in every sense (Figure 3.1). Diffused lighting,
muted excitement generated by proximity to automotive icons from 1929 to
1996 resulted in an event that fulfilled the Musée's charter of 'the beautiful
in the useful'. The fundamental utility of the vehicles was indisputable but in
each instance historical and cultural resonance combined, creating an aura
not unlike that of religious relics; in the Musée, from April to August of 2011,
these icons were venerated.

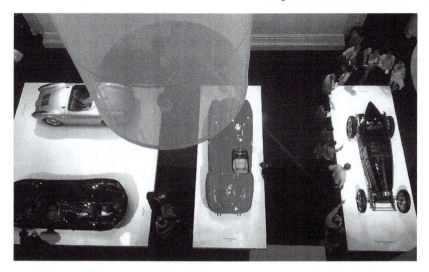

Figure 3.1 The art of the automobile: masterpieces from the Ralph Lauren Collection.

Source: G. Best

Reverence and veneration are, indeed, particularly focused responses but not exclusive to religious contexts or settings. Encountering an acknowledged masterpiece for the first time is thrilling for the acolyte, and while there is truth in the adage that 'beauty is in the eye of the beholder' such beauty can take many forms. This leads, inevitably, to the issue of why these cars are in a museum with decorative arts as its focus or, for that matter, in any museum.

The obvious corollary is that cars have been exhibited for public delectation, male and female, almost since their inception. Automotive displays have attracted crowds since the 1898 Automobile Club of France and Chicago shows, followed in 1900 by the first National Auto Show in New York City (Georgano 1992: 19). Similarly, an automobile museum for early vehicles and historical printed material was proposed for London in 1902, and November, 1906 saw a parade of pre-1901 vehicles in Paris, all indicative of an early consciousness acknowledging the value of collecting and curating what was then the 'motor-car' (Jeremiah 1998: 93). Museum displays and growing public interest in attending what were to become an annual event – *the motor show* – highlight the enthusiasm of an embryonic motoring public keen to experience new designs, styles, and fashions. While gender assumptions here may privilege the male, women had attended the early shows and actively participated in the new automania. 1899 saw the first US driver's license issued to a Chicago woman, and women in society clubs driving decorated cars in a Newport, RI parade (McShane 1997: 26). In 1909, Alice Ramsey, with three female companions, became the first woman to drive across the USA (Nelson 2009: 4, 60–70).

The history of very early twentieth century motor shows reveals a fore-grounding of the latest models and developments, and startling visions of *future* styles in increasingly glamorous locations on an annual basis. Apart from increasing the scale and range of highlights, the motor show as a ded-icated, targeted event has operated largely unchanged for more than a cen-tury. In contrast, museums, without the perceived beneficial ritual of annual updates, face having to regularly develop new strategies that reconfigure exist-ing collections to offer new perspectives, as well as presenting themed block-busters to attract new visitors.

Having cars as the sole focus of museum exhibitions (other than in dedi-cated automotive museums) is not a new phenomenon. In autumn 1951, New York City's Museum of Modern Art (MoMA) offered *8 Automobiles*, the 'first exhibition anywhere dealing with the aesthetics of automobile design' (MoMA 1951: 1), and has since organized eight further automotive exhibi-tions, with six cars now in its permanent collection. In 1970, the Musée des Arts Décoratifs, Paris, presented a selection of competition cars in *Bolide Design*. A jury of designers and artists selected models inspired by the concept of the car as a design object and a work of art, showing that 'art and tech-nique ... are the expression of man and his relationship with design' (www.automuseums.info). Los Angeles' Museum of Contemporary Art opened in 1984 with *Automobile and Culture*, a show devoted to the reality that 'living in a thoroughly motorized society has an impact upon the way that Southern California artists and their local patrons experience the world' (Finch 1992: 361–362).

The first museum show of twenty-nine cars from Ralph Lauren's automo-bile collection was at Boston's Museum of Fine Arts (MFA) in *Speed, Style, and Beauty: Cars from the Ralph Lauren Collection* March 6 to July 3, 2005. In the preface to the exhibition's book, Darcy Kuronen of the MFA writes:

> Rather than create a collection in a systematic way, Mr. Lauren has taken a more individual approach, acquiring particular cars that appeal to his personal sense of aesthetics, much as would any other private collector of fine art. Consequently, the shape and contents of his collection are very much the result of his own keen perception of style and form.
>
> (MFA 2005: ix)

The exhibition's title offers key Lauren indicators of style and beauty, just as Kuronen associates Lauren with aesthetics, fine art, and style and form. It is apparent that these cars (they become *automobiles* seven years later in Paris) are to be taken very seriously.

From March to June, 2010, Atlanta's High Museum of Art, Georgia, showed *The Allure of the Automobile: Driving in Style, 1930–1965* with eigh-teen classic cars, which then moved to the Portland Art Museum, Oregon, from June 11 to September 11, 2011. Michael Shapiro, Director of the High Museum of Art, writes of the exhibited cars: 'Created for the privileged few, these luxurious, custom-built automobiles embodied speed, style, and elegance, exerting influence on art, fashion, and design' (Gross and Labaco 2010: 9). Again the value-laden indicators are cited in yet another celebratory paen to the (now) automobiles – their style and elegance influencing art, fashion, and design past, present, and future. As symbols of power, wealth, and prestige in times of global hardship, the 'luxurious, custom-built automobiles' were revered by owners and aficionados apparently without irony.

Diverse, ironic perspectives on automobilia are evident in the pop-cultural works of Andy Warhol (1928–1987), ranging from advertising sketches of the 1950s to the multi-hued screen printed car crash photographs beginning in 1962, and perhaps culminating in his painting of an actual BMW M1 Art Race Car in 1979. More than thirty years later, in 2012, The Andy Warhol Museum, Pittsburgh, mounted the exhibition *Warhol and Cars: American Icons* that explored the iconic qualities of both artist and subject. A 1966 quote attributed to Warhol offers a modest explanation for his art as well as conveniently identifying a nexus between art and fashion: 'I just paint those objects in my paintings because those are the things I know best ... I've heard it said that my paintings are as much a part of the fashionable world as clothes and cars' (quoted in Bunyan 2012). Warhol's reference to clothes and cars being elements of 'the fashionable world' draws attention to the schism evident when Lauren dismisses the short shelf-life of fashion and applauds the enduring rewards of style. Despite his assertion that fashion is over very quickly, the reality is that particular fashions and styles experience revivals often aligned with a *retro* sensibility, such as Volkswagen's New Beetle, recently reinvented as just the Beetle, and BMW's 'new' Mini in all its permutations.

Fashion, style, and automobile *classics* endure, with dedicated events continuing to both consolidate their status among the cognoscenti, and engage the neophytes encountering, for the first time, the icons in the fabric, paint, or metal.

Learning from Lauren – oeuvre, ethos, and a car collection to die for

> For almost four decades, Lauren ... has been more than a fashion designer; he has been a canny reformulator of Wasp finery ... So when his designs quote from the past, it's always in the lyrical mode. His tropics are never sweaty. His American West has got the once over with a feather duster. And millions love him for it. Because Lauren has summoned them to a past that was never theirs.
>
> (Lacayo 2006: 140)

Ralph Lauren's carefully constructed advertising vision is that of an imagined world of old money and chic sensibility, exemplified by elegant mannequins languidly populating ancestral estates; think here of Mrs. Kennedy and her Oleg Cassini neo-classicism, all country club and Park Avenue. Yet the seventeen cars on display at the Musée had different characteristics in common that at first may appear to counterpoint Lauren's informing design spirit.

Curator Rapetti noted two critical characteristics shared by all the cars – their capacity for speed, and the small number of automotive brands (Meagher 2011: 82). Competition, speed, and classic status combined to offer a 1929 Bentley Blower; a 1955 Porsche 550 Spyder; a 1996 McLaren F1 LM; two Bugattis – the 1933 59 Grand Prix and the breathtaking 1938 57 (C) Atlantic; two Alfa Romeos – the 1931 8C 2300 Monza and the 1938 8C 2900 Mille Miglia; two Mercedes-Benz – the extraordinary 1930 SSK 'Count Trossi' and the 1955 300 SL 'Gullwing'; three Jaguars – the 1950 XK 120 Roadster, the 1955 XKD, and the 1958 XKSS; and four Ferraris – the 1954 375 Plus, the 1958 250 Testa Rossa, the 1962 250 GTO, and the 1964 250 LM.

These, then, are some of competitive racing's grand tourers and supermodels, fêted, adored, worshipped, and still lusted after. The brands have resonated internationally since the end of the 1920s. Records and reputations were earned through fast, furious racing on the legendary *Grands Prix* circuits but no vestige of speed, hot metal, or burning rubber remained; each car was flawless, the only patina that of Laurenesque perfection. One significant aspect of the exhibition's *reality* was the politics of presenting an immaculate past; what, exactly, does any given visitor want and/or expect to see? Would period mud, worn tyres, dented bodywork, and split leather create a more convincing verisimilitude? The Ralph Lauren milieu, as evidenced by advertising campaigns and the condition of these seventeen classics on display, would seem to necessitate a very particular lens through which the past can be observed, imagined, and experienced – no trace of hardship or challenge is permitted to blemish that which has both endured and, more importantly, succeeded.

The fact that all eight legendary brand names continue to be manufactured is a telling indicator of not only demand for expensive and, perhaps more importantly, exclusive automotive experiences but also the powerful and resonant historical cachet that such ownership both connotes and imparts. The dynastic families of many of the original companies may have long since vanished but the brands continue to grow and diversify. The legends, both real and constructed, are skillfully sustained through sponsorship and selected multi-media advertising, ensuring that via ownership and aspiration, carefully targeted messages of style, elegance, and exclusivity are always being communicated.

One significant characteristic of this rarefied sector of the automobile world is that throughout their history, most of these marques, and certainly those in the Lauren exhibition, did not offer an annual new model. Consistent with the craftsmanship involved in their production, these marques were only updated when new features and mechanicals improved the overall quality, performance, and style of the vehicle. It should be noted, however, that current notions of fashion were often an influence, particularly regarding exterior coachwork (an endearing anachronism for styling) and interior fittings.

Rolls-Royce, from 1907 until 1939, only built a rolling chassis which was then delivered to a specified coachbuilder: 'In theory, a customer could specify whichever body style and whatever coachbuilder he desired, although Rolls-Royce usually made their own preferences, and their opinions of a chosen style, discreetly but definitely clear from the outset' (Robson 2000: 11). While Roll-Royce has for decades offered a range of vehicles in standard specification, the client can always choose a bespoke approach to personalizing their chosen motorcar, essentially perpetuating the coach-built experience of yore.

Prestige manufacturers displayed at major annual national and international motor shows but without all-new models each year. Incremental changes and improvements were made but belied annual changes decreed by the likes of Alfred P. Sloan, Jr., of General Motors (GM) who believed the primary function of the annual model change was: 'to create demand for the new value and ... create a certain amount of dissatisfaction with past models as compared to the new one' (Pettifer and Turner 1984: 13; see also Sloan 1965: 261–270). Further, Packard cites articles in two 1934 issues of the *Journal of the Society of Automotive Engineers* stressing the 'desirability of building automobiles with a limited life' and that 'parts ... might be designed for "controllable wear" as well as imperceptible wear' (1960: 64). Packard had earlier explored the advertising drama of what he termed 'The Upgrading Urge', by then an entrenched phenomenon, the roots of which are directly traceable to Sloan's mid-1920s machinations.

Despite the two major international upheavals of the Depression and World War II, the American automotive industry had basically taken the form by the late 1920s that would endure largely unchanged until the end of that century. While the critical element of GM's organizational strategy was the annual model change, the socio-cultural imperative was solely aspirational – if not buying a brand new car, then at least a newer car, all the while ensuring regular progression up Detroit's artfully constructed status hierarchy. Writing on fashion, Kawamura notes that: 'No matter which time period ... one is talking about, the definite essence of fashion is change' (2005: 5) and also proposes that: 'the newness which is the essence of fashion is the typical condition of modernity and post-modernity' (2005: 25). The automobile continues to be an exemplar of the modern and post-modern experience, with society embracing the latest, then abandoning it for the newer model, the process being adapted in both socio and economic terms to covertly underpin planned obsolescence.

Bigger, brighter, and better: meet me at the motor show

Success in any industry is contextual, conditional, relative, and usually very specific, depending on delivering on the promise; it is not, however, always sustainable. Two excellent examples of such a cycle brought to vivid, successful life in twentieth century USA were Hollywood and the American motor industry. Each produced distinctive and enduring commodities that, annually, exemplified the latest, newest, most fashionable, most stylish, most desirable and most glamorous movies and cars, must-sees and must-haves. Of the two, the annual trend of new car releases in October of next year's models became one of the most anticipated of American socio-cultural rituals, enduring still but in a diminished form. US manufacturers, as well as most others internationally, are unable – not to mention disinclined – to bear the costs of major annual changes; global economic impacts have also profoundly compromised mass-market consumer spending.

Annual motor shows became an institutionalized mainstay of both the automotive industry and the car-buying public, particularly in twentieth century America, with Los Angeles, New York City, and Chicago as well as many other cities hosting annual events that became self-proclaimed extravaganzas.

Chicago first exhibited cars in late 1898, with a larger show the next year offering driving demonstrations. The first Chicago Automobile Show ran March 23–30, 1901 with a reported sixty-five firms displaying vehicles that visitors could ride in. By 1905 the show had a reputation for elaborate themed decorations – 'nature' in 1906, an English garden in 1910, classical antiquity in 1913, and an English cathedral in 1917 with an opening day crowd of 40,000 (Flammang and Frumkin 1998: 42, 47, 50, 52, 54, 58). Attending the show:

> was an all-out event, one that warranted dressing for the occasion. Men were likely to wear suits, ties and hats; women dressed in their most stylish attire … Even in the 1950s … it was common for families to visit the auto show garbed as if they were attending a wedding or ceremony. This was a family-focused occasion and looking 'proper' was part of the preparation.
>
> (Flammang and Frumkin 1998: 6)

Here, then, is another glamorous intersection, with 'dressing for the occasion' being an individual and familial socio-cultural obligation, the black leather of contemporaneous teenage rebels without a cause notwithstanding. Shifting trends in what was considered, as opposed to what actually constituted, 'proper' motor show hostess/model attire would also shift from the Chicago neighborhood and community 'beauty queens' in gowns and sashes to two naked young women draped over an aptly named TVR Vixen at the London Motor Show of 1971 at Earls Court (Cardew 1971: 48; Pettifer and Turner 1984: 163). China's August 2012 Chengdu Motor Show similarly had young women wearing only adhesive ornaments pasted strategically on their bodies (Campbell 2012), perhaps further perpetuating the cyclical nature of motor show fashion but only briefly, as they were quickly ushered off the stand by vigilant motor show authorities.

The informing spirit of the motor show has always been the thrill of beholding the newest (or nudest), the latest, the most innovative, and the most exciting. The challenge, of course, is when the offerings are not new but still have to face intense consumer scrutiny – enter the *facelift* that has freshened last year's model with new colours, interior trims and features. Here, once again, the American shows were the exemplars of such smoke and mirrors, thereby meeting customers expecting 'new all over again'. Sloan offers a lengthy explanation of, and justification for, the annual model change from the manufacturer's perspective, the essence of which is: 'Since its earliest days, long before the expression "annual model" was used, the process of creating new models has generated the progress of automobiles' (Sloan 1965: 270). There is, of course, so much more to the dynamic that Sloan avoids, particularly as the developments that constitute 'progress' do not necessarily occur on an annual basis. In the parallel world of fashion, the 'mass market was driving the production of a number of different lines of goods, based on a fashion theme, and directed towards particular market shares' (Craik 1994: 212), the obvious link being the identical economic and manufacturing strategies of automobile and fashion producers alike.

The conditioning created by American car manufacturers, advertising agencies, and sales teams coalesced into a national mindset that not only understood the status benefits accruing from an annual update of the family car but also that ownership of particular models in each manufacturer's clearly delineated vertical hierarchy contributed to perceptions by others of an individual's prestige and overall success. Cadillac, Lincoln, and Imperial were marketed as the swankiest US models for GM, Ford, and Chrysler respectively, as well as being ranked similarly in sales. Advertising for each of the three took status, as well as the trappings of success and the latest fashions and styles, very seriously indeed.

Fantasy, fins, and *la femme*

The 1902 Cadillac was the first sold, then marketed as the 'Standard of the World' from 1903 (Van Bogart 2003: 12). For most years from 1949 to 1962, each Cadillac advertisement featured one car against a luxurious fabric background (brocades, velvets, and embroidery) or Cadillac-appropriate scenery (embassy party, nightclub, the opera, and famous hotels) with the sometimes bejeweled Cadillac crest centered, and underneath a similarly jeweled necklace in a V shape echoing the bonnet emblem, both always positioned above the car. Jewelers were acknowledged, with regulars Harry Winston, Van Cleef & Arpels, and Cartier. Soothing copy informed that Cadillac is 'More Eloquent than Words', 'Worth its Price in Prestige', and 'Magnificent Beyond all Expectations'. Needless to say, 'Everybody served Cadillac aristocrats. They always wore formal evening wear and were waited on at five star restaurants' (Dregni and Miller 1996: 33).

Cadillac's fantasy realm has probably been the most sustained in automotive advertising history, consolidated by high profile owners, socialites, legitimate (and otherwise) business operators, and regular movie and TV appearances. Cadillac's most significant and instantly recognizable styling feature from 1948 until 1964 was fins on the rear fenders, modest bumps in 1948 that by 1959 had reached their soaring apotheosis; Marling notes that the '59 Cadillac tail fin had 'acquired a life of its own: it towered three and one-half feet above the pavement' (1994: 141). Robinson's engaging fashion analogy is: 'The tail fin – supposedly derived from the airplane tail – may be interpreted as the last resort of over-extension, an outcropping that quite seriously serves much the same purpose as the bustle or the train' (1958: 136), adding few Detroit designers were prepared to confirm the claim that fins stabilized moving cars in cross-winds, although Chrysler's Maury Baldwin asserted that: 'Wind tunnel tests proved conclusively that they added to stability over 60–70mph' (Langworth and Norbye 1985: 165). Such tests notwithstanding, after 1959, an annual reduction of the Cadillac tail fin began, ending in the final shaved-off vestiges of 1964; Cadillac's fashion of fins was finished. In 'Behavioral Science Theories of Fashion' (1985), Sproles proposes his 'Conceptual Framework for a General Fashion Theory'. This model further informs 'new styles' of clothing, their dissemination by fashion leaders resulting in broader acceptance among fashion-conscious consumers creating social visibility for the style, followed by social saturation, and eventually decline and termination (65–67); once again, the rise and decline of fashion styles echoes those of the automotive domain, and vice versa.

Throughout the 1950s, all Big Three cars became lower, longer, and wider, thereby creating a new range of challenges for consumers and cities alike. Evoking the long, low look of ranch houses, Walter M. Schmidt, executive stylist of the Chrysler Corporation asserted that: 'To fit into its surroundings gracefully, the automobile also must have a contemporary appearance' (quoted in Robinson 1958: 135). The 'contemporary appearance' of 1958 cars continued the lower, longer, and wider approach with Packard emphasizing that: 'The sight line of drivers has dropped nine inches below the sight line of pre-war autos' (1960: 85) and at GM's annual meeting of shareholders in July, 1959: 'An average-sized man from Massachusetts exclaimed that he couldn't sit in a 1959 Buick with his hat on. And he added: "It's a disgrace for a woman to have to get in and out of such low cars"' (1960: 86). Among other sins, Detroit designers were also compromising polite societal practices, according to Chrysler's President K.T. Keller who back in 1948 pronounced: 'Many of you … may have outgrown the habit, but there are parts of the country containing millions of people, where both men and the ladies are in the habit of getting behind the wheel, or in the back seat, wearing hats' (quoted in Langworth and Norbye 1985: 138). Keller's insistence on headwear-friendly, boxy, functional designs lasted into the early 1950s but Chrysler trumped the burgeoning fin market with 'The Forward Look' of its 1957 range, a design imperative that had completely disappeared at Chrysler five years later. By 1959, DeSoto had swivel seats, with grateful advertising announcing: 'Bless DeSoto for making seats that let you step out like a lady!'

One final, fabulous targeted special event for the ladies: 'By Appointment to Her Majesty, the American Woman: La Femme by Dodge'. In 1955 and

1956, Dodge offered the 'La Femme' trim package on its Custom Royal Lancer. A Heather Rose and Sapphire White two tone exterior was matched to rosebud cloth fabric and white vinyl bolsters. The La Femme came with special seat back pouches with room for the supplied rain-bonnet and pink calf-skin purse (handbag) with compact, cigarette case and lighter, lipstick case, and change purse, all by 'Evans' of Chicago. The 1956 was even more femme in Misty Orchid and Regal Orchid, with seats in Orchid Jacquard with Gold Cordahyde bolsters, as well as specially designed rain gear only, all on pink and burgundy woven carpet.

The La Femme brochure, a cheap, three colour fold-out, did not suggest Dodge considered it to be 'America's most glamorous Car – Designed with the ladies in mind!' Profits were probably more in mind, given the design was superficial feminine appliqué, so the 'La Femme' was only a Dodge Custom Royal Lancer in drag, despite *Popular Mechanics* being sure: 'Dodge's La Femme Is First Automobile With a Gender – It's Female' (1955: 133). So there.

Designers doing the Continental

Edsel Ford's love affair with all things Continental resulted in a personal bespoke design that, on his 1939 Palm Beach winter holiday, caused a furore. Returning to Detroit with 200 requests, 500 cars were hand-built to gauge market response – and a legend was born (Langworth 1987: 131). Evoking European coach-built automobiles, the Lincoln Continental eclipsed the rest of Ford's 1940 range. The original has remained the best, as heavy-handed facelifts in 1942 and 1946–48 compromised the original design's purity. One advertisement picturing the 1947 Cabriolet stated simply 'Nothing could be Finer', with the significance of the 1941 Lincoln Continental further validated by inclusion in MoMA's exhibition *8 Automobiles* in 1951.

1956 saw the Continental Mark II (*sans* 'Lincoln') debut at the 1955 Paris Motor Show. It was elegant and devoid of excessive decoration; one designer noted it was an: 'all-out luxury car of impeccable design and exquisite taste' (Langworth 1987: 179). Priced at almost $10,000 – the cost of a Rolls-Royce, or two Cadillacs – it attracted celebrity owners such as Elvis Presley, Frank Sinatra, and the Shah of Iran. The Mark II was only in the spotlight for two years, as Ford incurred a loss on each sale and production halted in May, 1957.

A third attempt was the 1968 Continental Mark III, promoted as 'The most authoritatively styled, decisively individual motorcar of this generation'. Individuality and exclusivity had always been the Continental's basis of appeal but one rather overt plea for status association was the Mark III's 'tribute' to the Rolls-Royce grille. Familiar styling cues such as the spare-wheel hump in the boot-lid evoked that of previous Marks and while production lasted for four years, the Mark III was much more a Mark for the masses. It was also blessed with a Cartier timepiece, a chic harbinger of fashion packages to come.

The most stylish option of the bigger Mark IV was saved for the final 1976 model that could be optioned with one of four Designer Editions themed packages – Bill Blass, Cartier, Givenchy, and Emilio Pucci. Designers deigning to embellish mass-produced cars was not new – American Motors had also tempted fashion-savvy buyers with a Gucci Hornet Sportabout (1972–73), a Levi's Gremlin (1973) and Pacer (1977), a Pierre Cardin Javelin (1973), and an Oleg Cassini Matador (1974). Cadillac's compact Seville also got a Gucci going-over for 1978–79, but Lincoln's remained the major commitment to designer special editions.

As well as those listed, Versace and Valentino later contributed their own versions but the Designer Series were in no sense bespoke; the extent of buyer engagement was essentially limited to instructing a salesperson to tick a box on an order sheet. There were no appointments in chic offices, no discussions, no preliminary design sketches, no swags of fabric, no fittings, no sense of an original being created; nothing of what being the client of a designer might be like, apart from a 1977 advertisement showing Mr. Blass, Messieurs Cartier and Givenchy, and Signor Pucci developing their design proposals.

This reductive, superficial experience, lasting until the final Cartier Lincoln of 2003, was, perhaps intended, to bring more women into showrooms – 'Bring the little lady in, she'll love choosing all that crazy designer stuff' – and maybe there were enough women content with these Continentals. Who, then, constituted the Lincoln buyer's male demographic? Brooklyn bosses goggle-eyed over Gucci? Texan oil barons validating Valentino? Cool Californians crazy for Cartier? At Lincoln, fashion and style had become, once again, an add-on. The glory days of the elegant Marks I and II were long gone, now evoked only through garish colors and dubious detailing. And the final triumphant touch? The quintessence of anti-chic: the owner's name on a 22 carat gold finished nameplate on the instrument panel. Classy.

Everything new is old again

Barthes wrote in 1957 of the new Citroën: 'It is obvious that the new Citroën has fallen from the sky inasmuch as it appears at first sight as a superlative object' (1973: 88). Barthes' breathless rhetoric may seem to overstate the case of what was, after all, just another in a long history of new car releases, but the essence of his observation identifies the transformative qualities of the truly new, consistent with what Robert Hughes, in an art context, termed 'the shock of the new'.

The Lauren exhibition, however, was not about the new in the 'motor show' sense; the seventeen cars were all freighted with historical and cultural significance but manifested a complex contemporary resonance and allure as well. The cars, the manufacturers, and the drivers embodied not only a battle for supremacy on the race track and the showroom but also for admission to an exclusive social echelon where the winner takes all, in every sense – enter Mr. Lauren.

Each of the cars on display in the elegant, muted gallery exemplifies the transfiguration of refugee Ralph Lifshitz into ersatz Wasp Ralph Lauren, a masterpiece of his own creating. Collecting masterpieces, according to curator Rapetti, is 'also a definition of the self' (Meagher 2011: 83), so the triumphant, beautiful cars and the lovely gallery and the hushed, subdued tone contributed to a tangible reverence that may not have been lost on those who were there to behold seventeen masterpieces but discovered one more than expected.

References

Barthes, R. (1973) *Mythologies*, St. Albans, UK: Paladin.

Bunyan, M. (2012) 'Exhibition: "Warhol and Cars: American Icons" at The Andy Warhol Museum, Pittsburgh – Exhibition Dates: 5th February–13th May, 2012', http://artblart.com/2012/05/06/exhibition-warhol-and-cars-american-icons-at-the-andy-warhol-museum-pittsburgh (accessed: November 6, 2012).

Campbell, M. (2012) 'Crackdown on Showgirls', http://news.drive.com.au/drive/motor-news/crackdown-on-show-girls-20120911–25p8w.html (accessed: December 11, 2012).

Cardew, B. (1971) *Daily Express Motor Show Review A-Z 1971*, London: Daily Express Newspapers.

Craik, J. (1994) *The Face of Fashion: Cultural Studies in Fashion*, London: Routledge.

Dregni, E. and Miller, K. (1996) *Ads That Put America on Wheels*, Osceola, WI: Motorbooks International Publishers and Wholesalers.

Finch, C. (1992) *Highways to Heaven: The AUTO Biography of America*, New York: HarperCollins.

Flammang, J. and Frumpkin, M. (1998) *World's Greatest Auto Show: Celebrating a Century in Chicago*, Iola, WI: Krause.

Georgano, N. (1992) *The American Automobile: A Centenary 1893–1993*, London: Prion.

Gross, K. and Labaco, R. (2010) *The Allure of the Automobile: Driving in Style, 1930–1965*, Atlanta: The High Museum of Art, in association with Skira Rizzoli.

Jeremiah, D. (1998) 'The Formation and Legacy of Britain's First Motor Museum', *Journal of the History of Collections*, 10 (1): 93–112.

Kawamura, Y. (2005) *Fashion-ology: An Introduction to Fashion Studies*, Oxford: Berg.

Lacayo, R. (2006) 'Ralph Lauren', The 2006 TIME 100, *TIME*, May, 8: 140.

Langworth, R. (1987) *The Complete History of the Ford Motor Company*, New York: Beekman House.

Langworth, R. and Norbye, J. (1985) *The Complete History of the Chrysler Corporation 1924–1985*, New York: Beekman House.

Marling, K. (1994) *As Seen on TV: The Visual Culture of Everyday Life in the 1950s*, Cambridge, MA: Harvard University Press.

McShane, C. (1997) *The Automobile: A Chronology of Its Antecedents, Development, and Impact*, Westport, CT: Greenwood.

Meagher, D. (2011) 'Show of Speed', *Wish* magazine, May, *The Australian*, Melbourne: 82–83.

Museum of Fine Arts (MFA), Boston (2005) *Speed, Style and Beauty: Cars from the Ralph Lauren Collection*, Boston: MFA Publications.

Museum of Modern Art (MoMA) (1951) Press release, New York.

Nelson, K. (2009) *Wheels of Change: From Zero to 600 M.P.H. The Amazing Story of California and the Automobile*, Berkeley, CA: Heyday Books/ California Historical Society.

Packard, V. (1960) *The Waste Makers*, London: Penguin.

Pettifer, J. and Turner, N. (1984) *Automania: Man and the Motor Car*, London: Collins.

Popular Mechanics (1955) 'Dodge's La Femme Is First Automobile With a Gender – It's Female', July: 133.

Robinson, D. (1958) 'Fashion Theory and Product Design', *Harvard Business Review*, 36, November–December: 126–138.

Robson, G. (2000) *Rolls-Royce Silver Cloud: The Complete Story*, Marlborough, Wiltshire: Crowood.

Sloan, Jr., A. (1965) *My Years with General Motors*, London: Pan.

Sproles, G. (1985) 'Behavioral Science Theories of Fashion', in Solomon, M. (ed.), *The Psychology of Fashion*, Lexington, MA: Lexington.

Van Bogart, A. (2003) *Cadillac: 100 Years of Innovation*, Iola, WI: Krause.

4 National dress and fashion trends of a royal Bhutanese wedding

Paul Strickland

In 2011, the Fifth King of Bhutan, His Majesty, Druk, Gyalpo Jigme Khesar Namgyel Wangchuck, married his commoner bride now titled 'Her Majesty, the Druk, Gyaltsuen Jetsun Pema Wangchuck' (Yeewong 2011: 4). To the Bhutanese, this was one of the most joyous celebrations the country had seen in recent years. The Wangchuck monarchy has been revered by the Bhutanese people for over a century as the family dynasty has bought peace, happiness and increased prosperity to Bhutan. More importantly, the dynasty has been able to maintain their traditional culture. This has not been an easy task, since the opening of Bhutan's borders to Westerners in the 1970s meant the country has been prone to external influences that can be seen to have had both a perceived positive and negative effect. To ensure these influences are more positive than negative, individual decrees by the reigning Kings meant the distinctive culture of Bhutan was preserved. One such declaration was the announcement that all Bhutanese must wear the national dress of the Bhutan; a *kira* for females and a *gho* for men. Not only has this provided the Bhutanese people with a sense of identity and pride, it also has also sustained the traditions and culture that the ever growing tourism industry has come to expect. Coupled with elaborate costumes, make-up and masks for festivals and events, the Bhutanese national dress has become iconic around the globe and uniquely fashionable throughout Bhutan.

The Royal Wedding in 2011 paved the way for Bhutanese clothing to become a spectacle in itself and, as such, re-invigorated their tapestry industry in creating an eye catching treat for tourists and spectators from around the world. Tourists have now come to expect the elaborate costumes presented during the annual religious festivals that are seen to be such important expressions of the Bhutanese faith (Berthold 2005). However, an unexpected outcome of the Royal Wedding was the purchase of so many new outfits just for the Royal Wedding by Bhutanese commoners. The excitement of the Royal Wedding did not merely start on the actual day of the ceremony. Many textile weavers of Bhutanese national dress are lucky to sell one or two outfits to locals annually. This is typically due to the high prices and generally low incomes. However, six months prior to the Royal Wedding, a textile weaver commented that she 'has already sold 16 weaves that buyers will wear on the day of the

Royal Wedding' (Dema 2011: 2). This kept some weavers working long hours for months to ensure they could fulfil orders. It was not just the weavers who benefited. Dema (2011: 8) points out that: 'A traditional shoe making shop … has ten employees working overtime to meet demand making fifty-one hundred products per day, when generally it is less than twenty.' It appears that many Bhutanese would like to look their best by purchasing new outfits and shoes just for the event.

As financial stability and wealth is still in its infancy, such purchases are uncommon. Not only did the Royal Wedding increase the demand for locally produced clothing, it also assisted in boosting the sale of fashionable yet traditional clothing. This was predominately led by the youth of the country whose disposable income was increasing.

Brief history of Bhutan

Bhutan is a mountainous, land locked country with a population estimated to be between 800,000 and 1.3 million (Collister 1987). It borders India and China (Sharma 2002). The Kingdom of Bhutan is a constitutional monarchy, however the fourth Druk (known as the Dragon King) Gyalpo Jogme Singye Wangchuck abdicated his throne to his son in 2008 (Lawson 2011). This decision created a new constitution which allows the monarchy to remain while giving the power to operate the country's affairs to government ministers; so, effectively, introducing democracy (Pek-Dorji 2007). Both the fourth and fifth Druks have overseen the introduction of television, the Internet and mobile phones (BBC News Online 1999: para. 3); however, with regulations (BBC News Online 2004: para. 2). They have also been responsible for important infrastructure development, including new roads, and invested heavily in public health, tourism and education among other initiatives; consequently, they are highly regarded by their Bhutanese citizens (Planning Commission 1999).

The Kingdom of Bhutan, known by the locals as Druk Yul (Land of the Dragon), was created in 1907 with Ugyen Wangchuck being elected as the first, hereditary monarch of Bhutan and the first Druk. This family monarchy has continued with the Fifth King (Jigme Khesar Namgyel Wangchuck) currently on the throne. As aforementioned, despite having a monarchy, much of the power has been given to the government with democratic elections. A unique attribute of Bhutan is its power sharing arrangements and the development of five year planning cycles. Although official policy is developed by the Royal Government of Bhutan (RGoB), most *Dzongs* (original fortresses) house a seat for the King, the Prime Minister and the spiritual leader of Bhutan as they are all considered equals. Known as one of the last Shangri-las, Bhutan is one of the last developing countries to open its borders to other cultures. As a result, it has many historical precedents from which to learn so that it has been given the opportunity to choose which external influences will be rejected and which influences will be embraced. It has not squandered this opportunity.

Gross National Happiness – the concept

Bhutan has a unique philosophy of Gross National Happiness (GNH) which was first penned over thirty years ago and finally implemented by the fourth ruler in the year 2000. It is a philosophy which underpins many of the government's policies. GNH is a unique concept that aims to increase the happiness and satisfaction of the people, shifting the focus of growth from monetary value or gain (Bauer *et al.* 1999; Ritchie 2008). His Majesty stated that 'Gross National Happiness is more important than Gross National Product' (Beyul Dewaling 2012: 1). The inherent belief of GNH being that if the people are happy, the flow on effects will naturally help stimulate economic development and environmental conservation, promote culture and meet the spiritual and emotional needs of the people (Ministry of Finance 2000). GNH is a 'balanced development philosophy which seeks to integrate equitable and sustainable socio-economic development with environmental, conservation, cultural promotion and good governance' (Beyul Dewaling 2012: 2).

Even though GNH places the people and the country's happiness first, it still allows for economic development including employment creation and making the country less reliant on foreign aid (Du 2003). This has led to the introduction of many educational programmes with the most challenging being the proposed development of the GNH centre known as Beyul Dewaling which is based in the middle of the country in Bumthang. The GNH centre may take many years to complete depending on financing; however, plans are under way. The GNH concept will be incorporated into all domestic education programmes with the idealistic vision that the GNH centre concept can be replicated in other countries. Traditional attire has an importance place in this process. Having the Bhutanese people dress in traditional attire is one element which is believed will keep the culture alive, instil pride in the people and satisfy tourist expectations. This in turn enhances the GNH philosophy.

National dress code

Traditional dress (*Driglam Namzha*) is worn by all the locals (*Drukpa*) and is extremely important to Bhutanese culture. So much so that the RGoB declared in 1989 that it must be worn by all local inhabitants while working for the government, in offices, schools and on formal occasions. It was also mandated that members of the National Assembly would also wear national dress during daylight hours. However, most locals choose to wear the national costume outdoors, regardless of their profession or legislation. The *gho* is worn by the males, and is a long robe hoisted to the knee and held in place by a belt known as the *kera* (Druk Air 2012). The large pouch at the front is used as a carrying aid. The *kira* is worn by the females, and consists of a full length dress secured by a chain at the shoulder (*komo*) and a belt at the waist (*kera*). A blouse (*wonju*) is worn underneath the kira and a cropped jacket called a *toego* is worn over the top. The kira is usually made of bright coloured, fine woven fabric with traditional patterns (Druk Air 2012). Ceremonial kiras and ghos are hand woven in traditional patterns and are highly prized. As a form of respect, additional scarves must be added when entering Dzongs and monasteries (Ritchie 2008). Although to some, the national dress may appear impractical and perhaps uncomfortable (especially in the hospitality industry) the insistence that it is worn helps Bhutan retain its cultural identity and national pride as well as adding to the overall perception of the tourists' experience. Consequently, almost all workers wear the kira or gho at work, especially in office buildings and tourist attractions and hotels (Morgan 2011). There is little resentment towards the national dress except from the small number of ethnic minority groups that have emigrated from other regions and are forced to wear clothing that is not culturally theirs.

Bhutanese design

Bhutan has a long tradition of textile design and manufacturing, and the handlooms have played an important role in Bhutanese society, both culturally and economically (Wangchuck 1994). It has been noted that: 'Textiles are a rich and complex art form deeply embedded in the culture and history of Bhutan' (Bean 1994: 13). The female weavers are considered artists while the male embroiders (usually monks) follow a religious tradition and are viewed as extremely skilful. The basic materials have always been wild silk, cotton, nettle, yak hair and wool. Today, other materials and fibres from India and China and wool from Australia have become ubiquitous (Bean 1994). Although the traditional materials and available colours may be changing, the methods of producing them have remained unchanged for centuries (Aris 1994).

To champion the Bhutanese textile industry and showcase designs and fashion, exhibitions have been occurring over the last few decades. The Royal Wedding, for example, has inspired a new generation of affection for these industry events with the latest exhibition housing over fifty designs of traditional clothes dating back to the nineteenth and twentieth centuries. This included Royal Family attire. Many of the costumes on display were purchased back from foreigners and locals at high prices. These included silk garments valued at US$10,000 an outfit. It was hoped the exhibition would 'sensitize, inspire and inculcate a sense of pride, empathy and appreciation for Bhutanese textiles among the Bhutanese' (Choden 2012: 3). Based on visitor numbers, it appears to have been successful.

As with many televised Royal Weddings, keen observers focus on the bride's outfit and a great deal of information is given about the background of the design. There is also continuous commentary throughout the broadcast. The Fifth Bhutanese Royal Wedding was no different and was also televised to a global audience; the first in the Kingdom's history. Once again, like many other royal weddings, very little information was revealed about the bride's dress prior to the wedding day. What was known was that: 'Several famed weavers were competing for the honour of clothing her on the big day' (Philomena

Figure 4.1 King and Queen of Bhutan in ceremonial dress
Source: Yeewong (2011), front cover

2011: 7). The only information released to the public was that the Queen 'will wear according to her element. There are five elements in our culture. For example, red is fire and earth is yellow ... her element is earth, so it will probably be mostly yellow' (Philomena 2011: 5).

One designer was named prior to the event. This was 'Lhadrip (Scroll Painter) Lopon Ugyen, who designed the Crown and had it embroidered in Hong Kong. He noted that the frame of the Crown was carved in such a way that it accommodated all the strokes of different colours' (Yeewong 2011: 84). The Queen's crown had many significant depictions such as the auspicious colours, the phoenix and longevity birds, the wheel of Charma symbolising power between the King and Queen for peace and prosperity and the lotus flower symbolising love and devotion (Yeewong 2011).

Being a modern monarchy, the Royal Bhutanese Wedding organisers also commissioned Western designers: 'The shoes worn by the Gyaltsuen during the Royal Wedding are said to have been designed by the New York Footwear Designer, Steve Madden. The designs on the shoes include Ja Tsherings (phoenix) and the longevity birds' (Yeewong 2011: 85). This was important as it indicates that aspects of both Western and Bhutanese culture can be blended and that while Bhutan is modernising, it is still maintaining its traditions. For example, the King wore a traditional gho that was also worn at the Third King's wedding. Clearly this was to portray a modern union based on traditional Bhutanese values. The front page of *Yeewong*, Bhutan's first and only women's magazine, showcased the King and Queen of Bhutan in ceremonial attire on their wedding day (Figure 4.1). The page also included inserts of the King openly demonstrating his affection for his new bride. The combination further reinforced the mix of traditional and modern features.

The event

The Royal Wedding (*Gyaltsuen Trashi Ngasoel* Ceremony) was conducted in Punakha at the Pungthang Dewa Chhenpoi Phrodrang which is a fortified monastery (*Dzhong*). This location also has symbolic significance as Bhutan's old capital city, spiritual heartland of the country and the main seat of the monarchy. The 2011 Royal Wedding was the first ceremony that retitled the King's wife as the *Queen* of Bhutan (*Druk Gyaltsuen*) as opposed to *Ashi* which is a lesser title shared by the Queen Mothers and the Princesses. The retitling was at the Command of his Majesty. The auspicious day for the Royal Wedding was the 13th of October 2011, which the majority of the nation's population watched on television. The ceremony was beamed around the sovereign state with thirteen other countries around the world also having media broadcasts of the event. Although some dignitaries attended the formalities of the occasion, it was still considered quite a sedate and intimate affair (Yeewong 2011). According to Pindarica (2011: 2): 'About 70 invitations were sent to foreign guests. No foreign VIPs or fellow Royals were on the guest list.' The Royal Wedding was the first to be televised. This is not surprising as electricity was only introduced into Bhutan in 1966 and it is still only a few areas such as the capital Thimpu and Paro that have a permanent electricity supply. The majority of the population rely on generators, candles and fires for warmth and power although this is rapidly improving.

The religious ceremonies started at dawn with His Holiness the Je Khenpo (Bhutan's spiritual leader) initiating the prayers that were followed by an esti-mated one hundred monks. It was during these prayers that the Royal family arrived and the first glimpses of their national dress and costumes were tele-vised around the world. The festivities continued with the lighting of golden lamps and the arrival of the future Queen. This was followed by the *Chhipdrel* ceremony. This is a ceremonial procession to receive and honour distinguished patrons. The lead person astrologically has an auspicious quality of life, body, power, luck and intelligence and is a respected religious figure. A white stal-lion followed as a good omen and legend suggests the horse is a manifestation of Chenreyzi who has rescued many people from demons and bought them back to Earth. Following this was a person carrying a *Chogdar* that ensures protection against any bad omens. As the morning unfolded, further cere-monies continued including the Druks' purification ceremony, this being a sacred blessing that only four men were allowed to witness. This was held in front of the remains of Zhabdrung Ngawang Namgyel who was the founder of Bhutan and considered sacred.

Members of the Royal family then went on to pray with His Holiness presenting Jetsun Pema with a sash showcasing five auspicious colours embroidered on it. His Holiness then announced the Royal union to the crowds outside and the Druks ascended their thrones in the Kuenra. At this point, the Royal Bride prostrated to the King and offered him The Golden Bumpa which is a vase filled with ambrosia signifying eternal life and her devotion to the Royal family. After the symbolic gesture of offering a drink to the Triple Gem and Guardian Deities of the Kingdom, the King took a sip and placed it next to the throne. His Majesty then bestowed the silk Crown of the Druk Gyaltsuen on his wife's head and proclaimed her as the Queen of Bhutan. She then ascended to her throne which was positioned next to the King's. He also donned the Raven Crown. Various other chants and blessings continued, represented through many symbolic gestures. At the completion of the official ceremonies, the entire Royal family moved outside for the public celebrations (Yeewong 2011). It took almost twelve hours for the Royal couple to travel back to the capital the next day: a trip that usually takes about two hours. Many people lined the streets to see the royal newlyweds who continually left their vehicle to greet them. Some of the walks on this occasion stretched for a number of kilometres. These long walks were an excellent opportunity to showcase the couple's new outfits.

Festivities continued in Thimpu and the atmosphere was filled with a sense of national pride. Agence France-Presse's (2011) prediction that thousands of Bhutanese 'are expected to turn out in colorful national dress', is exactly what happened. This image was what the Royal family wanted beamed around the world:

> The capital is all decked up, festooned with flags, flowers, huge por-traits of the Royal couple and glittering lights. A frenzy of some sort

has captivated the whole nation. To the outside world represented and wired by about hundred international journalists, tweeting every other second, the marriage of the King to a commoner is a fairy tale wedding, at its best.

(Business Bhutan 2011: 11)

Some international reports remarked that Bhutan had Royal Wedding fever (*Calgary Herald; The Indian Express*) and that this was the biggest event many Bhutanese would see for a very long time.

Bhutanese fashion

As Bhutan is a developing country with an increasing number of tourists and exposure to other media such as television and the Internet, there is a strong movement to embrace fashion. However, the interest appears to be in Western fashion. Television was introduced into Bhutan in June, 1999 for the World Cup (BBC News Online 2004). Initially, the majority of channels were relayed from India, which is one of Bhutan's closest geographic neighbours. India's television stations broadcast many channels including those which not only screened Bollywood movies and local content but also programmes from the United Kingdom (BBC) and the United States of America (CNN). Seeing Western fashion on television and internet programmes and witnessing the attire of visiting tourists, the young people of Bhutan developed a desire to purchase garments other than their traditional costumes. Shops and clothes markets were able to supply items such as jeans, baseball caps and designer shoes. Tourists were also giving away items of clothing and showcasing their wardrobes to the locals. A shift in local dress code was appearing. Even His Majesty was succumbing and often referred to as the 'Asian Elvis' because of his Western hair style (Agence France-Presse 2011; Harris 2011).

Influence of Royal Wedding fashion on the Bhutanese people

It is events such as the Royal Wedding that 'provide an opportunity for Bhutanese villagers to take a break from their work, dress in their finest clothes and mingle with the crowds' (Berthold 2005: 41). This also develops a sense of pride and nationalism in the Bhutanese. Although the Wangchuck Dynasty is seen as revolutionary in its embrace of modernism, it still maintains traditional values. This can be illustrated by the new Queen's choice of a wedding dress which included traditional designs with a modern flair. This was very much anticipated by the public. An online article asked the question: 'Can Jetsun Pema change fashion in Bhutan?' (Zimbio 2011: 4). It appears that the answer is yes:

The Bhutanese royal bride, Jetsun Pema, is really a fashion icon for the people who love to see different styles with the latest fashion trends in the world. People of Bhutan are really shocked by the fashion of their queen because the television has been banned in the country since 1999 and they have been disconnected from the fashion world but now there are youngsters who are changing their fashion. Their Facebook pages show they are demanding the latest fashion trends in the country.

(Zimbio 2011: 2)

As Misener (2011: 5) notes, 'interest in Bhutanese fashion is growing in a nation with a historically isolated culture'. The Facebook pages of *Bhutan Street Fashion*, for example, showcase Bhutanese men and women asking for more images of the Queen of Bhutan to see what she is currently wearing. However, this does not mean that it is only Bhutanese trends that the people want. Some younger Bhutanese are curious as how to obtain Western clothing such as cargo pants and baseball caps. Although this may be a coincidence, these questions were only posted online after the Bhutanese Royal Wedding in 2011.

Local Bhutanese people who were interviewed on the streets of Thimpu by the author between 2 and 16 July 2012 offered comments such as: 'The Queen is very glamorous', 'I like what she wears', 'The King looked very handsome in his father's gho' and 'I want to dress like her'. When asked: 'What did you wear for the Royal Wedding?' responses included; 'I wore my best kira', 'I had a new dress made … it cost me almost a year's wage' and 'I had new shoes made and the King commented on them when he walked past'. Other comments included: 'I couldn't afford to buy anything new but I wanted to', 'I just wanted to see what they wore on TV' and 'I want to copy her dress'.

To assist in showcasing new designs based on history and tradition, three Bhutanese designers purposely launched a fashion show six months prior to the Royal Wedding, stating: 'the goal was basically to create an image of how the Gho and Kira have changed and evolved through time becoming today not just a dress but a personal stamp and statement' (Kash and Tals 2011: 50).

Impacts of Bhutanese fashion on international fashion and tourism

In 2007, *Marie Claire* undertook its first, international photo shoot in Bhutan. Since then, very few, if any more have occurred. However, that changed following the Royal Wedding when two international fashion houses indicated they would use Bhutan as a fashion shoot location. The Royal Wedding also had an impact on tourism in Bhutan. The world-wide media focus on broadcasting and reporting the event increased the number of international travellers booking holidays to the country. In 2010, the average length of stay was 7.6 nights with about 23,480 visitors annually. Post-wedding projections indicate international visitors will increase by over 40,000 per year (Tourism Council of Bhutan 2010: 31). In reality, as Figure 4.2 shows, over 64,000 tourists visited Bhutan in 2011 and this is seen to be largely due to the Royal Wedding (Tourism Council of Bhutan 2011: 17).

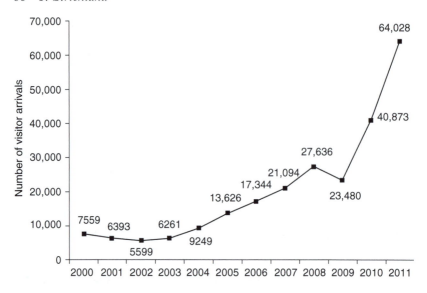

Figure 4.2 Visitors to Bhutan, 2000–11
Source: Bhutan Tourism Monitor (2011)

Textiles has always been a vital industry for international tourism as exit polls conducted at the airport indicate 65 per cent of international tourists suggested *culture* as the number one reason for visiting Bhutan (Tourism Council of Bhutan 2011) with 37.8 per cent of international tourists report-ing they had visited textiles/weaving facilities (Tourism Council of Bhutan 2010). The Royal Wedding has simply drawn attention to the country, tourism and fashion and this has had an impact on international fashion.

Local fashion designer Sonem stated that her shop in Thimpu 'is doing very well since the Royal Wedding. The Queen wore one of my dresses, now I am in high demand' and 'I have orders for at least a year as one of the Queen Mothers wore my Kira' (Sonem Penam, fashion designer, pers. comm. 11 July 2012). Interviewing the General Manager of a prominent Thimpu International Hotel, he stated: 'The gift shop [clothing sales] is doing better with the official [wedding] photo of their Majesties on display' (pers. comm. 4 July 2012). Two more Bhutanese fashion designers commented that: 'Young women want to dress like the queen' (Penang 12 July 2012) and 'I think the [Royal] wedding made more locals focus on accessories and shoes. This will mean more sales and keeping our traditions alive' (Dorji 9 July 2012).

Conclusion

The Fifth Royal Wedding of the Wangchuck Dynasty has had a major influence on the entire Kingdom of Bhutan. Not only did it bring national pride, joy, tradition and reinforce religious custom to the Bhutanese people, it re-invigorated the local textile industry by increasing production as a result of the increase of demand before and after the wedding. The main difference with this event to previous Royal Weddings was that it was televised to the entire country and reported globally. Given both the King and Queen of Bhutan were educated in both Eastern and Western cultures, the couple could incorporate core traditional values with a modern twist through their choice of wedding attire. This was especially apparent in the media reporting on the Queen's choice of wedding dress. Although the Bhutanese people have great affection for the King, the Royal Wedding was more focused on the Queen and her perceived modern fashion sense. It appears that many of the young Bhutanese women would like to emulate the manner in which she superimposed her modern style on essentially traditional designs. This event also paved the way for large, international fashion houses to view Bhutanese clothes and incorporate them into modern, Westernised designs that are being showcased in the fashion capitals of the world. If future orders are anything to go by, it has also meant local Bhutanese designers can modernise traditional designs and these will be accepted into Bhutanese culture.

References

Agence France-Presse (2011) 'Bhutan counts down to a Royal Wedding', *Inquirer News*, 11 October, http://newsinfo.inquirer.net/74249/bhutan-counts-down-to-royal-wedding (accessed 4 April 2012).

Aris, M. (1994) 'Textiles, text and content, the cloth and clothing of Bhutan in historical perspective', in D. Myers and S. Bean (eds), *The Land of the Thunder Dragon*, London: Serindia Publications (pp. 27–32).

Bauer, J., Brunet, S., De Lacy, T. and Tshering, K. (1999) *Milk and Cheese Always: Proposal for collaboration in education, training and research for conservation and sustainable tourism in Bhutan*, Co-operative Research Centre for Sustainable Tourism, Griffith University Gold Coast Campus, Australia.

BBC News Online (1999) 'World South Asia: Bhutan TV follows cyber launch', June 2, http://news.bbc.co.uk/2/hi/south_asia/358230.stm (accessed 19 April 2013).

BBC News Online (2004) 'Has TV changed in Bhutan?' 17 June, http://news.bbc.co.uk/2/hi/entertainment/3812275.stm (accessed 3 April 2012).

Bean, S. (1994) 'Introduction. Bhutan, its textiles, and the world', in D. Myers and S. Bean (eds), *The Land of the Thunder Dragon*, London: Serindia Publications.

Berthhold, J. (2005) *Bhutan. Land of the Thunder Dragon*, Boston: Wisdom Publications.

Beyul Dewaling, Gross National Happiness Centre (2012) [Brochure], Bumthang, Bhutan.

Business Bhutan (2011) 'The crowning moment', 15 October, http://www.businessbhutan.bt/?p=7867 (accessed 2 April 2012).

Choden, S. (2012) 'Woven, cut and stitched', Kuenselonline.com http://www.kuenselonline.com/2011/?p=28746 (accessed 2 April 2012).

Collister, P. (1987) *Bhutan and the British*, Boston: Serendia Publications.

Dema, T. (2011) 'Gearing up for Bhutan's Royal Wedding', *Asia News Network*, 12 October, http://www.asianewsnet.net/home/news.php?id=21598 (accessed 4 April 2012).

Druk Air (2012) *Dress*, http://www.drukair.com.bt/COMMON.aspx?Type=Dress. htm (accessed 2 April 2012).

Du, J. (2003) 'Reforms and development of higher tourism education in China', *Journal of Teaching in Travel & Tourism*, 3(1): 103–113.

Harris, D. (director/producer) (2011) 'Bhutan Royal Wedding: a commoner becomes a Queen', *Australian Broadcasting Commission, ABCTV, NEWS*, 13 October, http://abcnews.go.com/international/bhutan-royal-wedding-commoner-queen/story?id=14727724 (accessed 3 April 2012).

Kash and Tals (2011) (Mar–Apr) 'On the catwalk', *Tashi Delek*, 16(2): 17–19.

Lawson, A. (2011) 'Profile: Jigme Khesar Namgyel Wangchuck', *BBC NEWS Online*, http://www.bbc.co.uk/news/world-south-asia-15287281 (accessed 21 March 2012).

Marie Claire (2007) 'Bhutan fashion', *Marie Claire Online*, 6 October, http://www.marieclaire.com/fashion/trends/fashion-bhutan#slide-5 (accessed 4 April 2012).

Ministry of Finance, Royal Government of Bhutan (2000) *Development Towards Gross National Happiness*, Thimpu: Bhutan.

Misener, J. (2011) 'Jetsun Pema, Queen of Bhutan: A newlywed style icon', *The Huffington Post*, 27 October, http://lharikhamba.blogspot.com.au/2011/10/bhutan-street-fashion-in-huffington.html (accessed 7 May 2012).

Morgan, J. (2011) 'Bhutan spruces up for fairytale Royal Wedding', *The Age Online*, 1 October, http://www.theage.com.au/world/bhutan-spruces-up-for-fairytale-royal-wedding-20110930-1l1gw.html?gclid=CPCxiaLHl68CFeJKpgodnw5i3g (accessed 3 April 2012).

Pek-Dorji, S. S. (ed.) (2007) *The Legacy of a King. The Fourth Druk Gyalpo Jogme Singye Wangchuck*, Thimpu, Bhutan: Department of Tourism: Royal Government of Bhutan.

Philomena, S. (2011) 'Bhutan: Royal Wedding fever', *MeDIndia*, 12 September, http://www.medindia.net/news/Bhutan-Royal-Weddiing-Fever-90448-1.htm (accessed 4 April 2012).

Planning Commission, Royal Government of Bhutan (1999) *Bhutan 2020: A vision for peace, prosperity and happiness*, Thimpu, Bhutan.

Pindarica, Y. (2011) 'Friend of Bhutan who made it to the wedding', 5 October, http://www.businessbhutan.bt/?p=7911 (accessed 2 April 2012).

Ritchie, M. (2008) 'Tourism in the Kingdom of Bhutan: a unique approach', in J. Cochrane (ed.), *Asian Tourism: Growth and change*, Oxford: Elsevier (pp. 273–283).

Sharma, N. (2002) *Nepal's Relations with Sikkim and Bhutan 1770–1900*, Kathmandu, Nepal: Himshikhar Publications.

Tourism Council of Bhutan (2010) *Bhutan Tourism Monitor: Annual Report*, Thimpu, Bhutan.

Tourism Council of Bhutan (2011) *Bhutan Tourism Monitor: Annual Report*, Thimpu, Bhutan.

Wangchuck, A. S. C (1994) 'Foreword – Her Majesty Ashi Sangay Choden Wangchuck, Queen of Bhutan', in D. Myers and S. Bean (eds), *The Land of the Thunder Dragon*, London: Serindia Publications.

Yeewong (2011) 'Bringing her forward', December.

Zimbio (2011) 'Jetsun Pema Bhutan fashion icon', 18 September, http://www.zimbio.com/King+Jigme+Singye+Wangchuck/articles/RSC9bM8jeXA/Jetsun+Pema+Bhutan+Fashion+Icon (accessed 4 April 2012).

5   Female Civil War reenactors' dress and magic moments

Kimberly Miller-Spillman and Min-Young Lee

Introduction

Historic reenactments attract millions of participants and spectators, and are popular events across the globe (Shanks 2009). Despite their popularity, reenactments have been criticized for allowing individuals to focus on their own experience rather than on the historic events that are being reenacted (Agnew 2007). Reenactments have been growing in number and popularity over the last two decades, and appeal to individuals regardless of income level, occupation, or education (Miller 2000). Given their broad appeal and amount of resources from spectators, reenactors, event planners, corporate sponsors, government agencies, and retailers, reenactments warrant the continuing attention of scholars.

Historic reenactments are events in which dress plays a central role. Reenactors are unpaid hobbyists who have a passion for history and provide costume scholars with rich opportunities to research the experience of being in costume. In this context, *dress* is defined as 'an assemblage of body modification and or supplements to the body' and *costume* is defined as 'the body supplements and modifications that indicate the "out-of-everyday" social role or activity. Examples include dress for acting in the theater, folk or other festivals, ceremonies, and rituals' (Roach-Higgins and Eicher 1992: 1).

Dressing in historic costume provides reenactors with the possibility of experiencing a *magic moment*. This is when an individual is no longer reenacting but feels as though s/he is participating in the actual moment in history. Magic moment, *period rush*, or *being in the bubble* all refer to the feeling of time travel, which is a pinnacle experience for reenactors. Using symbolic interaction theory from the field of sociology and the *Public, Private, and Secret Self Model* (Eicher and Miller 1994; see Table 5.1) we investigate the interest in American Civil War (1861–1865) reenactment dress among a sample of female reenactors and examine what connections, if any, these reenactors make between reenactment dress and magic moments.

Table 5.1 The Public, Private, and Secret Self Model (Eicher and Miller 1994) was the theoretical basis of the present study to examine magic moments and reenactment clothing in a sample of female Civil War reenactors (Miller-Spillman 2008).

	REALITY Dress	*FUN/LEISURE* Dress	*FANTASY* Dress
PUBLIC Self	Gender Uniforms Business Wear **Male Reenactors' Love of History (Miller 1998)** **(1)**	Office Parties Dating Sports Events Reenactors' Public Performances **(2)**	Halloween Living History Festivals **Male and Female Reenactors' Public Performances (3)**
PRIVATE Self	Housework Gardening Novelty Items **(4)**	Home Exercise **Male Reenactors' Interests Shared with Family (wives) and Friends (present study) (5)**	Childhood Memories Sensual Lingerie **(6)**
SECRET Self	Tight Underwear **(7)**	Some Tattoos Novelty Underwear **(8)**	**Female Reenactors Connect Dress to their Sexual Fantasies (Miller 1997) Female Reenactors want to Assume Another Persona (Miller 1998) All Reenactors' Magic Moments (9)**

Note: Highlighted boxes and bold print indicate areas of focus for the present study.

Reenactments

A typical Civil War reenactment takes place in a farmer's field, a historic battlefield, or a living history site. However, due to National Parks Service policy they are not allowed to take place at Battlefield National Monuments or National Military Parks such as Gettysburg (Frost and Laing 2013). Reenactment organizers publicise events in Civil War publications and provide supplies such as hay, chopped wood, and water. Reenactors arrive on a Friday afternoon and begin setting up both military and civilian campsites (women, children, and men past the age of portraying a soldier are referred to as civilians). Since the era being presented is from 1861 to 1865, efforts are made to ban modern items that would spoil the 1860s atmosphere.

Figure 5.1 Female reenactor at Ashland: The Henry Clay Estate, 2012
Source: K. Miller-Spillman

Meanwhile, *Sutler's Row* is being constructed in an area away from the battlefield and campsites. Civil War merchants or sutlers set up tents to sell books, magazines, clothing, historic spectacles, etc. to reenactors and spectators. There may be a speaker's tent, an actual wedding between reenactors, a ladies tea, and a dance – with period music and dances – for reenactors after spectators have left. Male reenactors outnumber female reenactors (Stanton 1997) by as many as seven to one. This estimate is based on the subscriber lists to two popular Civil War reenactor publications: the *Camp Chase Gazette* targets military reenactors and lists 7,000 subscribers while the *Citizens' Companion* targets female reenactors and lists 1,000 subscribers.

Reenacting battles appeals to male reenactors in which they play active (*agonic*) roles. Female reenactors, typically civilians, participate in passive (*hedonic*) roles. Women often admit that the hobby is an interest of their husband and in order to not be left out women take up the hobby. At a reenactment, women observe the battles while playing a supportive role cooking meals (Figure 5.1). Exceptions to this are female reenactors who serve as battlefield nurses or cross-dress as male soldiers in order to participate in the battles (Stanton 1997).

Theoretical background

Symbolic interaction. The theoretical basis of the study is symbolic interaction. George Herbert Mead (1934) founded symbolic interaction and used verbal discourse to illustrate how individuals communicate through the use of symbols. Stone (1965) added appearance to Mead's work in his pioneering article 'Appearance and the Self'. Stone stated that since individuals see one another's appearance prior to verbal discourse, appearance precedes verbal discourse and is therefore primary. Stone also created the concept of fantastic socialization as important for both children and adults. Fantastic socialization encourages imaginative play and social development. Stone indicated that adult fantastic socialization is more private than that of children. However, historic reenactments represent times when adults can indulge their fantasies in public while dressed in costume.

PPSS Model. Eicher (1981) built on Stone's work by creating a model for researching dress and the public, private, and secret self (PPSS Model). Eicher's 1981 model was based on her observations of dress rather than empirical research and was quite simplistic. Eicher and Miller collaborated in 1994 to revise the PPSS model to create a grid form (Table 5.1). The PPSS model states that the public part of the self is the part that everyone can see, the private part of the self is the part that only close friends and family can see, and the secret part of the self is the part that no one or only intimates can see. Dressing for reality is roughly equivalent to 9-to-5 dress, dressing for fun or leisure equates to dress after 5 p.m. and on weekends, and dressing for fantasy is dress that expresses a dream or desire. The nine cells in the grid format lead to research possibilities on dress that is not seen in public.

Women and costuming. Reenactments have been a popular topic of research since the late 1990s. Examples include: reenactments as a consumption experience (Belk and Costa 1998), effect of reenactments on Black southern identity (Davis 2009), reenacting and history on television reality shows (Agnew 2007; Rymsza-Pawlowska 2007), and debate among academics, reenactors, and historians (Frost and Laing 2013; Shanks 2009). Few studies have focused solely on women's experience of costuming. One study (Miller *et al.* 1991) reports how costumes influenced college students' perceptions of their identity and role on Halloween. Female students surveyed were less likely than male students surveyed to disguise their identities in Halloween costumes. Females were also less likely than males to believe they had new identities with their costumes or to believe they could play different roles at Halloween.

The private and secret parts of the self were tested with a *Dressing for Fun and Fantasy* questionnaire by surveying adults who costume for historic reenactments and ethnic dance groups (Miller 1997). Results indicate that women who dress in costumes reported more sexual fantasies (*secret self*) about dress and more detailed descriptions of dress worn during childhood memories (*private self*) than men who wore costumes (Miller-Spillman 2005). Reasons why individuals dress in costumes were explored in another study (Miller 1998). The top two reasons why these individuals dress in costume is because of a love of history (men's first choice) and an opportunity to assume another persona (women's first choice).

Another study (Miller-Spillman 2008) examined magic moments reported by male Civil War reenactors. Eighty-three percent of men surveyed reported having magic moments while reenacting. Male respondents also felt that historical accuracy in their costume and the costume of others was essential to setting the stage for a magic moment to occur. There is some evidence that men in costume may be more prone to fantasies (magic moments) than women. This would support Stone's (1959) findings that boys tend to select Halloween costumes for fantastic socialization while most girls' costumes represent anticipatory socialization.

Lastly, magic moments can be described as liminal experiences. Liminal is a term used by anthropologists to describe a transitional period or phase of a rite of passage, during which the participant lacks social status or rank, remains anonymous, shows obedience and humility, and follows prescribed forms of conduct and dress. This definition describes the anonymous nature of reenacting, especially at very large events such as the Battle of Gettysburg. Reenactors show obedience (in military matters) and humility (as part of a historic code of ethics) and they follow a prescribed form of dress and conduct. During a magic moment a reenactor feels they are between the present and the past. In addition, liminal experiences can occur during transitions such as dawn and dusk.

Given the lack of research on female reenactors in general, and female Civil War reenactors in particular, we formulated the following four research questions to guide the study:

1. Who are female reenactors in terms of age, occupation, income, and education?
2. How much do female reenactors invest in their reenactment clothing and where do they acquire it?
3. How many female reenactors report having a magic moment and can significant relationships be identified between magic moments and other variables?
4. How do female reenactors describe the connections, if any, between magic moments and reenactment clothing?

Method

Sample and procedure. A mail survey following Dillman's (1978) total design method was sent to a random selection of subscribers to *The Citizen's Companion*, a popular Civil War reenactor publication targeting female reenactors. The mailing list included 1,000 subscribers from across the United States. Two hundred and fifty subscribers were selected at random to participate through two mailings. The first mailing included a cover letter, a questionnaire, and a postage paid return envelope. The second mailing was a reminder postcard.

Instrument. The *Civil War Reenactor Survey* was developed by the authors using symbolic interaction theory and the PPSS model (Eicher and Miller 1994). Ten items from the questionnaire were included in the study; four demographic items and six reenactment clothing items. Twelve individuals pretested the questionnaire and were not included in the final sample. Two sections of the questionnaire are relevant to this study and are described below.

Reenactment clothing. Six items from the questionnaire addressed:

1. how reenactment clothing was acquired;
2. the amount of money spent on reenactment clothing;
3. level of interest in reenactment clothing;
4. participation because of a Civil War ancestor;
5. whether or not individuals have experienced a magic moment while reenacting;
6. what part, if any, reenactment clothing played in the magic moment.

Personal information. Four items from this section were included in the present study including age, occupation, education, and household income.

Data analysis

This study used a combination of quantitative and qualitative methods. Quantitative data analysis included descriptive statistics and Pearson's chi-square. A grounded theory approach (Strauss and Corbin 1990) was used to analyze the qualitative data into a continuum format ranging from 5 = clothing plays a critical part in a magic moment, to 1 = clothing plays no part in a magic moment.

Quantitative results and discussion

Sample characteristics. Responses were received from 148 female reenactors; a return rate of 59 percent. All respondents were subscribers to *The Citizen's Companion*. See Table 5.2 for demographic information about the respondents.

Sixty-six percent of the respondents are between the ages of 36 and 55. Forty-one percent of the sample is employed in professional occupations (e.g., nurse, teacher, lawyer). Nearly one-third of the sample had some graduate work or completed a graduate degree. Thirty percent of the sample had an annual household income between $50,000 and $74,000 (see Table 5.2).

Around 33 percent of the sample spent between $1,000 and $3,999 on Civil War clothing (see Table 5.3). When asked to check all that apply from choices presented of where they acquire their Civil War clothing, 106 respondents said from sutlers, 121 said clothing custom made by themselves, and only 20 said from purchases on the Internet (see Table 5.3).

Table 5.2 Demographics of a sample of female Civil War reenactors who responded to the *Civil War Reenactor Survey*

Demographic	Frequency	Percent
Age		
18–35	31	21.0
36–55	98	66.2
56–65+	19	12.8
Total	148	100.0
Occupation		
Executive, admin, manager	14	11.2
Professional, nurse, teacher, lawyer	52	41.3
Technician, sales, admin support	30	23.8
Service, farming, machine operators	9	7.1
Transportation and other	21	16.6
Total	126	100.0
Education		
High school	13	9.1
Some college	42	29.6
Completed college	43	30.3
Some graduate work to a graduate degree	44	31.0
Total	142	100.0
Household income		
Up to $24,999	16	11.7
$25,000 to $34,999	17	12.5
$35,000 to $49,999	31	22.6
$50,000 to $74,999	41	29.9
$75,000 to $99,999	18	13.1
$100,000 & up	14	10.2
Total	137	100.0

Respondents were asked to check the number on a continuum that corresponded with their level of interest in reenactment clothing and were instructed that this interest might include collecting, making, or wearing reenactment clothing. The continuum ranged from 0 to 5, where 0 = minimum interest in reenactment clothing and 5 = very interested in reenactment clothing. The data yielded a mean score of 4.46 (SD = 0.803). Fifty-four percent of respondents (n = 81) reported their level of interest as 5 ("very interested in reenactment clothing"); 18.8 percent (n = 28) indicated 4; and 6 percent (n = 9) indicated 3.

Magic moments were addressed through this questionnaire item: 'Have you had any "magic moments" (or "period rush") while reenacting?' Two options were offered: no and yes. Usable responses for the magic moment item came

Table 5.3 Responses from female reenactors on questionnaire items of the *Civil War Reenactor Survey* regarding clothing purchases

Questionnaire item	Frequency	Percent
Amount spent on Civil War clothing		
Less than $500	23	16.3
$500 to $799	29	20.6
$800 to $999	19	13.5
$1,000 to $3,999	46	32.6
$4,000 to $6,999	15	10.6
$7,000 to $9,999	8	5.7
Over $10,000	1	0.7
Total	141	100.0
How Civil War clothing is acquired (check all that apply)		
Sutlers (civil war merchants)		
No	41	27.9
Yes	106	72.1
Total	147	100.0
Custom made by a specialist		
No	85	58.4
Yes	62	41.6
Total	147	100.0
Custom made by yourself		
No	26	17.7
Yes	121	82.3
Total	147	100.0
Mail order catalogues		
No	86	58.5
Yes	61	41.5
Total	147	100.0
Internet purchases		
No	127	86.4
Yes	20	13.6
Total	147	100.0

from 143 respondents. Forty-six percent ($n = 66$) of women surveyed reported they had not had a magic moment. Fifty-four percent ($n = 77$) reported having had a magic moment (see Table 5.4).

When the magic moment item was compared to other survey items, one yielded significant results. The item was 'I participate in Civil War reenactments because one of my forebears/ancestors fought in the War Between the

Table 5.4 Participation in Civil War reenactments because ancestors fought in the Civil War and the occurrence of magic moments while reenacting

| | | | Have you had any 'magic moments' while reenacting? | | |
			No	Yes	Total
I participate in Civil War reenactments because one of my forebears/ancestors fought in the War Between the States	**No**	Count	47	44	91
		% w/in ancestor	51.6%	48.4%	100.0%
	Yes	Count	19	33	52
		% w/in ancestor	36.5%	63.5%	100.0%
Total		Count	66	77	143
		% w/in ancestor	46.1%	53.8%	100.0%

Note: Pearson Chi-Square = 3.040, df = 1, p = 0.058

States'. Responses to this item were also no or yes. A significant association was found between the occurrence of magic moments and having an ancestor who fought in the Civil War (chi-square = 3.040; df = 1; p = 0.058). The largest number of respondents (n = 47) fell in the no magic moment and no ancestor cell (see Table 5.4) while the smallest number of respondents (n = 19) fell in the yes to ancestor and no to magic moment cell.

Qualitative analysis and discussion

Written responses to the question 'Please describe what part, if any, reenactment clothing played in your magic moment' were analyzed using a constant comparative approach (Strauss and Corbin 1990). Constant comparisons of coded materials generated the concepts presented in this study. Rather than having defined categories prior to data collection and fitting the data to predetermined categories, categories emerged from data analysis. Therefore, 'two analytic procedures are basic to the coding process; that of *making comparisons* and *asking questions*' (Strauss and Corbin 1990: 62, emphasis in the original). A continuum arrangement was used to organize the statements from 5 to 1, where 5 = clothing critical to a magic moment, 3 = magic moment described but no clothing mentioned or ambiguous comment, and 1 = clothing played no role in a magic moment.

Seventy written responses were received and all seventy were included in the analysis. Forty-three quotes (61.4 percent) were rated a 5 and illustrated the importance of reenactment clothing to the reenactor's magic moment. These forty-three quotes were further broken down into four categories: general statements, temporal setting, spatial setting, and dressing for a role. Sixteen quotes (22.8 percent) represented the midpoint of the continuum by not including clothing in their description of a magic moment or providing contradictory statements about dress and a magic moment. Eleven comments

(15.7 percent) indicated that reenactment clothing makes no contribution to a magic moment.

Clothing crucial to magic moment. General written comments rated a 5 on the continuum which indicates that clothing is crucial to a magic moment. The following comments indicate the essential nature of dress, however they do not provide a specific example of a magic moment. Consider these examples:

> [Clothing] very much plays a part. A [magic moment] happens only when I am completely authentic and all around me are too! (41 year old respondent).
>
> There is a difference. You can put yourself in that time period, see the moment and feel the moment if you are in the clothing. The clothing helps to make the experience real, not just an outsider. You are there (34 year old respondent).
>
> Sense of being in another time would not have been possible otherwise (48 year old respondent).
>
> Without the clothing there would be no 'moment'. Costuming makes the experience more realistic (35 year old respondent).
>
> Only as much as they [clothes] set the scene. And they were generally other people's clothing. In a magic moment, you are, in a way lost in it, you are more conscious of what is going on around you rather than what you look like yourself. You are the eyes (45 year old respondent).

Criticality of the temporal setting. The following responses also rated a 5 and deal with dress and specific times of day that contributed to a magic moment. The time setting added an additional element to make a magic moment possible. Liminal experiences, such as during a magic moment or during a specific time of day/night can enhance a magic moment. Examples include:

> Wearing a ball gown and dancing at a period ball, you find yourself transformed in the candlelight. Wearing refugee work dresses and shawls strolling through a smoke filled camp at dusk. Wearing black mourning clothes at a period funeral (57 year old respondent).
>
> Early morning at a reenactment I arose and felt as though I were in another time as troops gathered in the mist to go off to an early battle – all those around me were in dress and very solemn (52 year old respondent).
>
> In one of my first reenactments, I approached Union pickets just at dark, along with my daughter grasping my hand (also in her period cloth-ing). It seemed so much like I was really there I felt fear of the enemy, covered my secession badge with one hand and grasped my daughter's hand tighter with the other (48 year old respondent).
>
> [Clothes] contributed to the ambience of the mood during the sunrise at the apex of a hill at Gettysburg (47 year old respondent).
>
> We were all in capes and undergarments rushing to 'see' a 5 a.m. battle that was fog covered – very mystical (51 year old respondent).

Spacial settings critical to magic moment. In addition to clothing and time of day, the immediate surroundings added to the occurrence of a magic moment as illustrated below:

> On or near major battlefields, the reenactment clothing allowed me to 'return to 1860s' as though it was actually occurring. I could truly 'feel their pain' (57 year old respondent).
>
> When I began doing male impressions – a private soldier on the battlefield – I had 'rushes'. It is hard not to be moved by the thousands of soldiers, the camaraderie, the blaring and smoke of the guns. Very spiritual (18 year old respondent).
>
> At Oak Alley [Plantation in] Louisiana as I stood on the top story veranda in period costume and looked out over the avenue of oaks and felt I had stepped back in time (47 year old respondent).
>
> During a Christmas program at a Historic Site (where I volunteer) we had a Christmas Caroler on the front porch of the antebellum home while a woman portraying a slave in the cabin next to the big house was celebrating Christmas with her type of singing and clapping. I stood between the two – without lights or any modern distractions. This is what a plantation must have sounded like (45 year old respondent).
>
> [The magic moment] was in a historic house and we were decorating a period tree at Christmas and baking in a wood stove – the clothing and Xmas decorations were vital to the 'rush' (40 year old respondent).

Criticality of clothing when playing a role. Dress that defines a specific role, or role dress, is crucial to the magic moments mentioned below. Roles of these reenactors included a battlefield nurse, spy, or a *Vivandiere*. The last were women who traveled with soldiers for little or no pay as mascots, sutlers and nurses, while some fought alongside their male counterparts. The term originated in France and the idea was later picked up during the American Civil War. Examples of Vivandieres include:

> I am a Civil War nurse, with aprons, etc., just like they had. I have done events where I end up covered in blood, with wounded and dead all around me, just like they did. I have tried to keep true to what they wore and I feel like I am really on the battlefield like they were (33 year old respondent).
>
> I was in my Vivandiere uniform serving as a powder monkey for a gun crew when the first 'magic moment' occurred. I've had several [magic moments] (18 year old respondent).
>
> I was very nearly executed in Liberty, NY when dressed as a Confederate spy! (40 year old respondent).

Midpoint of the continuum. Several comments described a magic moment, but did not include a connection to clothing or their comments were ambiguous.

Ambiguous quotes began by stating that clothing played no part but continued to give an example of how important clothing is. Examples include:

> When I stepped into antebellum homes, I felt I belonged – I could feel and see the people of that era moving about the house (48 year old respondent).
>
> No part – except one must be in uniform to participate in an event. No uniform, no participation – no magic moment (41 year old respondent).
>
> None other than being allowed to be the lady/women that we are no longer allowed to be (25 year old respondent).
>
> Walked thru camp at night when all was quiet – there was a full moon shining off the white [tent] canvas rows: very eerie, very magical – very peaceful. Felt like I was back in time (46 year old respondent).

Clothing played no role in magic moment. Several female respondents said that clothing played no part in their magic moment. Examples include:

> Clothing had nothing to do with the period rush (57 year old respondent).
>
> Clothing did not play a part of it (35 year old respondent).
>
> It [clothes] didn't really, it is purely auditory for me. The sounds, not the visions, can do me in! (47 year old respondent).

Summary of qualitative analysis. Reenactments appear to provide unique and personal experiences to a large number of diverse male reenactors (Miller-Spillman 2008). In comparison most female respondents may only have a strong interest in Civil War clothing. Women who described the general contribution that clothing makes to magic moments provided thoughtful and evocative responses with statements such as 'the clothing helps to make the experience real' and 'you are, in a way lost in it and more conscious of what is going on around you than what you look like yourself'. It is interesting to note that two quotes mentioned 'real' or 'realism' in conjunction to their magic moment. An ironic explanation for a magic moment although the experience was obviously very real to these women. Also, the average age of the respondents in this category is 41 years old. Perhaps a mature reenactor can best provide these insights.

Temporal and spatial contributions were also noted more often in women's responses than in men's responses (Miller-Spillman 2008). Liminal moments were keenly described by respondents as 'strolling through a smoke filled camp at dusk' and 'clothes contributed to the ambience of the mood during sunrise'. Respondents providing these comments were an average of 51 years old. Spatial contributions to a magic moment involved a particular place when a magic moment occurred. Statements such as 'on or near major battlefields, the reenactment clothing allowed me to 'return to the 1860s as though it was actually occurring' and 'decorating a period tree at Christmas ... baking in a wood stove … the clothing and … decorations were vital to the rush' provided excellent spatial examples of their magic moments. The respondents who provided these insights were an average of 47 years old.

Taking on a specific role and the associated dress contributed to the magic moments described by female respondents. Women in specific role dress had a defined and active role to play. Given that most female reenactors are civilians, their role as a passive observer is much more common. However, responses such as 'and I feel like I am really on the battlefield like they were' and 'serving as a powder monkey for a fun crew when the first "magic moment" occurred' draws us into the active role these women were experiencing during the reenactment.

At the midpoint of the continuum, some respondents gave ambiguous responses such as 'No part – except one must be in uniform to participate in an event. No uniform, no participation – no magic moment.' This response starts off stating that clothing played no part, but then it goes on to state that one must be in uniform to participate and participation leads to a magic moment. Another respondent mentioned being in an antebellum home where she could 'feel and see the people of that era moving about the house' contributing to her magic moment.

Women who believed that clothing played no part in their magic moments, for the most part, made direct, unambiguous statements. One respondent indicated that the sounds surrounding her contributed more to her magic moments than the visual of clothing.

Conclusions

The purpose of this study was to investigate female reenactors' clothing and connections, if any, to magic moments. Data from our sample gives us this portrait of female reenactors: the average female reenactor was 44 years old; held a professional position; had some graduate work or a graduate degree; had a household income between 50K and 75K; spends between 1K and 4K on Civil War clothing; and acquired reenactment clothing from sutlers or made it themselves.

Overall, female respondents in our sample hold a strong interest in reenactment clothing ($M = 4.46$, on a scale of 1–5, 5 being the highest). Eighty-two percent ($n = 121$) custom make their own reenactment clothing. Making Civil War era garments requires a high level of expertise in construction techniques. One could argue that this level of expertise goes beyond a hobby and becomes a vocation for these reenactors.

When addressing magic moments, 46 percent of our sample reported no magic moments and 54 percent reported having magic moments. When you compare these findings to men in a similar study of reenactors, you find that 85 percent of men surveyed had a magic moment, while 15 percent of men did not (Miller-Spillman 2008). Further, while we would have expected that having an ancestor that served in the Civil War would have increased the likelihood of experiencing a magic moment, this did not appear to be the case. Instead that cell representing women with an ancestor in the Civil War and experiencing a magic moment (see Table 5.4) had the next to lowest number of women (*n* = 33). Perhaps this finding is similar to the findings of Miller *et al.* in 1991 with respect to college students in Halloween costumes. Female students were less likely than male students to disguise their identities and were less likely to believe they had new identities with their costumes or to believe they could play different roles at Halloween. This suggests that women don't always let themselves go while in costume and costume allows for personal experiences among women.

Written responses from female reenactors indicate that dress sets the scene for a magic moment. Written responses from female reenactors surveyed represent a smaller range of clothing connections to magic moments than male reenactors (Miller-Spillman 2005). Males' comments were more spread out along the resulting continuum (5 = clothing very critical to a magic moment, 1 = clothing not necessary for a magic moment) while more than half of the sample of female comments were rated a 5. This indicates a stronger connection between clothing and magic moments for women than for men. However, men talked more about how the clothing felt on their bodies compared to women. This is interesting since female reenactors wear corsets and hoop skirts.

Women noted their surroundings in addition to clothing as a precursor to a magic moment. Temporal examples include daybreak and dusk with fog, mist, or a smoke filled camp. Spatial examples include a battlefield, an antebellum home, historic site cooking on wood stove, and auditory examples such as hearing a caroler at the big house and a slave celebrating by singing and clapping in a nearby cabin.

Taking on a specific role helps magic moments to occur. Given that women's roles within reenactments are less defined than men's, women have to define a role for themselves or be content as an observer. A Vivandiere or a spy are examples of active roles for women. Overall, we believe that fantastic socialization through costume at reenactments is important but is often taken for granted by reenactors. Female reenactors often want to portray wealthy women during the Civil War. This is comparable to the idea that men of wealth gravitate towards playing generals, whereas poorer men are often playing ordinary soldiers. The lack of social status during a magic moment may also appeal to participants who have professional jobs and relish the opportunity to escape their responsibilities temporarily.

References

Agnew, V. (2007) 'History's affective turn: Historical reenactment and its work in the present', *Rethinking History*, 11(3): 299–312.

Belk, R. W., and Costa, J. A. (1998) 'The mountain men myth: A contemporary consuming fantasy', *Journal of Consumer Research*, (25): 218–240.

Davis, P. G. (2009) 'Ripping the Veil: Collective memory and Black southern identity', Unpublished dissertation, University of California, San Diego.

Dillman, D. (1978) *Mail and Telephone Surveys: The Total Design Method*, New York: Wiley.

Eicher, J. B. (1981) 'Influences of changing resources on clothing, textiles, and the quality of life: Dressing for reality, fun, and fantasy', *Combined Proceedings, Eastern, Central, and Western Regional Meetings of Association of College Professors of Textiles and Clothing*, 36–41.

Eicher, J. B., and Miller, K. A. (1994) 'Dress and the public, private, and secret self: Revisiting a model', *Proceedings of the International Textile & Apparel Association, Inc.*, 145.

Frost, W. and Laing, J. (2013) *Commemorative Events: Memory, Identities, Conflict*, London and New York: Routledge.

Mead, G. H. (1934) *Mind, Self, and Society* (Charles W. Morris, ed.), Chicago: University of Chicago Press.

Miller, K. A. (1997) 'Dress: Private and secret self-expression', *Clothing and Textiles Research Journal*, 15(4): 223–234.

Miller, K. A. (1998) 'Gender comparisons within re-enactment costume: Theoretical interpretations', *Family and Consumer Sciences Research Journal*, 27(1): 35–61.

Miller, K. A. (2000) 'A national profile of Civil War reenactors', *ITAA Proceedings*, Proceedings of the International Textile and Apparel Association, Inc.

Miller, K. A., Jasper, C. R., and Hill, D. R. (1991) 'Costume and the perception of identity and role', *Perceptual and Motor Skills*, 72(3): 807–813.

Miller-Spillman, K. A. (2005) 'Playing dress-up: Childhood memories of dress', in M. L. Damhorst, K. A. Miller-Spillman, and S. O. Michelman (eds.), *The Meanings of Dress* (2nd edn.), New York: Fairchild (pp. 274–283).

Miller-Spillman, K. A. (2008) 'Male Civil War reenactors' dress and magic moments', in A. Reilly and S. Cosbey (eds.), *Men's Fashion Reader*, New York: Fairchild (pp. 455–473).

Roach-Higgins, M. E., and Eicher, J. B. (1992) 'Dress and identity', *Clothing and Textiles Research Journal*, 10: 1–8.

Rymsza-Pawlowska, M. (2007) *Frontier House: Reality Television and the Historical Experience*, Georgetown University, Monograph.

Shanks, M. L. (2009) 'Very civil wars: Reenactors, academics, and the performance of the past', Unpublished dissertation, University of California, Santa Barbara.

Stanton, C. (1997) 'Being the elephant: The American Civil War reenacted', Unpublished master's thesis, Vermont College of Norwich University, Northfield, Vermont.

Stone, G. P. (1959) 'Halloween and the mass child', *American Quarterly*, 2: 372–379.

Stone, G. P. (1965) 'Appearance and the self', in M. E. Roach and J. B. Eicher (eds.), *Dress, Adornment and the Social Order*, New York: John Wiley & Sons (pp. 216–245).

Strauss, A. and Corbin, J. (1990) *Basics of Qualitative Research: Grounded Theory Procedures and Techniques*, Newbury Park, CA: Sage Publications.

Part II
Industry and destination perspectives

6 When the event is insufficient

An apposite story of New Zealand Fashion Week

Peter Shand

In April 2001, *Apparel* – the New Zealand garment industry journal of record – announced that the inaugural *New Zealand Fashion Week* (NZFW) would be held the coming October (*Apparel* 2001: 9). A short statement noted the formation of NZ Fashion Week Ltd, its securing of sponsorship and the confirmed presence of international buyers and media. Company Director and event organiser Pieter Stewart was well known and well regarded in the local industry, having previously developed collection shows for prime-time television broadcast. Moreover, the development and realisation of a New Zealand variant of the Fashion Week model both capitalised on and advanced the considerable local attention that had been given to the industry in the wake of a series of successful international runways shows culminating in the invitational presence of four New Zealand designer labels (Karen Walker, NOM*d, WORLD and Zambesi) at both London Fashion Week (LFW) shows in 1999.

Twelve NZFWs have since come and gone and NZFW faces not inconsiderable challenges to its continued viability. Causative factors include: pressure on competitive pricing and high currency rates, challenges to manufacturing, decline in meaningful international participation, lack of substantial long-term sponsorship of the event, cost to designers of showing and apparent lack of innovation or responsiveness to the event model in order to mitigate these. Each exacerbates the inherent challenge of a small-scale creative industry; collectively, they reinscribe the particular difficulties faced by such an industry geographically isolated from major international markets.

This chapter considers NZFW as an example of the challenges that face small, often territorialised fashion-producing communities. It focuses on a narrative of peaks and troughs pertinent to New Zealand designers' participation in Fashion Weeks at home and abroad over the past fifteen years. It identifies a suite of pertinent issues that point not only to the inevitable external challenges but also to the demands on a creative event or service business, the primary *raison d'être* of which is to advance the economic and creative reach of creative professionals.

NZFW did not emerge from a vacuum for the industry, the participating designers or Stewart (for a broad historical overview of NZ Fashion 1979–2009 see Shand 2010). Karen Walker and WORLD each showed at separate Hong Kong Fashion Weeks in 1998. Karen Walker's *Daddy's Gone Strange* collection of reworked men's suiting garnered attention and the label was picked up by Barneys, the New York department store. There was also early critical success in national presentations at the second and third Australian Fashion Weeks (AFW) in Sydney in 1997 and 1998. AFW 1997 saw collections presented by Moontide, Wallace Rose, WORLD and Zambesi. Prominent, influential members of the international fashion press Hilary Alexander (*The Daily Telegraph*), Elsa Klensch (CNN) and Anna Piaggi (*Vogue Italia*) praised WORLD and Zambesi. The following year, they were joined by Blanchet, Karen Walker, Kate Sylvester and Workshop. Patty Huntington in *Women's Wear Daily* called the New Zealand contingent 'a formidable design force' (Hammonds *et al.* 2010: 328) and Maggie Alderson of the *Sydney Morning Herald* commented: 'a group of Kiwi designers is emerging with a distinctive, fresh style'. She also captured the attention of the industry with the rather singular appellation: 'the New Belgians' (*Apparel* 1998: 13) – a highly complementary comparison to the *Antwerp Six* (Walter Van Beirendonck, Dirk Bikkembergs, Ann Demeulemeester, Dries Van Noten, Dirk Van Saene and Marina Yee who showed as a collective renegade event at Westway during the British Designers' Show in March 1988 having been declined a place on the official calendar). The inference of shared characteristics of independence and youthful verve, small scale of production and a long national history of excellence in textile production seemed to promise similar success for leading New Zealand designers.

The following year represents a watershed in contemporary New Zealand fashion when the *New Zealand Four* (as they came to be known domestically) presented their A/W 1999–2000 collections in a joint catwalk show at LFW in February 1999. Their inclusion on the schedule was by way of juried selection by representatives of the British Fashion Council, the designers securing one of three slots from seventy other applicants. In this they were championed by *Liberty* Head Ladies Buyer Angela Quaintrell, who had travelled to New Zealand in 1997. Endorsing its contemporaneous trans-Tasman reception, she described New Zealand fashion as 'fresh and new' (*Apparel* 1999: 6).

In parallel to the development of the industry, public attention to LFW did not spring fully-formed in 1999. Vibrant counter-culture scenes developed in the 1960s and 1970s and these involved not only the manifestation of different modes of dress but also led to diverse fashion events – from public shows to marginal fashion events as happenings or at dance parties. Televised broadcast of the *Benson & Hedges* (later *Smokefree*) *Design Awards* in whole or part from the late 1970s to 1998 and *Style Pasifika* from the 1990s to 2011 is indicative of a prime-time audience for contemporary fashion design and attendant exposure for featured designers. In addition to these competitions, fashion broadcasting in New Zealand in the 1990s included in-season preview programmes. These were inaugurated by Stewart in 1990 and ran for the remainder of the decade as the Corbans then Wella Fashion Collections then the Wella Fashion Report. Importantly for NZFW it is from this platform that Stewart developed the industry relationships, knowledge and credibility that assisted in the realisation of the first event.

Beyond the specifics of LFW or of Stewart's previous work, the timing of NZFW's inauguration was prescient. There was in 2001 a real sense of possibility for the creative sector. The then Prime Minster, Helen Clark, held the Ministerial Portfolio for Arts and Culture, an unheard-of endorsement of the importance of arts and creative industries in a Westminster-style government. With Vice Chancellor of the University of Auckland, John Hood, she hosted *The Knowledge Wave* Conference that August. This was intended to examine New Zealand's future in a predicted economic and social environment that would privilege education, innovation and knowledge generation in the realisation of enhanced goods and services for international markets – a classic rhetorical formulation for creative economies at the time. An example of a platform for a creative industry, NZFW occurred two months later. It also fell between two other critical events for New Zealand's international cultural profile: artists Jacqueline Fraser and Peter Robinson were the first to represent New Zealand at the Venice Biennale, opening in June of that year; and *The Fellowship of the Ring*, the first of director Peter Jackson's *The Lord of the Rings* trilogy of films, was released in December. The time was ripe.

What Stewart recognised was the absence for fashion of a galvanizing event of national scope but with international reach. Contemporaneous developments included those in Dunedin and Wellington. *iD Dunedin Fashion Week* was established by a group of independents in 1999 and the *Wellington Fashion Festival* (2001–2003; re-launched as *Wellington Fashion Week* in 2012) provided opportunities for local designers to show collections publically. In that sense, they were more fashion festivals than fashion weeks as such, with a clear focus on the consumer audience and connection to specific metropolitan location, as distinct from the Fashion Week model of an advance-season, trade-focused event with cosmopolitan ambitions. The choice of Auckland, the country's only globally connected city, as a location reflected its strategic and logistical advantage for the international trade ambition of NZFW as much as its commanding position in the domestic market.

Fashion Week is a marquee event providing a consolidated platform for the display of high-quality designer fashion. For the major markets it is a biannual event that enables the majority of participating designers to preview ready-to-wear collections in advance of the season. That characteristic of preview is a core component of the agglomerated fashion event. It serves both a creative advantage (presenting current design propositions) and an economic one (generating orders prior to production together with the additional impetus of fuelling consumer desire). It is exclusive in nature, both insofar as access is limited to trade or individuals of status within or related to the industry and in that the design propositions shown are current formulations of a particular creative language. In this sense it is a quintessential example of a creative industry at work: the close, mutually sustaining embrace of creativity and commerce; profit (financial and reputational) sustained by the apprehension of quality by the critical cognoscenti; a distinct orientation toward media; and communication to interested consumers. As an event, particularly its major incidents in New York, London, Milan and Paris, it is carefully choreographed. This is true not only of the often lavish, spectacular, technically rigorous and creatively audacious of the very best collections in a season, it is also a condition of the consolidated Fashion Week schedule. It is a high-profile, high-status spectacle that, in its promulgation in print, broadcast and on-line media, is rendered publically available even though its exclusion of the hoi polloi is of central importance to its perceived cultural value. In a manner of speaking, it is a short period of stillness in the otherwise steady diachronic march of fashion, a moment for comparative analysis and consideration by a community of practitioners.

Of course, NZFW was not and is not intended to operate at that global level of self-valorising creative corporate activity. Nevertheless, its inauguration with Southern Hemisphere A/W collection previews in October 2001 represents a conscious scaling of its commercial and cultural allure. In its first years, performance data was positive across the board. From studies commissioned in 2003 and 2006, the company showed NZFW 2003 was worth NZ$23.2 million to the New Zealand economy overall and NZ$19.2 million to the Auckland region; values that rose NZ$10 million in each case for NZFW 2004. Those same reports noted steadily increasing attendance from buyers (up to 190 from 11 countries in 2004) and 110 media representatives from 10 countries (Lewis *et al.* 2008: 48). Importantly, early attending buyers included representatives of *Selfridges* in 2002–2003 as well as influential independents. Clearly building on the showing at LFW, early high-profile media delegates included fashion luminaries Hilary Alexander in 2001 and the leading British fashion historian Colin McDowell the following year. Their presence added weight to the event while securing valuable, networked international attention and advocacy. That capacity to drive international growth (through attracting buyers or promoting recognition) is of central importance to designers in a geographically isolated country such as New Zealand. A company press release summarising the 2006 report gave the value of foreign exchange earnings to designers as NZ$13.1 million.

Nothing succeeds like success and in response to the perceived economic cut-through achieved on the back of the event and the exponential growth in national media interest, the number of participating designers increased steadily from fourteen individual designer shows at NZFW 2001 to a 2008 peak of twenty-nine. These were complemented by group shows, including (from the event's inception) the *New Generation/Breakthrough Shows* of selected young designers, *Style Pasifika* showcase (2003–2005, 2007) and from 2009 a showcase of winners from the *Miromoda Designer Fashion Awards* for Maori fashion run by the Indigenous Maori Fashion Apparel Board. The largest single NZFW in terms of labels showing was 2009, with forty-eight New Zealand and three international designers on the schedule.

Nevertheless, what began to emerge from 2005/2006 were risks to the event model's capacity to generate sustained success for New Zealand designers. As the initial waves of buyers and influencers gave way to less influential counterparts, concrete international success became increasingly elusive. In response, there has been little obvious attempt to extend or innovate that basic model. As a criticism this is double-edged. On one hand, it is important to bear in mind that NZFW is a platform for the work of the designers – a business with the purpose of creating additional business opportunities for the fee-paying designers who show. In that respect it ought not to outshine the fashions. On the other, the business requirement of NZFW is not only as a service business or platform for presentations but one for which connection and reputation are critical value attributes. As challenges mount that remain unanswered, the business's capacity to serve its clients is eroded. The loss of named sponsorship (Air New Zealand withdrew in 2010 and no replacement was secured) can suggest to a vulnerable, volatile industry that the event is inadequate for its commercial purpose. If this coincides with a decline in international connectivity (fewer buyers, fewer orders; less international media, less exposure) then labels will reconsider continued participation.

This reflects more than the normative requirements of an industry hungry for overseas markets but a very specific characteristic of the New Zealand fashion industry. With a national population of a little over four million, the local market is small. The majority of designer fashion businesses in New Zealand are vertically structured; an obvious indicator of this is almost all have eponymous retail stores. The majority have stable representation in local boutiques that provide additional national reach, and these relationships tend to be managed in-house rather than secured and managed by agents. Few, however, have significant international representation and only a limited number of mostly younger labels are represented on aggregator fashion retail websites. Hence, international expansion is of vital importance to almost every New Zealand designer label and this requires not merely an international presence at NZFW but a presence that affects results. In the face of the marked downturn in the global economy since 2007, New Zealand is less and less a viable prospect for international buyers or agents, especially when the allure of novelty is no longer a claim the local industry can credibly mount.

The territorial particularity of New Zealand fashion has remained challenging – *the tyranny of distance* as it is locally described. Southern Hemisphere A/W presentations in September are inevitably perceived as being behind their Northern equivalents, which for a future-focussed industry further disinclines international attendance. The premise of the preview show is that a limited number of sample garments are made coincident to the show: one to be worn, one in the sales room for buyers to see, for instance. What this affords the designer is the opportunity to test a design – both on the runway and with prospective clients. If, however, the label is not reliant on buyers or agents for the local market and there are few international commercial contacts to be made, then that function all but disappears. Simultaneously, the impact of digitisation on the presentation, viewing and purchase of fashion garments throws into question the very assumption that the traditional fashion preview has value.

Indeed, what has become increasingly apparent over the past NZFWs is that designers in this country are less inclined to ape the determined rhythm of the preview collection. There are three contributing reasons. First, a significant number of the labels showing at NZFW are not designer fashion as such but middle-market or streetwear producers for whom international timeliness is less of a concern. Second, the majority of New Zealand fashion designers are essentially trans-seasonal; New Zealand has a temperate climate and its population is proportionately highly urbanised, which informs habits of dress where seasonal shifts are margins of subtle degree. Third, consumer demand is speeding up business and contracting traditional production lead-times. In response, an increasing number of labels at NZFW show in September garments that can be purchased that September.

The geographic distance of NZFW may be mitigated by the collapse of temporal space wrought by digitisation. That reconfiguration of proximity and distance fractures the nationalist position adopted for LFW and, 'despite the nationalism implicit in New Zealand Fashion Week, by the early 2000s the collective "New Zealand Fashion" brand seemed to be nearing its use-by date' (Hammonds *et al.* 2010: 350). That said, small, idiosyncratic labels like most in New Zealand will struggle with the incessant demands of the industry should they successfully internationalise their brands. To one way of thinking, NZFW serves that interest – the bringing together of numerous brands in a single event that provides the level of critical mass that might attract international contacts of influence or industry heft. When that attraction fades, however, a significant component of the model also dims. What appears missing from the entrepreneurial model is a strategy for long-term development that secures robustness for the event. In the same way that the underlying format of the *Corbans and Wella Collections* broadcasts remained static in the 1990s a similar structural assumption has emerged with respect to NZFW: a model is established but there follows little interrogation of its continued relevance or fit. The problem for a small event such as NZFW is that it lacks the self-validating scale and significance of the Fashion Weeks or the connection to rapidly growing markets as served by those in Beijing, Jakarta, Mumbai or São Paulo.

Exacerbating these challenges is a commercial imperative that inhibits company organisers mediating the calibre of designers or shows. Schedules are remarkably inconsistent in terms of quality and are padded with shows that add nothing to staple items. Shows of manufactured garments rather than designer fashion further compromise the attractiveness of the NZFW ticket for those travelling from far afield. For designers it reflects a closing down of the audience for the collection to a tiny coterie of local pundits and celebrities mixed with a loyal customer base and limited walk-ins. Again this is double-edged. From one perspective, it generates a broadly celebratory environment that cements relationships with clients and customers. From another, it inhibits critical engagement and response, dumbing down discourse that would provide valuable feedback to designers. Together, such features risk circumscribing individual designers' visions with an attendant risk that they become myopic rather than maintain a clear point of view, reiterative rather than directional.

Added to this, the gap of credible critical fashion journalism in New Zealand is palpable. With the notable exceptions of Stacey Gregg and Michael Lamb's runwayreporter.com (March 2006–January 2009) and emerging writer Zoe Walker in national newspaper *The New Zealand Herald*, the bulk of local media coverage has proven to be uncritical and largely uninformed. Enthusiastic rhetoric or gushing praise increasingly holds sway over informed commentary, with diminishing returns. If one considers the New Zealand Four, for example, well-received as those collections may have been, their impact on global fashion does not remotely approach that of the Antwerp Six; similarly, the lasting influence of Hussein Chalayan's extraordinary A/W 2000–1 collection *After Words* that showed at LFW six months after the New Zealanders. Such an observation serves as a corrective appraisal of lasting influence as distinct from passing interest. At the same time, it does not diminish the significance of the Four and other leading labels' contributions domestically, as the rise of public institutional interest in the form of curated exhibitions indicates. Pertinent examples of exhibitions of contemporary New Zealand fashion include: The First New Zealand Fashion Week curated by Angela Lassig at Te Papa Tongarewa, The Museum of New Zealand, Wellington, 2002–2003; 'We fought fashion – and lost!' WORLD 1989–2005 and Zambesi: Edge of Darkness curated by the author for the Auckland War Memorial Museum, 2004 and 2005 respectively. The point however is that a pervasive lack of criticality stifles development.

The participation of the New Zealand Four in NZFW focuses attention on these and other relevant factors. Although not unique in and of themselves, their various engagements with and reaction to the event over its twelve-year history chart a gamut of response to its sufficiency – from expedience to sustained aspect of the design practice. They also indicate the particular experience of established fashion labels with local authority, as distinct from younger brands for which breakthrough domestic exposure would be a successful outcome.

Of the Four, Karen Walker was the only label not to participate in the inaugural event, which was taken at the time for disdain as to the relevance NZFW might hold for the label. Similarly, in London, it had traded from an official LFW hotel and had engaged a New York-based PR firm to handle business (the other labels had traded directly from Trade New Zealand rooms in New Zealand House). It followed that Walker was viewed as not being a team player, not contributing to a collective leveraging for the industry. While factual, the inference mistakes the motivation. Walker was very clear about the role of any fashion event when she noted: 'I'm not in this business to express my love for my country. It's got nothing to do with patriotism and everything to do with buyers and media – that's all fashion shows are for' (quoted in Gregg 2003: 33) Subsequent participation in NZFW (2003–2005, 2007–2011) suggests a shift of mind, whereby the local market is recognised as a secure base for a label still working to maintain international purchase. Shows included the launch of an accessory line of jewellery (2003) and to support the label's involvement in *The Department Store*, a fashion and beauty venue (2010–2011). In 2012, the label did not show. This in part was due to the dates of NYFW, which opened within the week of NZFW closing. Karen Walker had first shown there in September 2000, the first New Zealand label to do so. The obvious expedient commercial decision was to prioritise retaining that presence.

Similarly, WORLD's mode of engagement reflects a fitful relationship (showing in 2001–2004, 2008, 2010 and 2011). It is also the only label on the schedule most likely to present experimental or conceptual components of a collection, not solely ready-to-wear lines. That capacity to stretch the normative expectations of NZFW has contributed to its reputation as the leading avant-garde label in the country. A WORLD show is accompanied by a sense of demand; much as there is spectacle to be experienced, it also posits questions that are not necessarily resolved in the minds of an audience within the duration of the runway presentation. It also signals a tension with the more commonly held reception of the collections presented. The theatricality of garments and presentation is easily mistaken as non-commercial, whereas a more sophisticated sense of commerce is at play. For example, at NZFW 2002 the label mounted the first demi-couture show by a New Zealand label, which included maquillage featuring thousands of Swarovski crystals, adhered to the faces of the models. That partnership coincided with the revitalisation of the Austrian luxury brand and initiated a partnership that endures – notably a suite of seven crystal encrusted silhouettes of the *There is No Depression in New Zealand* A/W 2009 Collection that was the centrepiece of NZFW 2008. The relationship continues, which reflects its long-term value to both rather than a one-off pageant.

This sort of approach reflects a label that holds the event at arm's length. WORLD tends to engage with NZFW quite obviously on its own terms. That can result in spectacle that is the most public face of its brand identity (Figure 6.1). The label plays to that reputation and essentially turns its uniqueness on the NZFW calendar to mutual advantage, albeit to the label's privilege. A pertinent example was in 2011, when the WORLD A/W 2012 collection was used for the finale of the *New Zealand's Next Top Model*, the local variant of the televised modelling competition franchise. The show (from host Buckwheat, a drag artiste who had modelled for WORLD in the 1996 *Wella Fashion Collections*; to the opening suite of LED piped garments starting on an unlit stage; to a finale ensemble commissioned by Te Papa Tongarewa, The Museum of New Zealand) (Figure 6.2) was conspicuously oriented towards extending brand awareness afforded by the broadcast. Since 2010, the label

Figure 6.1 NZFW 2011, WORLD 'Good vs Evil' show A/W 2012.
Source: N. Hindin

has developed an independent relationship with an Auckland hotel and has moved to open-ticketed, in-season presentations with a mix of press, long-time supporters and paying members of the public. It chose this independent event over participation in NZFW 2012.

2011 was the first NZFW at which NOM*d did not show. The critical issue for this label was the impossibility of securing sufficient sponsorship, as so many creative enterprises face in an economic recession. In a television current affairs programme broadcast on the eve of the 2012 event, founder Margarita Robertson candidly spoke of the relationship of sponsors to the success of a runway show (Television New Zealand 2012). Sponsorship was terrific when markets were buoyant, she noted, but the capacity to secure sponsorship had

Figure 6.2 NZFW 2011, WORLD 'Good vs Evil' show A/W 2012 (finale silhouette: Wedding Dress commissioned by Te Papa Tongarewa, The Museum of New Zealand).
Source: M. Ng

declined sharply since the onset of the recession in 2007. If a presentation cost NZ$50,000 then NOM*d would need approximately 50 per cent from sponsors to make participation possible, a not-insignificant sum in a small market. What was especially pertinent about her comments is that she openly declared that not showing in 2011 had made no impact on sales in the following twelve months. While that business picture is damning, Robertson shares a creative's zeal for the individual show as an event of value for the designer and the label. She recognises the satisfaction of the runway show, the moment where the component parts of the presentation (models, styling, maquillage, location, music and light) breathe life into the designs. Coincident with the availability of its A/W 2012 collection *Do Not Disturb* and in replacement of a runway show, NOM*d commissioned a six-minute video that was posted on YouTube. Such an approach served the label well; it maximised atmospheric characterisation, expanded the availability of the collection launch to a wider audience and realised a remarkably positive solution to the sticky problem at hand. While such postings lack the immediate thrill of applause at a marquee event, the prevailing characteristic of the Internet enables a responsive and commercial reach concomitant with the expanded viewing audience.

Of the New Zealand Four, the most consistent participant in NZFW is Zambesi, one of only two labels to have presented individual shows at all twelve events. Three conjoined goals form the basis for that engagement: attracting new clients (particularly international ones); maintaining the label's place in the market; and showing what Zambesi can do. In recent years the client focus has moved closer to enhancing existing relationships with buyers and stockists. Mindful of the ongoing investment they have made in the label, founder Elisabeth Findlay recognises the value of its Australasian home market and existing clients and customers' reception of the creative propositions of each collection. Foregrounding the creative driver of the design practice, Zambesi's presence at NZFW is important because of what is learned from showing at scale. The shows are uplifting achievements for the label, provide closure and completeness of the collection realised and germinate new ideas for the following collection.

This reflects the precision of the label's position. Since inception it has been a niche brand. With runway presentation honed in in-house, capsule and venue events for twenty years before London and a wide array of local and international presentations prior and subsequently, Findlay is very clear not only as to her design vision but also to its relationship to the runway show. Zambesi also has certain advantages in showing at NZFW that mitigate some of the challenges raised in this chapter. The business is vertically structured; it does not have an agent so maintains closeness to stockists; is essentially trans-seasonal (both in the sense of cross-over within the A/W S/S cycle and building a consistent look and feel year-on-year); and it always puts every garment shown into production. Such characteristics of the label helped mitigate the impact of the drought of new and overseas buyers at NZFW. They also complement the label's motivation to contribute to where it is based and that shapes what it does. There is a clear pragmatism attached to the creative position – one makes it work.

In different ways, then, the New Zealand Four have enjoyed freedom enough to stretch the assumed conditions of the event. What is most valuable about that activity is that it clearly separates the structure of the event from what it is they do. It brings back to mind the purpose of NZFW as a commercial business, to prove its value to producers, bridging producers, intermediaries and consumers in order to enhance its own value and reputation. It keeps in the forefront of that consideration that designers are the drivers of the event.

Although the currency of design is a flexible commodity, the fact that of the New Zealand Four, only Zambesi, showed at NZFW 2012 carries inescapably negative implications for the event.

The others' absence exposes the inherent management challenges for a small, independent operator such as NZ Fashion Week Ltd. Those challenges have been drawn into focus with the decline of sponsorship and financial certainty in recent years but it is worth reflecting that problems such as those with sponsorship can be as much symptomatic as causative. The steady decline of international participation, the lack of modification of the underlying structure and the absence of meaningful updating in the conduct of the event are not necessarily insurmountable problems in and of themselves but they are indicative of an incapacity to innovate. As it stands, NZFW seems to lack impetus, content to roll out essentially the same event year on year but without clarity of vision or direction. In this respect, the event begins to lose vibrancy and relevance, with a correlative erosion of reputation that threatens its continued viability.

At the time of writing, its lifeline comes from local government. The Auckland City Council agency Auckland Tourism, Events and Economic Development (ATEED) is charged with realising an ambitious set of economic and socio-cultural goals predicated on the wider value to the city of major cultural and sporting events and contributed NZ$225,000 to NZFW from a total Council development budget of NZ2.25 million (ONE News 2012). NZFW is one of five regular major events named in the agency's Auckland Major Events Strategy document (the others being the Pasifika and Lantern cultural festivals, the Auckland Arts Festival and the Auckland Marathon). Interestingly, it is the only demonstrably trade-oriented event of the five. While that is indicative of a favourable view of the event, it also infers a misinterpretation of Fashion Week as it is experienced globally. It is less a visitor-attracting event such as those listed by ATEED than an economic leveraging one, with obvious benefits to the businesses based in the host city as well as an enhancement of the cosmopolitan reputation of that city (and the investment potential that generates).

In this context, NZFW might productively give attention to elements of the event that have proven insufficient in recent years. Consider timeliness and the runway show, for example. The seasonal preview is manifestly anachronistic in the local environment. The majority of labels are either trans-seasonal or have turned to showing in-season collections. That reality better reflects how collections are communicated to the public. Digitisation has collapsed a preceding system of delayed authoritative arbitration and contributed to an unprecedented level of immediacy. Fashion pundits and buyers are not only aware of that shift but they now contribute directly to it. The explosion of on-line retail (whether label-specific or aggregated) is thoroughly overhauling the scope and diversity of garments available to consumers. Manufacture lead-times have collapsed in direct relation to the temporal changes in the industry. This closes the circle of production and consumption so that the most effective contemporary strategy for smaller labels is to show collections that are in stock – capitalising on the *see it, like it, buy it* approach that underpins modern fashion production and consumption.

Add to this a complicated spatial relationship to the fashion world. With international visitation having fallen off in New Zealand, the strategy for engagement in the global fashion economy is better served by two different approaches. The traditional one is participation by New Zealand labels in international shows, not only costly front-end events of Fashion Weeks but also the attendant trade shows. After LFW, with support from New Zealand Trade and Enterprize, NOM*d, WORLD and Zambesi and two other labels showed for two seasons at the Tranoï trade show attached to Paris Fashion Week and attempted to maintain a presence after support was discontinued. Other labels, too, have rightly assessed that their better strategy is to take samples to potential markets, not remain at home waiting for a visit that without structure is unlikely to eventuate. The more contemporary approach is to understand the operation of the digital environment and harness it to individual labels' requirements. In the past, NZFW has addressed this by inviting bloggers but that approach underestimates the scale of the opportunity social media in particular provides and misapprehends the mechanisms by which designers can recruit that opportunity. It gets right the marketing focus of fashion's connection to the blogosphere but remains wedded to the assumption that successful digital marketing is predicated on the physicality of encounter. In effect, exchanging a magazine elite for an Internet one misunderstands what digitisation of media, cultural and social relations effects: a comprehensive rejection of the concept of a distant hierarchy of fashion arbiters. That is complemented by a decoupling of the physical product to any single real-world location for purchase.

To those matters, one can add audience agency. Widespread interest in fashion and the fashion industry is part of the zeitgeist. It is not driven solely through passive consumption but, increasingly, through active engagement. Fashion Weeks share characteristics of an *Experience Economy* (Pine and Gilmore 2011) but potential audience engagement is not contained by the runway; it is independently created and developed. As opposed to maintaining sector insularity, it is worthwhile to consider how public interest spills over into other domains and how it may relate more broadly to creative ecologies. A crude example is that fashion is increasingly a key social expression of personal individuality, and people desire to be active participants in the production of fashion, not simply its passive recipients.

What these questions propose is the broadening of the scope of NZFW. This is in part a reaction to the waning effectiveness of the model implemented in 2001 and in part a suggested review both of purpose and how to meet that purpose once redefined. Such a review ought also to encompass governance. Stewart has repeatedly advocated for a national fashion council, which might be a productive innovation if it were to extend the developmental scope to yearlong support of the industry rather than the stop/start model of NZFW. However, it is not immediately clear how its activities would differ from the existing industry advocacy group Fashion Industry New Zealand. Alternatively, like a number of other leading Auckland developmental organisations and cultural venues and events, an event trust could be established. What either a council or trust can achieve that even the strongest of small businesses can struggle with is the breadth and length of reach. They are in a better position to withstand the vagaries of particular political or funding horizons and are also more likely to adopt a more complicated long-term view of future viability of a particular strategy or flagship event and act promptly with respect to that view. Without an internal commercial imperative, they are better able consciously to shape events, including the who, where and what is shown. That seems valuable at this juncture.

In concluding, I want to be clear that this chapter is not intended to be an excoriation of NZFW. Its contribution to the development of the local industry has been marked and its value to the visibility of New Zealand fashion significant. Nevertheless, it is also clear that its current contribution is more ephemeral than substantive, suggesting the event is no longer sufficient for the industry's needs. Hence, the necessity of a review. I wish also to posit a model I think demonstrably better suited to a fashion event in a small nation. Chapter 8 of this book provides a case study of the annual Melbourne Fashion Festival written by Karen Webster, for five years the Festival Director. Since its governing Trust's inception in 1996, this remarkable event has consistently realised long-term benefits for the local and national industry, advanced critical inquiry in the fields of design and creative business and their relationship to place and people, focused tourist attention on the city of Melbourne and, perhaps most importantly, engaged actively with a broad demographic of citizens. A multi-tiered event, it contrasts markedly with the traditional fashion week formula but in a similar timeframe to NZFW has helped secure a sustainable industry and a connected public. It is expansive rather than insular. In this respect, it offers a salient example of event sufficiency that NZFW, ATEED and the New Zealand industry at large would do well to regard.

Acknowledgements

I am grateful to Benny Castles (*WORLD*) Elisabeth Findlay (*Zambesi*), Francis Hooper (*WORLD*) and Margarita Robertson (*NOM*d*) for discussions about NZFW and other matters of pertinence to the industry over a long period of time, including in preparation for this chapter, and to my colleagues Elizabeth Aitken-Rose (University of Auckland) and Sally-Jane Norman (University of Sussex) for timely observations.

References

Apparel (1998) 'The Hottest Place on Earth', 30(5): 13.
Apparel (1999) 'NZ Designers for London Fashion Week', 31(1): 6.

Apparel (2001) 'NZ Fashion Week is on the Calendar', 33(3): 9.

Gregg, S. (2003) *Undressed: New Zealand Fashion Designers Tell Their Stories*, Auckland: Penguin.

Hammonds, L., Lloyd-Jenkins, D. and Regnault, C. (2010) *Dress Circle: New Zealand Fashion Design Since 1940*, Auckland: Godwit.

Lassig, A. (2010) *New Zealand Fashion Design*, Wellington: Te Papa Press.

Lewis, N., Larner, W. and Le Heron, R. (2008) 'The New Zealand Designer Fashion Industry: Making Industries and Co-constituting Political Projects', *Transactions of the Institute of British Geographers*, 33(1): 42–59.

ONE News (2012) Broadcast 7 September 2012.

Pine, J. and Gilmore, J. H. (2011) *The Experience Economy* (rev. edn.), Boston: Harvard Business School Press.

Shand, P (2010) 'Pieces, Voids and Seams: A Introduction to Contemporary New Zealand Fashion Design', in A. Lassig, *New Zealand Fashion Design*, Wellington: Te Papa Press (pp. x–xxxvii).

Television New Zealand (2012) *Close-up*, September 3.

7   Wedding hats, intellectual property and everything!

Paul Sugden

The wedding of HRH Prince William and Miss Catherine Middleton, billed by the media as yet another wedding of the century, was the event at which a fashion creation by Philip Treacy, worn by HRH Princess Beatrice, stole the public imagination and media attention. The creation of a hat of a stylised bow and ribbon loop galvanised media criticism as tasteless (Huffington Post 2011), crass and received as much comment as the wedding itself. The hat found fame, spawned its own website, launched fridge/car magnets, party hats (Gilbert 2011), cartoons and memes, paintings and copies for sale. Finally, the hat was auctioned for charity at the value of £81,000 (UK Telegraph 2011). The hat became its own event and was often more memorable than the wedding itself! As Sarah Gilbert said:

> This hat did its job. Not only did it give rise to a flurry of attention about Beatrice – which perhaps has not been quite flattering – it has also inspired a renewed interest in British millinery and, indeed, millinery worldwide. According to the Hat Gallery in London, 'We're definitely expecting hats to start reappearing at weddings; sales have risen by up to 20% since the [royal] wedding'. Business at other hat shops in London is up as much as 60% since this time last year, and at Philip Treacy, sales have doubled.
>
> (Gilbert 2011)

The hat created a commercial windfall for milliners, leading to further creations. However, others with an irreverent attitude to the hat and some entrepreneurial skill created different forms of the hat that produced short-run products for general mass consumption. These products copied the *essence* of the hat without any development of creativity or investment, except to apply it in a different form. In marketing and economics terms, the products spawned by the hat are *free riding* on Treacy's creativity and fame.

Should Treacy sue for infringement of his hat design when used as a fridge magnet or a party hat or toilet seat? Is the fame and publicity from the daring nature of the hat sufficient to provide recompense against copying? And how can fashion design be protected by a system which is fragmented by place, type, time and rules of protection? This chapter considers these issues, spawned by the Royal Wedding as a fashion event.

Characterisation of events and fashion under legal theory involves the protection of the economic constructive nature of these activities. Economic constructs are captured by intellectual property law, trade practices and the protection of goodwill. Ultimately, events and fashion at law are a patchwork composite of ideas, relationships, good and services, executed for commercial or altruistic purposes. An examination of events or fashion from all legal relationships is beyond the scope of this chapter, rather the current concentration of academic argument is about how to protect fashion and events as tangible expressions of intangibles. The intangible nature of rights expressed as tangible items has challenged law and its ability to protect the ephemeral nature of fashion. The inimitable Coco Chanel once said: 'Fashion should slip out of your hands. The very idea of protecting the seasonal arts is childish. One should not bother to protect that which dies the minute it was born' (Charles-Roux 2005: 377).

Introduction to intellectual property law

Chanel may believe that fashion should not be protected, yet the fashion industry in the twenty-first century has reignited the debate on fashion protection, particularly in the United States where Borukhovich (2009), Beltrametti (2010), Blackmon (2012) and others have debated the extent or lack of protection provided by new initiatives in the United States.

Ultimately, the twenty-first century, with its technological revolution, presents a more egalitarian consumer base than in Chanel's heyday. The consumers demand more innovation and more collections and technological broadcasts of these to an instantaneous international market. Designer clothes shown in Milan, Paris, New York and Tokyo are often reinterpreted and reproduced in various guises throughout the world in department stores within a matter of weeks or months. The speed and ability of computer programs to produce patterns versus the handmade individual *haute-couture* item has called into question the effectiveness of laws to protect fashion. This debate though is a segment of a greater debate about the extent or existence of strong intellectual property laws or weak intellectual property laws outlined by Dreyfuss (2010) who concludes that it is a matter of locating the divide between public and private interests of property and use.

Raustiala and Sprigman (2006) debate the need for strong intellectual property in an industry where copying is rife but competition and innovation and investment remain vibrant. They suggest that the innovation cycle of the fashion industry and its seasonal nature mean it is a counter-intuitive industry to intellectual property law protection and low levels of protection, even with high levels of copying, can support creativity. Howard (2009) criticises this view for two reasons – (1) advances in technology have changed the market and (2) their arguments are based on outdated views of consumer behaviour.

Technology has changed all industries, as exemplified by Philip Treacy's hat, which was unique and worn by one person at the couture end of a market, while the fascinator party hat version is in a humorous entertainment category. Technology though means the hat, once seen, can be dissected and created by others and sold in a short period, which leads the writer to consider that the property rights given by intellectual property generally adopt a *one size fits all* approach to legal protection. This approach does not provide adequate protection to an industry constructed of multiple layers catering to different needs and desires. In Raustiala's view, the fashion market pyramid is comprised of four layers, ranging from high-creative/high-cost/one off garments for women, to low creative mass demand basic essentials for all of us. Blackmon's (2012) alternative division describes a market of 12 different segments from haute-couture, couture, designer, young designer, bridge/better, contemporary, junior, upper moderate/lower bridge, moderate, budget, private label, and mass market. Each segment has its own demographic and production processes, meaning that creating certainty for a law applicable to each market through a one size fits all approach will be difficult. Blackmon simplified her model to two essential markets – *haute-couture* and *prêt-à-porter* (ready to wear), which will also be used in this chapter, as a characterisation for twelve individual market segments is beyond its scope.

Essentially the laws that protect creativity are patents, confidentiality, copyright, trade marks, designs and reputation (goodwill). These laws protect facets of fashion, not fashion itself, and have predominately long-term economic return philosophies, rather than the seasonal and extremely short-term outlook as is common in this industry. Conceptually, the law encapsulates the creative process of a fashion designer, given that each form of protection has its own individual requirements to attain protection. Some overlap, others exist independently, some require registration while others have international protection automatically upon creation. Copyright law applies internationally through the Berne Convention for the Protection of Artistic and Literary Works. The terms of protection also vary, and the ability to infringe depends on differing rules and national interpretations of the law. Even with international conventions establishing these forms of protection, there are idiosyncratic national variations. For example, *haute-couture* fashion in France is governed by rules set by the Chambre Syndicale de la Couture Parisienne. These rules do not apply to non-members in Milan or New York or elsewhere.

If fashion designers want an international protection system for their creativity expressed in their garments from the moment the models strut down the runway, and to extend this protection to include any substantial or derivative style of their work, they will be disappointed, as this will be unattainable. Such an absolute concept of property in their creations is beyond the ability of the law because all garments are derived and inspired from *previous creations*, and such creation revolves on facts that themselves are shades of grey, rather than black and white absolutes. If an absolute system were to be found, then how many current designers would meet an international test of absolute originality? How absolutely original is any garment, given current trends morph from reinterpretations of styles, methods of cutting, draping, corsetry or materials.

Protection of ideas – patents and breach of confidence

Absolute protection in law is only recognised conceptually in the patent system. The patent system described in this chapter is not the American design patent protection of shape but rather the patent system aimed at protection of ideas, as is found in Australia, for example. Patents for ideas relate to industrial applications within the definition of a manner of manufacture (see for example s18(1)(a) *Patents Act* 1990, which connects to the definition of manner of manufacture in the Statute of Monopolies 1623), being methods, processes, devices or products produced from processes that have an economically useful result (for Australia see *National Research Development Corporation v Commissioner of Patents* and see for the UK Norton's rules). Patents and fashion though have historically involved methods and forms of corsetry required to give the perfect figure, leading Burk (2006, 2007) generally and Swanson (2011) specifically to a feminist epistemological examination of patent law and corsetry. Corsetry though, with time, has given way to bias-cut figure-hugging materials and, in the modern era, fashion patents now create compression garments for core-stability and drag-reduction like the double-layer stretchable bonded fabric of the Speedo Rocketsuit (see Australian Patent Number AU200727872) rather than steel and laces, or $300g/m^2$ fire protection fabric (see Australian Patent number AU 2006224461) or shock absorption and ventilation processes for shoes (see United States Registered Patent 5224277). The suit caused controversy – see Tang (2008). Patents essentially protect *ideas* but do not themselves protect fashion designers' garments. Garments themselves are not a manner of manufacture, and the absolute novelty requirement for a standard means the idea must not have been disclosed prior to the application date. As Chanel said, fashion is seasonal, and timing-wise, the garments would require an average of three to four years from application to obtain patent protection, which is not suited to any segment of the fashion market.

The alternative provided by law to protect ideas or concepts is already utilised by the fashion garment industry to protect their designs before public display through utilising a legal obligation of *confidence*. This can arise through equity or contract. Most designers utilise this duty through contractual clauses in employment contracts to prevent disclosure of their designs before public display. The duty of confidence in the information being the garment is extinguished by the public display of the garment. In fact, David and Elizabeth Emanuel and their staff signed strict confidentiality agreements that required installation of additional security to protect the secrecy of Princess Diana's wedding dress in 1981 (Emanuel and Emanuel 2006). The great difficulty with the obligation of confidence is being able to cast a wide enough net to capture all subsequent people that see the garment who are not employees or restricted by a confidentiality agreement, as confidence is a *relationship* rather than a proprietorial right. Confidence thus only works until publication, in this case *public display*.

Ultimately, patents and obligations of confidentiality provide limited protection to the essence of fashion as the expression of a creative idea that conjures desire in consumers to possess, wear and display. Expression as an embodiment of intellect is the essence of copyright and design.

Copyright

Copyright does not protect an idea, but rather the form of expression embodied in a material form. Ideas in fashion revolve around descriptors of romance, sophistication, evening, morning, wedding, grunge, revival, austerity, carnival or flamboyance and other inspirational influences of mood or feelings relating to culturally orientated commodities, supporting Weller's (2007) belief that fashion is knowledge. Descriptors and knowledge themselves are not captured by copyright protection. The expression through an embodied form such as sketches, draping or sculpturing fabric on manikins, or creation of a template or pattern for the replication of the article is what counts.

Copyright protected expression in fashion occurs for an original artistic work produced in a material form. The concept of originality is assessed by the *sweat of the brow* doctrine. This doctrine assesses a work as original if a person used their own work, skill and effort to produce a copyright work and did not copy the expression from another (*University of London Press Ltd v University Tutorial Press Ltd* [1916] 2 Ch 601, and see also discussions in Loughlan 2006). The Copyright Act 1968 (Cth) specifically states that artistic works are protected regardless of their artistic merit, when coming within the definition of 'paintings, drawings, engravings and photographs'. Such a level of originality means that the ambit of originality captures not only the highly creative artistic works but also common functional hat forms created by others. This test has been criticised as too low and recent dicta from the *IceTV Pty Limited v Nine Network Australia Pty Limited* case ([2009] HCA 14), means the focus on economic value may be tempered by a consideration that *some* modicum of creativity will be required for protection (see the IInet case, HCA).

Princess Beatrice's hat, regardless, can be classified as a copyright artistic work under s10 of the Copyright Act (Cth) by various classifications; as drawings for the hat, as a sculpture and by itself as a work of artistic craftsmanship. These different interpretations occur as the term 'artistic work means (a) painting, sculpture, drawing, engraving or photograph whether of artistic quality or not; (b) buildings or model of a building; or (c) a work of artistic craftsmanship whether or not mentioned in paragraphs (a) or (b)'. The drawings of the hat that led to its creation are certainly artistic works and photographs of the hat are considered copyright works; furthermore the two-dimensional drawings would give protection to the three-dimensional hat (*King Features Syndicate Inc v O & M Kleeman Ltd* [1941] AC 417). The question of whether the hat is *art*, brings in an examination of sculpture, which again does not require artistic merit for protection. This argument begins with s10, which defines sculpture as including a cast or model made for the purpose of sculpture. Is the hat made for the 'purpose of sculpture'? A dictionary meaning of sculpture includes the making of abstract forms that can encapsulate a hat.

No court has debated this issue in relation to hats but the point arose in *Wham-O MFG Co.* v. *Lincoln Industries Ltd* ([1981] 2 NZLR 628), regarding Frisbees or flying discs. The claims related to three models of flying discs, including whether preliminary drawings and wooden models were artistic works as sculptures or engravings and further whether the Frisbees themselves were also covered by copyright protection as 'sculptures and/or engravings (print)'. The trial Judge Moller J. classed the wooden models as sculptures and the dies as engravings for the purposes of copyright protection, avoiding the difficulties of discussion of 'works of artistic craftsmanship'. As Grinlinton (1983: 408) said: 'This represents an interesting extension of the [New Zealand Copyright] Act to cover prototypes of a design and the dies from which they are to be reproduced as "artistic works".' Moller J. was overruled by the Court of Appeal finding that Frisbees are not sculptures. This appeal decision was followed in Australia by Pincus J. when considering a lawn mower drive shaft in *Greenfield Products Pty Ltd v Rover-Scott Bonnar Ltd* (1990, 17 IPR 417). His Honour held that sculpture had its ordinary meaning and that a drive shaft was not a sculpture for the purposes of copyright. The hat has more artistic features and equates more comfortably with sculpture than either a Frisbee or a drive shaft. What of garments made to drawings, as these are artistic works and would have protection except for policy objectives described below relating to copyright design overlap?

The more likely discussion is whether the hat comes within subsection (c) as a *work of artistic craftsmanship*. This alternative manner of protection for copyright works has been a fertile arena for debate arising with boat hulls, *Cuisenaire* mathematical rods, chairs, baby slings and knitting patterns for fabric (*Burge v Swarbrick* (2007) 234 ALR 204; *Cuisenaire v Reed* [1963] VLR 719; *George Hensher Ltd v Restawhile Upholstery (Lanc) Ltd* [1976] AC 64; *Merlet v Mothercare PLC* (1984) 2 IPR 456 at 465; *Coogi Australia Pty Ltd v Hysport International Pty Ltd* (1998) 41 IPR 593).

These cases demonstrate the difficulty courts have with the meaning of the words 'work of artistic craftsmanship'. These words offer the only protection for three-dimensional objects that are likely to be mass-produced and the words 'artistic craftsmanship' suggests that some artistic merit is required of the creative effort of the producer. The important case arising on issues in textiles is *Coogi Australia Ltd v Hysport International Pty Ltd*, where the court accepted that the way Coogi used stitch structures and colour to produce an unusual textured and multi-coloured fabric for a fashion garment satisfied two of the requirements, in that it was craftsmanship and had an aesthetic quality to it. Princess Beatrice's hat involves craftsmanship in its creation and is artistic in nature, even though some members of the public may think of it as vulgar, yet Pila (2008) considers that this orthodox approach, conforming to accepted case law, is part of a re-conceiving of categories of copyright works to ensure protection is given to individual objects. Regardless of this debate, Princess Beatrice's hat could obtain copyright protection as a work of *artistic craftsmanship*. It is a one-off original, and has not been mass-produced. The 'work of artistic craftsmanship' issue is an argument available for high fashion items and designer clothing. However, do the other items, such as the fridge magnets and associated items, infringe the copyright in the hat?

Copyright infringement

Infringement is an action stating that the hat or fashion item has been copied, and by statute and case law this occurs when a *substantial part of the work* has been reproduced into an object without the permission of the owner. It is unlikely that Philip Treacy was asked for permission for any of the various entrepreneurial examples that the hat spawned after the wedding. The issue for infringement that is always faced by fashion creators is whether a *substantial* part of the original has been produced. This is a question of fact that examines not just the quantity but the *quality* of the original work (see *Milpurrurru v Indofurn Pty Ltd* (1994) 30 IPR 209 and see also *Designer Guild Ltd v Russell William (Textiles Ltd)* [2001] FSR 11). Two prominent forms of copying arise: one where a definite portion of the work is copied; and the second where copying occurs by alteration. In the latter case, the test of infringement is 'has the infringer incorporated a substantial part of the independent skill, labour etc. contributed by the original author in creating the copyright work?' As Lord Hoffman said in the Designer Guild case:

> Although the term 'substantial part' might suggest a quantitative test, or at least the ability to identify some discrete part which, on quantitative or qualitative grounds, can be regarded as substantial, it is clear upon the authorities that neither is the correct test. *Ladbroke (Football) Ltd. v. William Hill (Football) Ltd.* [1964] 1 W.L.R. 273 establishes that substantiality depends upon quality rather than quantity (Lord Reid at p. 276, Lord Evershed at p. 283, Lord Hodson at p. 288, Lord Pearce at p. 293). And there are numerous authorities which show that the 'part' which is regarded as substantial can be a feature or combination of features of the work, abstracted from it rather than forming a discrete part. That is what the judge found to have been copied in this case. Or to take another example, the original elements in the plot of a play or novel may be a substantial part, so that copyright may be infringed by a work which does not reproduce a single sentence of the original. If one asks what is being

protected in such a case, it is difficult to give any answer except that it is an idea expressed in the copyright work.

([2001] FSR 11 at 18)

Such an assessment of 'substantial part' arises when fashion creations in the High Street resemble creations by high fashion designers. The Designer Guild case was approved of in the Australian decision of *Elwood Clothing Pty Ltd v Cotton On Clothing Pty Ltd* ('Elwood', [2008] FCAFC 197), where the importance lies in seeing the similarities and differences between the work and the original and then asking whether the essential features or a combination of features of the work have been copied. The Elwood composite t-shirt screen print comprising numerals '9' and '6', and slogans 'raging bulls' and 'durable by design' combined with the firm name in a central roundel and a small representation of a bull was infringed by the use of numerals '8' and '9', and slogans 'red lions' and 'reggae by reputation' with the use of words 'Kingston' in a roundel with a small representation of a lion. The Full Federal Court assessment examined the work as a whole and each element of the overall design had been so close to the original but changed to avoid being the same. They approved of Lord Hoffmann's comments in *Designer Guild v Russell Williams (Textile) Ltd*:

The more abstract and simple the copied idea the less likely it constitutes a substantial part. Copyright protects the detail within the basic idea as presented; the more and more of details that one takes from another person's work, the greater the chances are that one is taking too much.

([2000] UKHL 58)

This decision has been viewed by legal practice as increasing the protection given to designers, particularly for surface design or two-dimensional works on fabric in the mass consumer market.

Additional difficulties can arise with copyright, as this short aside indicates. If the hat were on permanent display, then there would be no infringement of the hat by the making of a painting, drawing, engraving or photograph of the work or by the inclusion of the work in a cinematograph film or in a television broadcast (s65 Copyright Act (CTH) 1968). The hat was not on permanent public display. Wearing it in public means it has been broadcast on television but the television transmission does not infringe copyright in the work. So individuals who take photographs of the hat while in public would not infringe the copyright in the hat. In addition, most of the uses of the derivate of the hat would fall under the exception to copyright infringement of being a parody (s41A and s103AA Copyright Act).

This copyright situation may appear straightforward but the devil is in the detail, because at law, the hat can be *either* a copyright or a design work but not both. The great difficulty for fashion at all levels is *copyright design overlap*.

Copyright design overlap

Fashion operates in the most conceptually difficult paradigm in intellectual property – that of *copyright design overlap*. This complexity has been the focus of the Australian Law Reform Commission Review Report on Designs (1995), which finally culminated in the Designs Act 2003 and changes to the Copyright Act and Copyright regulations. The intellectual property paradigm is to prevent industrial articles from having copyright protection, for example parts to hot water services and other items such as spare parts for cars. Ensuring this has led to difficulties that at various times enabled copyright and design protection to exist together, or at other times for it to exist for some items and not others. The current situation is covered by s75 of the Copyright Act. Where there has in fact been a registration of a corresponding design under the *Designs Act* 2003, copyright protection will be lost as soon as the design is registered.

This means the designer would be required to bring an infringement of designs action, rather than an infringement of copyright action. For uses of the design outside the design registration, copyright will still exist. For example, if a sketch is used as a two-dimensional surface use of the work on a T-shirt then this is protected by copyright, but making the three-dimensional garment infringes design registration. If the design is unregistered (the owner did not apply for registration) or unregisterable (they applied for registration but it was rejected as not new or distinctive), s77 provides that copyright will be lost if the design is applied industrially and the resulting products are marketed in Australia or elsewhere. Industrial application is deemed to have occurred if the design is applied to 50 articles (s77(4) Copyright Act and Reg 17 Copyright Regulations 1968, for example 50 copies of Princess Beatrice's hat).

Further, s77(1A) states that if the product illustration is published in a patent application or as drawings in a design application, it is deemed to be 'industrially applied' and loses copyright protection from the first day on which products are marketed or the application is published in Australia. Also, if casts and moulds are required, then it is not an infringement of copyright to make them. Examining Princess Beatrice's hat, it is a one off. Philip Treacy will fall under this provision as there is no registration of the hat in the design register, but he has not 'applied industrially' the design as 50 hats of this shape have not been made. He would have rights if he wished to sue for infringement for the party hats or fridge magnet versions of the hat as copyright protection would exist. Philip Treacy would therefore continue to own copyright in Princess Beatrice's hat. A prominent problem with copyright protection is the 70 years from the author's death protection period, which is longer than any fashion item survives without being reincarnated or reinterpreted, at least into multiple different versions. What of the fashion creator who wants to mass-produce their article? Is it necessary to register a design in your garment?

Design issues

The designs registration system aims to cater to the demands of fashion in the mass-production market. *Design* refers to the overall appearance of a product on the basis of one or more visual features being: shape, configuration, pattern or ornamentation (s5, s7 Design Act 2003) which can serve a functional purpose – s7(2). The product can be either manufactured or handmade (s6). To obtain a registration though, the design must be new (s15(1)) and distinctive (s16) when compared to the prior art. Prior art (s15) includes designs publicly available in Australia; design applications with an earlier priority date of filing or where the first public display occurs earlier than the filing date; as well as designs published in a document such as a catalogue either within or outside Australia. A design must meet the requirement of novelty as being new (s16(1)) and distinctive (s16(2)); *new* means not identical to a design in the prior art base and *distinctive* means not substantially similar to a design in the prior art base. The prior art base includes s15 (2) (a) – designs publicly used in Australia; (2) (b) – designs published in a document e.g. a catalogue within or outside Australia; and (2) (c) – designs in design applications with an earlier priority date than the design and where the first public display (s60) occurs before the date of the designated design.

Given these parameters, it would appear to the fashion world that these rights were worthless, but recent decisions demonstrate that these rights are effective in the mass-market clothing arena. In *Review 2 Pty Ltd v Redberry Enterprises Pty Ltd* ([2008] FCA 1588), Justice Kenny took into account that a designer has limited freedom to innovate a ladies' dress in a 'cross-over or wrap' style other than by reference to the shape and configuration of the skirt combined with differences in pattern including colour. Here, the imported dress did not infringe as there were sufficient differences in the shape and the skirt and the pattern. In *Review Australia Pty Ltd v New Cover Group Pty Ltd* ([2008] FCA 1589), Review succeeded in its infringement claim because while the pattern and colour of the Spicy Sugar dress differed from the Review design, it was substantially similar in overall impression to the Review design and so infringed. The test for distinctiveness ('substantial similarity') for registration is also used as the test for infringement under s71, so an infringing design is not a distinctive design and vice versa.

The informed user perspective has been adopted from the United Kingdom Registered Designs Act 1949 and the cases above accepted *Woodhouse UK Plc v Architectural Lighting Systems* ([2006] RPC 1), in that the informed user is a regular user of the items involved; not an expert, but not the 'man in the street'. Thus the consideration of an informed user is an objective test and looks at a person that knows 'what is about in the market' and 'what has been about in the recent past'. The focus is on the eye appeal of visual features rather than the issue of a 'nerd like' analysis of technical differences. Indeed, the *New Cover* case accepted the decision in *Application by Pauline Walton* (UK IPO, 0–027–07, 22 January 2007), that an informed user would be aware of the limited freedom of design of a poncho being either rectangular or square. This highlights the ALRC comments that the

> extent of difference required to make a design distinctive will depend on the state of development of the relevant prior art base. A more developed prior art base will mean that smaller differences will be sufficient to result in a finding that there is no substantial similarity.
>
> (ALRC Report no. 74 Designs p. 60 para 5.23)

Thus, new life has been brought to the design registration system for fashion in Australia and it is of particular interest that the firms utilising design protection are in a contemporary or upper moderate market segment aimed at the 20–25 year-old woman, not the *haute-couture* or upper bridge market segments. This helps confirm Hedrick's (2008) view that design protection is an underutilised method of protection.

The major problem for fashion designers is obtaining uniformity in protection internationally. France has specific rules for *haute-couture* ranges set by the Chambre Syndicale de la Haute Couture and the European Union has instituted design regulations to be harmonious throughout the European Union (see 31998L0071 Directive 98/71/EC of the European Parliament and of the Council of 13 October 1998 on the legal protection of designs, Official Journal L 289, 28/10/1998 P. 0028 – 0035). The directive gives protection to the form or shape of the article and uses the new and distinctive approach for the assessment of the shape configuration or ornamentation. Designs are not protected insofar as their appearance is wholly determined by their technical function, or by the need to interconnect with other products to perform a technical function (the 'must-fit' exception). Furthermore, the Design directive gives a protection period of 25 years in total, which is a longer period of protection than the Australian designs registration regime, which lasts for a maximum period of 10 years.

Failure to achieve international uniformity of design registration for fashion items means that ultimately an owner can be at the mercy of the economic free loader, resulting in the strongest legal weapons for a fashion brand in the past 20 years being those of trade mark and trade reputation infringements. This is particularly the case, as difficulties arise as identified by Suthersanen (2011) in the definitions in the European Union directive. The internationalisation difficulties though are further shown as the United States does not accept copyright or design rights in fashion garments or hats, no matter how artistic, as they performed a utilitarian function and so were outside the ambit of protection (Tsai 2005), though lobbying has increased. The issue of fashion protection has arisen with the introduction of the Design Piracy Prohibition Act and the subsequent innovative Design Protection and Piracy Act copyright protection and the possibility of a three-year design right is currently being debated. Ellis (2011) believes these legislative initiatives are a step towards controlling the counterfeit problems in fashion. Hemphill and Suk (2009) are for protection but Raustiala and Sprigman (2006) are against it, believing it will stifle innovation. The debate in America wrestles with the time periods of protection and classification between copyright and design and the appropriate form of protection, keeping many authors occupied discussing the benefits and disadvantages of the laws, like Adler (2009), Bennett *et al.* (2010) and Xiao (2010–2011). Beltrametti (2010) compares the Design Piracy Prohibition Act with the European Union regulations and asks whether the cure is worse than the disease, while Ferrill and Tanhehco (2011) support the view that design patents are underutilised in America and would be appropriate for protection of fashion. Obtaining international uniformity of protection of fashion designs is still further in the future and is a continual moving feast for debate.

Knock-offs

Princess Beatrice was one of 1,900 guests at Westminster Abbey. An estimated 1 million people lined the streets for the procession while 2 billion watched the broadcast via satellite, and syndications on televisions and computers globally. Protection of fashion has become more difficult as major technological shifts give the industry the ability to copy and transform designs quickly from images transmitted anywhere in the world. Even when Princess Diana was married in 1981, the first copies of her dress were appearing within hours in Asia. These copies were not to the Emanuels' standards of craftsmanship (Emanuel and Emanuel 2006), but were being sold as Diana-like dresses, and people purchasing them knew they were not getting Diana's dress. The transmission via internet and technology means that what is seen in Paris may be produced in Indonesia or other places within days.

The design laws and copyright laws do not protect a *style* of clothing or the style of a fashion creator. Thus the difficulty is that high fashion items displayed in Paris are then reinterpreted for middle income or lower consumer groups by other chains. This issue of style remains an essential difficulty in fashion as the essence of fashion which informed users associate with Chanel, Armani and Versace is their ability to tailor clothing to the female form. This essence is *reputation*. It is more than just a design issue but is not protected as a property right in the creation itself but in the name of the designer.

Goodwill is the intangible reputation that customers, attendants and participants associate with fashion labels themselves. The difficulty is that in such a high turnover market, this goodwill may not equate to a particular dress. Legally though, reputation is encapsulated in two forms of protection – through the use of trade marks under the Trade Marks Act and reputation actions as a tort of passing off or for conduct that misleads or deceives the public under the Australian Consumer law s18. Difficulty arises with trade marks raising two additional issues; there is an international trend towards the acceptance of criminal sanctions for counterfeiting of trade marked goods; and there are additional remedies provided regarding words of geographic origin under trade legislation and international law. The law requires an owner to prove they have a reputation for the goods and considers numerous issues, including length of time in the business, distribution, geographic area, whether there is a cross-over with other products, use of disclaimers and all things that support the arena of commerce in which the reputation is stated to exist. Ultimately, this is done through the tort of passing off or its statutory form under the Australian Consumer Law 2010 s18.

A tort of passing off occurs when the person sells the fashion item in such a manner that customers believe the item was produced by or is the product of the original creator and causes damage (*Reckitts and Coleman Products Ltd v Borden Inc* [1990] 1 All ER 873). According to Raustiala and Sprigman (2009), this is part of the 'knockoff economy' and how far this goes in the development of new products that escape the effects of the tort is very much a question of fact on how the item is sold and what reputation a designer can prove exists. With the example of the copies of Princess Diana's wedding dress in Asia, such an action would not be made out as there is only one dress that she could have actually worn to her wedding, and further the Emanuels could not show they lost sales of the dress because of the copies. Similarly, with respect to Princess Beatrice's hat, it is a one-off unique creation but Philip Treacy has not lost sales due to the other variations seen on eBay or because of the party hat fascinators people bought. If anything, both of these creators increased their workloads and demands because of the publicity given to the original items they created. Even in the lower end market, with respect to designer-inspired articles, it can be very difficult to prove that a competitor who produced a similar style of item is causing an original designer to lose a sale, such that the original designer can say that every sale the competitor made of that design is a sale that they should have made.

The statutory equivalent examines the representation made from the prospective of a consumer. Here, all the circumstances of the sales and its presentation must objectively indicate to the customer that it is the product of someone else such that they are misled or deceived into believing it is another's creation. Often this is overcome by appropriate labelling on the garment, clearly stating the designer or the appropriate fashion house. The advantage with this statutory equivalent is there is no requirement of proving *damage*. America provides similar protection in the form of dilution of trade mark actions but this falls outside the scope of this chapter and will not be covered.

Ultimately, one area of the law that does satisfy designers is trade mark infringement under the Trade Marks Act 1995 (Cth). This is an international arrangement that enables designers to register their brand to cover the goods and services that they produce in the countries to which they distribute. The essential aim is to differentiate goods in the course of trade by the use of a mark (s17) as a sign that includes (s6) name, logo, colour, brand, signature or scent from others in the same category or associated categories. The grant of a registered trade mark gives individual ownership of the name in the relevant category of goods or services to which the mark is applied. It is the recognition of property in the name and upon registration the proprietor does not have to prove they have a reputation. Chanel registered her name in 1933 as a trade mark.

The action for infringement asks: 'Does the item use a mark that is substantially or deceptively similar in appearance to the registered mark?' In fashion, the most common forms of trade mark are names and logos such as Chanel's double 'C' or Pierre Cardin's 'PC' combination. The trade mark infringement actions against counterfeit goods are common but also it is common to see specific places where infringing items are openly sold, i.e. Canal Street in New York, the Ladies Market in Hong Kong and Petaling Street, Kuala Lumpur, Malaysia. This action does not protect the shape of the garment or the idea but it is effective as a mechanism for removing items that have a trade mark applied without the permission of the owner.

This has become a major issue through the inclusion of intellectual property under the auspices of the World Trade Organization. There is increased recognition of the problems of counterfeit goods which people purchase at the markets mentioned above and there are even grades of counterfeit goods, ranging from production overruns that are as good as the original to cheap versions made of plastic (maybe someone should remind them that Chanel does not do plastic!). Thomas (2007) explores this as a multifaceted problem of desire, economics and culture but a complete examination of the issue is beyond the scope of this chapter. Suffice to say, trade mark protection is best seen and utilised by well-known, high-end and desired designers like Prada, Escada, Chanel, Louis Vuitton and Dior. Yet for those starting in the business, obtaining a trade mark when not well-known is important for when you do become well-known.

Reputation is as fickle an area of law as it is in the everyday life of the fashion trade. It is the method by which the law could allow a designer to own a 'style' but the difficulty is in proving to the satisfaction of the courts, in such a highly competitive market known for its re-interpretation of others' work, that a designer is known for a particular style. At a micro-level, this may be achievable but at the macro-level of international coverage, this is a more difficult if not impossible task.

Conclusion

The laws discussed in this chapter provide forms of protection that can be utilised at all levels of the fashion pyramid. Fashion has the shortest run for items other than basic essentials, and even in the Kmarts and Targets, limited numbers of items are produced as the seasons change. Cross-overs from different segments are increasingly common, and even international designers are producing mass-market limited edition apparel lines for such stores. Technology is not only assisting with just-in-time production of items but also in the distribution. On the flip side, it is also playing a part in the infringement of rights. Many debate the extent to which protection should or should not be given and whether the granting of property rights will stifle the creativity seen in the fashion industry that appears to survive in the United States even without protection. Ultimately, a fashion designer needs to know the patchwork existence of the law in this field, as being forewarned is forearmed. To answer the question posed at the commencement of this chapter, should Philip Treacy sue for the paper fascinators, the memes and the fridge magnets? No. These items may infringe but they do no harm; they are parodies of true creativity. In the life of fashion, they have died as new interpretations, fads and sensations have taken centre stage. If there is only one lesson from Princess Beatrice's hat, it is this – the more creative you are, the more the law will support you.

References

Adler, H. S. (2009) 'Pirating the runway: the potential impact of the Design Piracy Prohibition Act on fashion retail', 5 *Hastings Bus L J*: 381.

Beltrametti, S. (2010) 'Evaluation of the Design Piracy Prohibition Act: is the cure worse than the disease? An analogy with counterfeiting and a comparison with the protection available in the European Community', 8 *NW J Tech & Intell Prop*: 147.

Bennett, M. G., Buell, N., Cetel, J. and Perry, C. C. (2010) 'Vogue Juridique and the theory choice problem in the debate over copyright protection for fashion designs', 70 *MD L Rv*: 100.

Blackmon, L. (2012) 'The Devil wears Prado: a look at the Design Piracy Prohibition Act and the extension of copyright protection to the world of fashion', 35 *Pepperdine Law Review*: 107.

Borukhovich, B. (2009) 'Fashion design: the work of art that is still unrecognized in the United States', 9 *Wake Forrest Intell Prop L J*: 155.

Burk, D. L. (2006) 'Copyright and feminism in digital media', 14 *Am U J Gender Soc Pol'y & L*: 519.

Burk, D. L. (2007) 'Feminism and dualism in intellectual property', 15 *Am U J Gender Soc Pol'y & L*: 183.

Burk, D. L. (2010) 'Do patents have gender?' *UC Irvine Sch of Law Research Paper* No. 2010–17, http://ssrn.com/abstract=1652873 (accessed 15 February 2013).

Charles-Roux, E. (2005) *Chanel and Her World: friends, fashion and fame*, New York: The Vendome Press.

Dreyfuss, R. C. (2010) 'Does IP need IP? Accommodating intellectual production outside the intellectual property paradigm', *NYU Public Law and Legal Theory Research Paper Series* Working Paper No. 10–43, http://ssrn.com/abstract=1639590 (accessed 5 January 2013).

Ellis, S. R. (2011) 'Copyright couture: an examination of fashion and why the DPPA and IDPPA are a step towards the solution to counterfeit chic', 78 *Tenn L Rv*: 162.

Emanuel, D. and Emanuel, E. (2006) *A Dress for Diana*, London: Collins Design.

Ferrill, E. and Tanhehco, T. (2011) 'Protecting the material world: the role of design patents in the fashion industry', 12 *N C J L & Tech*: 251.

Gilbert, S. (2011) 'Hatters happy about Princess Beatrice's crazy millinery', *Daily Finance*, 19 May, http://www.dailyfinance.com/2011/05/19/hatters-happy-about-princess-beatrices-crazy-millinery (accessed 3 January 2013).

Grinlinton, D. P. (1983) 'Industrial design and copyright: recent developments', 4 *Auckland University Law Review*: 399 at 408.

Hedrick, L. (2008) 'Tearing fashion design protection apart at the seams', 65 *Wash & Lee L Rev*: 215.

Hemphill, C. S. and Suk, J. (2009) 'The law, culture, and economics of fashion', 61 *Stanford Law Review*: 1147.

Howard, L. (2009) 'An uningenious paradox: intellectual property protection for fashion designs', 32 *Colum J L & Arts*: 101.

Huffington Post (2011) Princess Beatrice's hat: worst ever?' *The Huffington Post*, April 29, http://www.huffingtonpost.com/2011/04/29/princess-beatrice-hat-worst_n_855657.html (accessed 3 January 2013).

Loughlan, P. (2006) 'Pirates, parasites, reapers, sowers, fruits, foxes ... the metaphors of intellectual property', *Syd LR*: 211.

Pila, J. (2008) 'Works of artistic craftsmanship in the High Court of Australia: the exception as paradigm copyright work', 36 *FLR*: 363.

Raustiala, K. and Sprigman, C. (2006) 'The piracy paradox: innovation and intellectual property in fashion design', 92 *Va L R*: 1687.

Raustiala, K. and Sprigman, C. J. (2009) 'The piracy paradox revisited', *Stan L Rev*: 1201.

Suthersanen, U. (2011) 'Function, art and fashion: do we need the EU directive?' *Queen Mary University of London Legal Studies Research Paper* No. 88/2011 http://ssrn.com/abstract=1945142 (accessed 13 January 2013).

Swanson, K. W. (2011) 'Getting a grip on the corset: gender, sexuality and patent law', 20 *Yale J.L. & Feminism*: 101.

Tang, S. K. Y. (2008) 'The Rocket swimsuit: Speedo LZR Racer', https://sitn.hms.harvard.edu/sitnflash_wp/2008/09/issue47–2 (accessed 13 January 2013).

Thomas, D. (2007) *Deluxe: how luxury lost its lustre*, New York, Penguin.

Tsai, J. P. (2005) 'Fashioning protection: a note on the protection of fashion design in the United States', 9 *Lewis & Clark L Rev*: 447.

UK Telegraph (2011) 'Princess Beatrice's Philip Treacy hat sells for £81,101 on eBay', *UK Telegraph*, 11 May, http://fashion.telegraph.co.uk/article/TMG8529823/Princess-Beatrices-Philip-Treacy-hat-sells-for-81101-on-eBay.html (accessed 13 January 2013).

Weller, S. (2007) 'Fashion as viscous knowledge: fashion's role in shaping trans-national garment production', *J Econ Geogr*, 7(1): 39–66.

Xiao, E. Y. (2010–2011) 'The new trend: protecting American fashion designs through national copyright measures', 28 *Cardozo Arts & Ent L J*: 417.

8 Creating wow in the fashion industry

Reflecting on the experience of Melbourne Fashion Festival

Karen Webster

> In the whirlwind of Fashion Weeks taking place across the world's top cities, it's easy to assume that those living outside of London, New York, Paris or Milan simply aren't as style-savvy as their city counterparts. But those well-established fashion capitals shouldn't take off their heels and get into their comfy clothes just yet; there's always room for the new kids. Fashion is making a home for itself in a whole heap of new places, with shows thriving and streets bulging with outfit inspiration.
>
> (Sampson 2012)

Every day around the world there is a city celebrating a fashion week. The spectacle of fashion has become a glamour-embedded and aspirational ritual to showcase designers so as to garner some presence on the radar of global media. The traditional big four fashion destinations still rule the calendar, with thousands flocking to New York, London, Milan and Paris for the launch of each spring/summer and autumn/winter fashion season and millions more connecting through a plethora of digital devices. Around the hectic scheduling of these four centres as the major drivers, other cities have explored opportunities to bring attention to their local fashion talent by programming runways and associated activities annually.

Amidst these cluttered global fashion forays, Melbourne, a city in Australia, albeit a destination for creativity, style and fashion, instigated a unique proposition around fashion events. This chapter explores a five-year period from 2005 to 2010 of the *L'Oreal Melbourne Fashion Festival* (LMFF) a time during which the author held the position of Festival Director of this event and was intimately immersed in the day-to-day delivery of what was asserted by the mid 2000s to be the largest consumer fashion event in the world.

LMFF celebrated and showcased the depth and breadth of all things *fashion*. The focus was based around key objectives including: stimulating retail-spend, instilling consumer confidence, developing the industry capability and capacity in a framework that stimulated tourism and the global branding of Melbourne as a fashion destination. The distinction of this event was evidenced by its diversity and accessibility.

Background and beginnings

In 1996, a group of Australian fashion industry visionaries gathered together to discuss the status of the local sector, which at the time was struggling within a recessed economy. An idea sprang forth to develop a festival that shifted the focus from the negative impacts to positive celebrations and acknowledged the attributes inherent in the local fashion industry.

In the mid 1990s, the fashion industry in Australia was in a tough and complex position. Emerging out of a previously protectionist position where Government tariffs and duties had cosseted local business, there was the demise in local manufacturing and an economy facing recession. Generally the industry was despondent and there was a tendency for those struggling to blame others in the fashion supply chain for the negative impacts. Manufacturers were blaming the designers, designers were blaming suppliers, retailers were blaming consumers and consumers were saying: 'What is good out there anyway?' The atmosphere at the time was creating a mood of anxiety, frustration and culpability among industry stakeholders. Interestingly there are parallels with a similar scenario being re-lived globally across the fashion industry in the past five years (with on-line retail and social media now added to the mix). The fiscal environment of the mid 1990s has parallels to the current international climate following the global financial crisis. Possibly this is a lesson that it is time to take stock and celebrate the positive options.

The first Board of Directors was a group of passionate leaders in the fashion sector across design, retail, education and government. This was a Board who were truly visionary, who were willing to take a risk and whose commitment and passion within the Australian industry went beyond the financial rewards of running a business and showed a dedication to progressing Australian fashion. The Board approached the Victorian State Government for start-up funding; the promise was that the industry would equally invest in the project so as to raise demand for local fashion product. The proposition supporting the first Festival was to showcase businesses across all tiers from micro to mass that were getting it right; the fashion sector had sparks of inspiration and these could be role models for the rest of the industry. An early memory – recalls Craig Kimberley, the first Chair of the Board of the Fashion Festival – was advocating 'to stop complaining about it and let's make a difference'. The ethos of the Festival from day one and testament to its success was to celebrate the industry, excite the person on the street and provide the inspiration to engage. This spirit has been a driving force in establishing the Melbourne Fashion Festival as a successful event model.

The Melbourne Fashion Festival was launched in 1997 with a minuscule part time management team who produced the inaugural events with the help of a host of volunteers and the commitment of a Board who gave significant time and resources to producing engaging and inspirational experiences. It evolved over the years as a valuable asset for the Australian fashion industry, with ever-increasing national recognition and international acknowledgement.

Figure 8.1 Connie Simonetti bridal couture on the catwalk during the 2010 L'Oreal
Melbourne Fashion Festival.
Source: Lucas Dawson Photography

The Festival ensured that for a period of time each year, the fashion spotlight shone on Melbourne, with each year gaining upward trends related to
economic impact, promotional exposure, cultural positioning and associated
retail expenditure. From its launch, with a programme of 20 events attended
by 30,000 people, fast-track 15 years and the Melbourne Fashion Festival was
by the mid 2000s purported to be the largest public fashion event globally. In
2010, the event attracted over 420,000 participants, included over 300 participating designers and brands and generated AU$48 million in national and
international media coverage, while contributing over AU$70 million to the
Australian economy (Unkles 2010) (Figure 8.1).

From those early years there was a heartfelt belief by those involved that this event could provide the opportunity to not only build the Australian fashion industry but nurture its development and position it globally. The Melbourne Fashion Festival's mantra was to promote Melbourne as a centre of fashion and style, stimulate ideas and highlight trends in design, innovation, business and the arts as they relate to fashion. The Festival's distinctive offering, in being consumer orientated, enabled it to be a leading fashion event on an international scale. By the late 2000s, it became established as a key event on the Melbourne events calendar, offering globally unique activities that celebrated the breadth and depth of fashion. As a multi tiered event, it offered a significant point of difference from the traditional fashion weeks that focussed on the designer category of fashion and, by contrast, it evolved as a true festival of fashion, providing a forum for the diverse sectors of the industry from mainstream chains to bespoke practices.

In retrospect, it was the Festival's ability to create a sense of community that became its greatest strength. It became a meeting place for all tiers of the fashion community no matter how large or small. What now seems to be an obvious need, in reality, was a difficult task to coordinate, requiring strength of vision to lead, inspire and garner an environment of collaboration and communication. When times are tough, most businesses will find it difficult to look beyond their own needs as the day-to-day dealings take all of their energy. Asking fashion brands and retailers to look beyond their immediate concerns, in a volatile economic environment, was a daunting proposition. The Festival required bringing together key influencers and advocates within the industry and beyond to encourage engagement. Once it started, the trajectory was upward and onward. Initially it was considered that it could have been a short-term project, to get the fashion industry reinvigorated. In 2013, the Festival was entering its 17th year and it continues to represent a major event in the Australian fashion calendar.

2005–2010

From 2005 to 2010, the Festival went through a considerable growth phase, exceeding year-on-year in relation to expansion in designer and brand participation, media coverage, attendance and economic impact. This upward trend countered the global shifts and economic conditions that saw reductions in consumer spending and a downturn in industry capacity. As reported in the independently commissioned Economic Impact Study of the 2006 Festival:

> The support for the Festival was very strong with independent surveys of patrons, sponsors and participants all indicating a high level of satisfaction with and a commitment to the LMFF events and operations. There continues to be a high degree of support for the professionalism of the LMFF staff and sub-contractors, for the overall management of the Festival and for the very high standard of event management and

Figure 8.2 Independent Runway – End of Show – 2010 L'Oreal Melbourne Fashion Festival.
Source: Lucas Dawson Photography

staging. The LMFF standards are generally seen as vastly exceeding the standards of Australian Fashion Week, for example.

(Unkles 2006)

The Festival's initial platform of supporting the local industry through growth opportunities and branding exposure expanded during this era to encapsulate the building of consumer confidence, evolving industry intelligence and stimulating global branding for Melbourne as a centre of style and innovation as well as creating positive perceptions around the Australian fashion industry. LMFF represented an exceptional celebration of all things fashion, giving the public unique access to world leading fashion runways and activities (Figure 8.2). The Festival was a vast array of creatively inspired activities encompassing fashion shows, exhibitions, business forums and celebrations; capturing the glamour and excitement of the world of fashion for the general public.

Experience, entertainment and engagement

The core fashion events were the *L'Oreal Paris Runway Shows* which had an emphasis on celebrating and promoting the exceptional and innovative fashion that is available in Australia. L'Oréal Paris Runway was staged over several nights and highlighted premium fashion collections of men's and women's fashion from approximately 40 leading Australian designers. Unlike the traditional shows of individual designers that are staged as part of international fashion weeks, these were group shows that highlighted the latest available collections across complementary labels. Every show evolved with a particular ethos so that the designers grouped together would have a reference point for the viewer and to provide an enhanced experience for those attending. Each of these shows was then aligned to a high profile fashion publication, such as *VOGUE* or *Harper's BAZAAR*, which not only provided the opportunity for editorial support but also endorsed the brands for the consumer.

These runway shows were housed in state of art infrastructures, seating an audience at each of 1500 people. This is contrasted with the global trade catwalk set-up, which though spectacles produced often as theatrical displays to garner global media attention, still generally have a sense of intimacy with a limited audience. Fashion is best viewed at eye level and at a relatively close distance; otherwise the intricacies of the designs are lost on the audience. This is difficult to achieve when accommodating an audience of 1500. To facilitate this, large-scale spaces were transformed where the catwalk was either exceptionally long or transfigured to facilitate additional front row and minimal tiered seating, enabling the audience to experience the catwalk as if it was an international calibre show.

The L'Oreal Paris Runways were deliberately slick, modern and stylish transforming purpose built infrastructures, providing a sense of drama as the high energy fashion shows inspired, excited and entertained the audiences. A typical set-up would include an extended catwalk, lean architectural lines and massive screens that suspended from up above the audience. The use of inspiring motion graphics would capture the mood of each runway show. Lighting and music were also key creative media used to generate drama on entrance into the space combined with atmospheric excitement throughout each presentation. These shows required significant back and front of house facilities to be built at the semi-permanent locations and needed professional teams to deliver the high quality productions to a captive fashion aware audience.

Tickets would sell out quickly, indicating a high demand for these productions by astute fashion spectators. The mood was generally exhilarating and inspiring; paramount to the success of the shows was the atmosphere that was created as it enabled the audience to experience the drama and delight of the catwalk experience; which is normally only available to industry buyers, media and selected celebrities. A driving vision for the team engaged in the Festival was to create the *WOW* factor. The purpose of the events was to engage and transport those participating into a realm of inspiration, enjoyment and delight.

The Festival celebrated the strengths of the Australian fashion industry, paying tribute to long established brands while also providing a forum to support future talent and recognising the global relevance of Australian designers. The intent was to establish the Festival as a globally relevant event that captured the diversity of the industry. This provided it with a distinction from the other traditional fashion events around the world. LMFF was a multi-faceted showcase for all tiers of the industry. The key fashion weeks around the world focus predominantly on the specific designer category of fashion. LMFF, by contrast, embraced activities that extended beyond the traditional designer catwalk and into the domain of promoting fashion by early stage independent designers, the mass large-scale clothing chains and specialist categories of childrenswear, hosiery, bridal and special occasion. The purpose of the Festival was to embrace the democratisation of fashion.

LMFF took seriously its ability to ensure there was also an investment in the future of the Australian fashion industry, providing opportunities for fashion designers and brands in the early stages of their business. The Festival championed emerging talent across a number of activities but most notably via the prestigious LMFF Designer Award, which established a reputation as the premium fashion award for early-stage designers in Australia. Additional to this, the Festival developed stand-alone events including *Independent Runway*, which provided a highly professional show for designers in the first 18 months of business (see Figure 8.2). In 2009, an additional initiative was developed to showcase the leading graduates from Australian fashion degrees.

Beyond the large-scale runway shows, the Festival incorporated activities including more discreet salon style shows that promoted broader areas of fashion. One of the more successful initiatives was the *POP-UP* series of fashion events. The concept of the POP-UP store was gaining some resonance in fashion from the mid 2000s. In retrospect today it is regarded as a viable retail option, however when they were first introduced it was a rather novel concept, spearheaded by more innovative brands like Comme des Garçons, which saw it as a version of *guerrilla retailing*. As explained by the website trendwatching.com, which developed the term Pop-Up in 2004:

> We've dubbed this trend POP-UP RETAIL, as these initiatives have a tendency to pop up unannounced, quickly draw in the crowds, and then disappear or morph into something else, adding to retail the fresh feel, exclusivity and surprise that galleries, theatres and Cirque du Soleil-adepts have been using for years. POP-UP RETAIL fits right in with the Entertainment Economy, the Experience Economy, the Surprise Economy, and so on. It's about surprising consumers with temporary 'performances', guaranteeing exclusivity because of the limited time-span.
>
> (Anonymous 2004)

In 2006, LMFF developed a concept for what is believed to be the first POP-UP series of runway shows; a concept that was deliberately non-exclusive and democratic. Titled *POP UP – POP IN – POP OUT*, this idea was championed because the Festival had reached relative saturation in terms of capturing a *fashion orientated* audience.

Compared to the key fashion activities already on offer, the Festival had missed out on a broader audience; the passer-by, the non-fashion punter. The formula of presenting similar large-scale runway shows annually, although spectacular projects, did mean that the same dedicated and loyal fashion fan base would attend each year. The challenge was to extend beyond this so as to really build profile, attract a wider audience and create something that touched on the fervour, excitement and experience of the large-scale shows as well as capture the attention of the general public. Fashion has a reputation for being elitist, yet, despite that, the majority of a society make daily choices on how they adorn themselves in deciding what they will wear. Individual fashion choices are intrinsic to personal representation and identity. Working on the principle that essentially everyone wears clothes, therefore we all make choices on how we present ourselves to the world, there was the possibility that the Festival could expand its audience by helping brands and local designers expose and showcase their work to the broader public. An experience that didn't require the viewer to buy tickets but hopefully captured their attention to consider fashion and what may be available through local retailers.

Not unlike the phenomena of a *Flash Mob* crowd attracting activities that evolved in the following years, the POP-UP catwalks were intended to take the commuter by surprise and entice them to take a few moments to get involved. A DJ or live music would start and the build-up would commence with activity around the infrastructure that had been specifically created. Outdoor staging was erected in venues like Federation Square, a central open-air community space in Melbourne, where the POP-UP activity would be pre-promoted and consequently would attract thousands of onlookers. In some cases, Federation Square would fill with an audience of over 4000.

On reflection, these events achieved a milestone for the Festival. It took fashion to the people in a dynamic, playful, engaging fiesta style, creating a highly desirable space where a broad audience could gather to socialise and view the latest fashions and trends. As they were free of charge to the public, there was a sense of community and goodwill that they evoked. The intent was multi-layered but focused on the ability to make fashion accessible and extend its reach through entertainment and experience. These events were conceptualised and designed to provide an easy entrée to fashion by the general public and have the opportunity to showcase Melbourne as a style orientated destination. It was important to fill the city with fashion activity so that wherever one walked or commuted they felt they were part of a major event. The Festival was by 2005 regarded as part of the *Major Event Calendar* in Melbourne, a significant feat considering Melbournians' passion for large-scale sporting activities and an accolade that was important to be preserved. In his speech for the Festival's Opening Night Launch in 2009, the then Premier of Victoria John Brumby stated, 'L'Oréal Melbourne Fashion Festival is an iconic major event, up there with the Australian Open, the AFL Grand Final, the Melbourne Cup and the Grand Prix. We can cut it with the best in the world!' (Brumby 2009).

Connections and collaborations

From broad appeal to specific know-how, the Festival also developed a global reputation for connecting the Australian fashion industry. As for many of the fashion sectors that exist around the globe, the Australian industry has been repositioned in the past three decades. It has moved from geographically connected clusters with centralised inner-city manufacturing bases to being disconnected and widespread, with companies housed in anonymous spaces across the country. Due to these shifts, which have seen the demise of local manufacturing, businesses now work in a framework of global supply chain connected through digital interfaces. This is a phenomenon that has had an impact on the fashion industry worldwide and has meant it works less as tight-knit communities within specific geographic locales. Recognising this major shift, the Fashion Festival developed a role of bringing the dispersed industry together by creating forums and seminars that provided industry intelligence, enabled networking and supported business growth. These events were perceived as world-class forums that added value to Australian businesses; they were intended to be informative and inspiring, bringing together industry leaders, designers and creative management teams to network and obtain fashion industry knowledge by building global relationships and attracting international visitors. To internationally position the Festival, a focus was on bringing the leading creative and business experts to Melbourne to shed light on opportunities and strategies for the fashion industry's future and addressed issues including brand sustainability, speed to market, digital engagement and creating a positive customer experience. The concerns of the present day were balanced by forecasting the excitement the future holds.

The Business Seminar established since the Festival's first year had a reputation for assisting the industry to become a community of like-minded professionals. From 2005 to 2010, some of the key presenters at these events included: Jane Shepherdson, who at the Business Seminar in 2009 did her first public presentation after leaving her senior role as Brand Manager of Topshop; Margareta van den Bosch – Creative Director of H&M; Francisco Costa – Women's Creative Director, Calvin Klein Collection; Paul Bennett – Chief Creative Officer of Ideo; Sir George Cox – author of the UK Government commissioned *Cox Report into Creative Industries* and ex-Chair of the British Design Council; Bob Isherwood – former World Creative Director, Saatchi and Saatchi; Jasper Conran – Designer; and Christian Blanckaert – former Executive Vice President, Hermes, to name a few.

International visitors attending generally became advocates for the creative culture of Melbourne and remained connected to the Australian fashion industry through the experience of participating. As captured in a testimonial provided by Paul Charron, Chairman Emeritus of Liz Claiborne Inc. and keynote speaker at the LMFF Business Seminar in 2007:

> There is no question that attendance at the 2007 L'Oréal Melbourne Fashion Festival was a superior expenditure of time and energy on my

part. Beyond renewing contacts and making new friends, I learned that New York, London and Paris are not the only fashion centers in the world. In particular, I found the Business Seminar enlightening and stimulating. The broad range of topics discussed, the notable presenters and thoughtful questions from the attendees made for a particularly beneficial day. I would recommend the Business Seminar most highly for retailers, wholesalers and fashionistas at all levels. If you come with an open mind, you are certain to be challenged and stimulated. I not only enjoyed myself, but I learned a few things as well.

The focus at the Business Seminar was predominantly on retail and big picture issues. The audience was diverse but had a strong leaning towards medium to large-scale organisations, vertical operators, independent businesses and educators. Another key event in the Fashion Festival calendar with a business orientation was the Marketing Breakfast. This was a 90-minute early morning session that brought together experts who would provide insight into the marketing, promotions and public relations aspect of the fashion industry. A third business event was developed in 2009: the Designer Forum, which evolved as a concept to support the plethora of micro to small businesses within the fashion design industry, providing intelligence and support to the creative and design sector. The intent of the Designer Forum, in the scheme of the overall Festival, was to be a micro event with a big heart. The Designer Forum hosted a selection of internationally renowned guests who imparted their unique knowledge and experiences to assist independent designers in making positive breakthroughs in both local and global markets.

LMFF built a reputation of developing solid industry networks and attracting the respect and commitment of designers, labels and brands across all market tiers. LMFF was the ideal forum to support Melbourne's position as a design centre, strengthen and expand the large-scale businesses in light of global chains entering the Australian retail landscape plus provide opportunities for increased export generation for micro to small businesses. The business events incorporated into the Festival schedule were less about showcasing (although it led to innumerable introductions and positive outcomes) but more about the sharing of industry intelligence from a global perspective. Less glitz, more wisdom.

As stated by Jane Shepherdson, ex-Brand Director of Topshop in a testimonial provided to the Festival after presenting at the 2007 Business Seminar:

> The Melbourne Fashion Festival is unique, in that it combines both great design and business, in a way that has not been done anywhere else in the world. It is a wonderful opportunity to get under the skin of this country's fashion scene. The Business Seminar was extremely well attended by highly motivated, ambitious and creative people from all aspects of the fashion industry in Australia, which made it a very exciting event to speak at. I also learnt a lot from the other speakers, who were from various different sectors of the business, and provided a real insight into global fashion today.

The creative vision

A major strategy was to evolve LMFF as a valuable asset for the Australian fashion industry, with ever-increasing national recognition and international acknowledgement. The focus was on attention to detail across everything that was produced. The events and activities associated with LMFF were renowned for their high level of professionalism and creativity; there was a healthy mix of risk taking and rational consideration of what could be achieved. One area that the Festival demonstrated leadership in was through its pivotal and forward thinking approach to creative branding.

One of the key tools that significantly contributed to the success of the Fashion Festival from 2006 to 2010 was the development of creative visuals that permeated through all collateral, sets and branding. Each of these Festivals evolved out of a theme centred on a narrative that was envisioned through intuition and developed insight into social and cultural trends, capturing a viable mood of the moment. Appropriate concepts were developed that would attract an audience, be pertinent to a number of applications and flexible enough to be adapted for differing events, market tiers and audience categories.

The creative branding of each Festival was the first interaction any stakeholder would have with the event. It was fundamental to distinguish each year from those that had been staged before although many of the activities and the framework of shows remained the same. Vital to fashion's existence is the belief in the *new*; the evolution of fresh ideas and the purpose for engaging with fashion is to align with the latest, most recent constructs. Parameters that were a guide for the creative branding and themes included having a graphic and bold handwriting, establishing a strong viewpoint that stands out from the visual clutter of other activities and branding messages. Each of the creative branding concepts that were developed year-on-year had a sense of fantasy, and played on the aspirational and other worldliness of fashion while being aesthetically engaging and vibrant. Media commentary referencing the 2009 creative branding states:

> The 2009 Festival imagery developed by the creative genius of Paper, Stone Scissors makes a bold statement; powerful, dramatic and visually enticing. When times are tough being bold and creative is vital to surviving. Webster comments, 'We need to make a stance against mediocrity and low risk principles. The images are clear, fresh, vibrant and optimistic – a pleasure to engage with.'
>
> (Anonymous 2009)

The theme for the 2010 Festival was titled *Get Happy!*, inspired by the Festival's success in creating a sense of delight among the fashion community. The imagery was developed to inspire people to celebrate fashion and as a consequence broke the unspoken rule of sophisticated fashion imagery and not only made the models smile (often a rarity in fashion), the intent was for them to look like they were having fun. The previous year leading up to the 2010 Festival had seen a cultural and economic shift for the industry, so the LMFF campaign message was deliberately optimistic and inclusive. The 2010 campaign received acclaim from industry, media and stakeholders. As captured by Melbourne blogger Kate Vandermeer, Director of i-SpyStyle:

> The official launch of the LMFF program was held yesterday at Federation Square. What is traditionally an invite only event made way for the 'welcome one and all' vibe adopted by the festival this year. It seems part of an overall strategy by LMFF to offer an 'inclusive, community' vibe to this year's festival. The 'Get Happy' campaign features models not only smiling but also laughing it up during the shoot! It's welcoming, infectious and fun. Gone is the typical, aspirational, come hither, you can't afford me international campaign style and in its place? Accessibility. How refreshing!
>
> (Vandermeer 2010)

The idea for the 2010 campaign was generated from the economic climate at the time. Business was tough, the world was reeling from the global financial crisis and it was envisaged this would be a difficult year to engage paying participants and sponsors. It was also vital to give the general public a reason to part with hard earned dollars to attend events and buy into fashion. In this environment there was a fundamental need to celebrate the industry, to applaud the creative strengths and showcase the positive. Although potentially a risk, in times of adversity, rather than a low key sombre approach, the perspective was to share goodwill and the positive experience that fashion can instill through confidence and self-esteem.

The sum is greater than the individual parts

The continued success and growth of the Fashion Festival was due to the engagement by diverse stakeholders, sponsors, brands, Government, designers and educators who shared a collaborative vision to make a positive difference for the Australian fashion industry. Accessibility, diversity and integrity were key mantras within the Festival's ethos. The team employed to facilitate the event were nicknamed the 'fashion family', and despite long hours and rigorous workloads, a passion for positive results connected all involved. This connection and collaboration were values that cannot be underestimated in the event's success, and as a consequence of the diverse mix of players across the multi-tiered and layered composition of the fashion industry, the Festival spearheaded new ideas in fashion activation, created powerful networks and evolved as the voice for the industry. Fundamental criteria instilled within the team included that everything we do should be about the *creation of magic*, and that to enable this we will *only work with nice people!* The creation of magic was more obviously aligned to the visual communication of the Festival branding but extended to all activities. The intent was to take the audience's breath away, to inspire and excite them about the fashion and provide an experience that created a sense of goodwill and engagement. The second mantra was an attempt to squash the impression that the fashion industry is cut-throat and bitchy. By contrast, if the team work in a harmonious environment with a common objective to achieve great results, it benefits all involved. There were of course moments that required management intrusion to placate the bullies that high-powered industries contain. As a manager I wasn't averse to taking some of the top CEOs of leading fashion groups to task if they or their teams put inappropriate pressure on the Festival staff to fulfil expectations.

The Festival was a prime example of the sum being greater than the individual parts. By bringing together approximately 75 sponsors each year with over 300 designers and brands connecting with an audience in excess of 400,000 the outcomes were significant and the results for all participants were enabled because of the collaboration of a number of stakeholders. LMFF from 2005 to 2010 successfully expanded opportunities for participating designers and brands; it showcased Melbourne building on its reputation as a creative hub and extended the reach of Australian fashion through an experiential engagement with the public. The focus for the Festival was to strategically bring the industry together, encouraging businesses across different tiers to support each other and reap the rewards of collaboration, mentoring and the sharing of ideas. As a major event, the Festival has had a proven record of generating millions of dollars in associated business activity and has been considered the most significant, proactive and responsive event that supports the Australian fashion industry.

References

Anonymous (2009) *Get Stylized*, January, http://www.getstylized.com.au/2009/01/loreal-melbourne-fashion-festival (accessed 19 March 2012).

Anonymous (2004) *Pop Up Retail*, January, http://trendwatching.com/trends/popup_retail.htm (accessed 15 November 2012).

Brumby, J. (2009) *Opening Night Address: LMFF* by the Honourable John Brumby, Premier of Victoria, March, Government House, Victoria, Australia.

Sampson, J. (2012) 'Alternative Fashion Week Trends From Around the World', *Sabotage Times*, http://www.sabotagetimes.com/ (accessed 20 December 2012).

Unkles, B. (2006) *LMFF Economic Impact Assessment*, Independent Research submitted to the State Government of Victoria, Saturn Corporate Resources Pty Ltd, Melbourne, Australia.

Unkles, B. (2010) *LMFF Economic Impact Assessment*, Independent Research submitted to the State Government of Victoria, Saturn Corporate Resources Pty Ltd, Melbourne Australia.

Vandermeer, K. (2010) *iSpy with My Little Eye … The Official LMFF Program Launch*, 11 February, http://lmff-blog.clientstage.com.au/2010/02/11/ispy-with-my-little-eye%E2%80%A6-the-official-lmff-program-launch/ (accessed 21 March 2012).

9 Millinery and events

Where have all the mad hatters gone?

Kim M. Williams

The twenty-first century is an era where mass production and inexpensive labour costs in developing countries have overwhelmed and perhaps consumed the manufacturing sector of the fashion industry. Many products are now sourced off-shore from countries in South-East Asia, predominately China (Kellock 2010). These developments in production have contributed to the demise of certain sectors of the fashion industry (Safa 1981; Wark 1991). Couture millinery is one such sector that has declined gradually over the last 60 years. The declining acceptance of hats and the changes in modern manufacturing techniques have seemingly placed hats of any kind as fashion accessories of the past, unless they are being worn for practicality; protecting the wearer from the harsh and unkind weather conditions (Cullen 2008).

McDowell (1992), a renowned fashion historian, stated: 'historically hats proclaimed the man – his status, attitudes and beliefs and the woman – her class, breeding and even matrimonial state' (1992: 97). Hats were considered to be a necessary part of a person's wardrobe and essential for strict dress protocols and societal regulations that were in place for both men and women prior to the Second World War. In addition, women's attire was expected to include all the correct and essential accessories: hats, gloves, bags, stockings and shoes (Harrison 2005; Mitchell 2010). However, that changed after the war: 'by the 1950s hats had become an unnecessary encumbrance and were considered to be out dated and inappropriate for the requirements of the modern lifestyle' (McDowell 1992: 160). Demand for exclusive, custom-made clothes and hats was shrinking in tandem with the growing informality of the 1960s (Leong and Somerville 2010). The freedom revolution of the mid to late twentieth and now into the twenty-first century has marginalised the hat as an item to be included as part of the basic fashion wardrobe. Modern consumers are searching for reasonably priced and value for money objects, rather than individualised, high quality and labour intensive couture items that may be acquired for only one occasion. Nowadays, a couture or even a mass production hat is an accessory that may only be worn on a particular occasion, such as a wedding, a funeral or perhaps a religious function (e.g. Bar Mitzvah). Then again, the modern woman may not deliberate about wearing a hat even at these significant, but infrequent occurrences.

Limited research has been conducted into the connection between the fashion industry and the events sector and even less focusing on millinery. This chapter makes a contribution to closing this research gap by exploring the influence and importance of the event industry to the sustainability of couture millinery. In addition, it will address the question: does the event industry, especially horse racing and the wedding sector, enable a struggling millinery trade to continue, thereby allowing some of the very talented to flourish in a depressed area of the fashion arena?

This chapter presents a discourse, providing the viewpoints and perspectives of four renowned milliners currently working in Melbourne, Australia: Richard Nylon, Serena Lindeman, Paris Kyne and June Edwards. All of these milliners have extensive industry experience and have each worked in the sector for at least 18 years.

Richard Nylon is currently the President of the Millinery Association of Australia (MAA) and has held this position for the last five years and June Edwards was a past president. The MAA is a not-for-profit organisation committed to generating public awareness of millinery and encouraging the wearing of hats. The association provides a range of educational classes and training for up and coming milliners along with creating and hosting events to showcase the work of established Australian milliners. Both Paris Kyne and Serena Lindeman are members of the MAA and furthermore they have completed training and have undertaken considerable millinery activities in the United Kingdom to hone and enhance their craft.

The discussion in the chapter will focus on seven themes:

1. Fashion and millinery: the hat concept;
2. The contemporary milliner;
3. The synergy of couture millinery and horse racing events;
4. Millinery events in Victoria, Australia;
5. Millinery and matrimonial events;
6. Royalty, celebrities and couture millinery; and
7. Potential new couture millinery markets.

Fashion and millinery: the hat concept

Clothing, dress, fashion, style and glamour are all synonymous with the garment industry. Each however invokes a different inference and there is no single meaning or sense that is common to them all (Barnard 2002). It therefore would be of benefit to provide an interpretation of these terms to provide clarity for the discussion within this chapter. *Clothing* refers to the requirement of protecting oneself from the elements and in many societies it has the function of providing modesty. Entwistle (2000) defines *dress* as 'an activity of clothing the body with an aesthetic element' (as in 'adornment') and *fashion* as 'a specific system of dress' (2000: 48).

Fashion can be divided into two market sectors: *high* or *haute couture*, and everyday fashion which is mass produced and is also known as *ready to wear* or *prêt-à-porter* (Craik 1994). 'Haute couture was founded by Charles Fredrick Worth (1870s–1880s) and coincidentally began at the same time as the invention of the sewing machine' (Martin and Koda 1995: 15). Haute couture garments are made to order for a specific client. They are usually from high quality, expensive fabric and are produced and finished by the most experienced and capable seamstresses. The manufacturing process is often time-consuming, utilising hand-executed techniques: embroidery, beading, feathers, lace and ribbon work. Troy (2003) specified that 'there can be a tension between orig-inality and reproduction, of a unique work of art and the mass-produced commodity' (2003: 7). *Style* is a complex and elusive concept and is connected to refined taste and the ability to select the best possible combination of items for the greatest impression for others and oneself. *Glamour* emerges from style and denotes beauty and opulence.

The style of dress and the selection of hat was said to supply the observer with information to be able to interpret a gentleman's profession and to what strata of society he would belong (McDowell 1992). Even now this accessory item provides a vehicle for self-expression and can exhibit social status within one's community (Reynolds 2003). To hat, or not to hat? That is a dilemma! In the contemporary era only a minority of individuals would ask this ques-tion. Nevertheless, a hat can be utilised as an expression of self and assist with personal identity, making a statement about an individual's fashion con-fidence. By wearing a hat today, an individual is able to stand out from the crowd. This portrays confidence in their fashion selection, which was not the case historically, because it was an expected obligation.

The contemporary milliner

Contemporary milliners create wearable art, and the very talented ones do not replicate but instead produce new and innovative designs (Reynolds 2003). The renowned milliners Philip Treacy and Stephen Jones belong to this league, and in Australia, Richard Nylon, Paris Kyne and Serena Lindeman are also among the desired milliners, winning awards and having celebrity clients.

The use of technology and social media for marketing purposes is common-place for most progressive businesses today. Many milliners have embraced this mode of communication and have employed the use of a website, Facebook, blogs and twitter to disseminate their merchandise. These technological plat-forms facilitate business transactions and promote and display a milliner's talents to interested consumers. In fact, because of the reduction in overheads it could be suggested that this new marketing strategy is better than having a traditional shop front on the high street. All of the interviewed milliners engaged in electronic commerce on some level and intended to broaden their engagement further in the future.

Seasonality has always affected the millinery industry across the globe. In the late 1800s, Blum (1993: 6) explains that:

> Due to the seasonal nature of the work and the low wages in the clothing sector many women in Paris and London were forced to look for alternative sources of income – one being prostitution or using their shop as a front for a brothel.
>
> (Gamber 1997)

It wasn't until the early 1900s that millinery was considered a respectable career choice for women, providing a potential job prospect for an ambitious person looking for self-employment.

All of the milliners interviewed indicated that the millinery season in Melbourne, Australia and even across the globe is strongly linked to racing events. In Melbourne, the high sales season for millinery is the spring (September and October), coinciding with the start of the main racing season. It was suggested that if a milliner desires a steady and continual income it is advisable for them to follow a number of racing carnivals across the globe. Paris Kyne supplies very little else other than the racing market. He produces racing millinery for racing events held in Tasmania and Victoria, Australia and the Kentucky Derby held in Louisville, USA. Thus he has access to three distinct seasons to generate sales of his millinery products.

As a result of the natural seasonality of millinery and the racing calendar it has been necessary for contemporary milliners to devise other income sources to provide them with a yearly income. Teaching their skills to others is one way of increasing their annual income. Many of the milliners conduct classes in their studios or deliver certified courses at a variety of Training and Further Education (TAFE) institutions, which belong to the vocational education sector in Australia. Serena Lindeman and Paris Kyne offer short courses at their studios in the central business district (CBD) and also work at Kangan Batman Institute of TAFE. Richard Nylon offers classes at his studio in Fitzroy and also works at RMIT. In addition, he has worked part-time with Myer for the last 25 years; a department store in the CBD of Melbourne. Many other Melbourne milliners operate their own milliner classes: Waltraud Reiner, Louise Macdonald, Phillip Rhodes and Rose Hudson to mention a few.

Serena Lindeman suggests that 'one of the reasons why so many milliners have turned to teaching is to spread their income over a broader period of time, to try to make a satisfactory living'. She believes, however that 'there is also a downside to teaching because milliners are training individuals who will potentially want their clients and become a competitor in an already small market place' (Lindeman, December 2012).

The milliners who conducted classes revealed that there were other motivation factors that attracted them to teaching, not only the financial gain. Historically there has been a shift in the Australian Textile Clothing and

Footwear sector, for which the millinery industry belongs, away from technical skills and craftsmanship; displaying hand-stitching and complex and intricate manipulation of millinery material (Kellock 2010). With the decline in the traditional apprenticeship and the introduction of certification many of these skills may be lost. Experienced milliners involved with training courses are the custodian of these skills. Each of the milliners explained that teaching was a financial incentive but they also recognised that their skills and knowledge base is often unique and some of their industry intelligence will be eventually lost if they do not hand it on to the next generation of milliners. Each of the milliners observed that they enjoyed teaching others and at times it was a two way street where the milliner might gain from the enthusiasm and new ideas of their students.

Richard Nylon indicated that he thought 'people will always want to learn millinery which is fantastic', however he is concerned about the career expectations of the up and coming milliner. He suggested 'a new entrant to this fashion sector requires access to a substantial amount of money to get started and survive in the first few years', because he has found the millinery industry a very challenging career path. 'There are only perhaps two or three milliners in Melbourne who devote their entire time to millinery and that might be because they have additional financial support and they do not really have worry about their actual annual income' (Nylon, December 2012).

The synergy of couture millinery and horse racing events

For a product to be successful it requires a flourishing market place and one of the very few examples for millinery is connected to the horse racing industry. In Australia only a minority of women wear or even own a hat in the twenty-first century. The major racing events around the globe have become the significant market place for milliners hoping to make a name for themselves and their business. Across the globe there are premier horse racing events that span the annual calendar attracting major punters and 'fashionistas' – these include: the Dubai World Cup (March); the Kentucky Derby (May); Royal Ascot (June); the Prix de l'Arc de Triomphe (October); and the Melbourne Spring Racing Carnival, culminating in the Melbourne Cup (October–November).

The Royal Ascot races in the United Kingdom have a long heritage of over 300 years. Royalty, celebrities and high society have attended this race meeting since 1711, making it one of the most famous and most fashion stylish events in the world of sport (Sherwood 2011). Royal Ascot is as much about the fashions and certainly the millinery as it is about the horse racing thoroughbreds on the track. According to Philip Treacy, who is a favourite at Royal Ascot: 'Hats are for everyone. We all have a head so we have the possibility to wear a hat. You feel better for wearing them' (Sherwood 2011: 142).

There has always been a tradition of a strict code of dress at Royal Ascot, however by 2012 it was considered that dress standards at the racetrack had deteriorated to such an extent that the 2012 Royal Ascot organisers perceived there was a requirement to provide two inaugural Style Guides for the Royal Enclosure and the Grandstand attendees. Both guides indicated that a headpiece should be worn as well as other formal dress prerequisites (Dow 2012). Considering these stipulated arrangements at Royal Ascot, Paris Kyne had the following comment concerning what might increase the interest in millinery in Australia:

> Horse racing in Australia is the answer to millinery. If we have more people going to the races, and the Victorian Racing Club introduced dress standards similar to Royal Ascot; making exact standards that you have to wear a hat with an enclosed crown in areas like the Birdcage or the Members enclosure of Flemington, I think it might help milliners. However, maybe the regulation could be a hindrance to creativity.
>
> (Kyne, December 2012)

Melbourne is renowned for its strategic development of a portfolio or calendar of hallmark events (Frost and Laing 2011). It is known as one of the most significant sporting event cities on the globe, hosting the Australian Football League Grand Final, a tennis Grand Slam, a Formula One motor race and the Spring Racing Carnival, just to name a few annual events. The world famous and very prestigious Melbourne Cup, promoted as *the Race that Stops a Nation* is held as a major component of the Spring Racing Carnival at Flemington racecourse. Held annually since 1861, it allows both rich and poor to partake in the enjoyment of a day at the races: 'Tens of thousands attend the race at the Flemington Racecourse in Victoria and millions more around the world watch and listen on television or radio' (Australian Racing Museum 2005b: 1). The fashion industry generates more than AU$15 million worth of revenue during the Spring Racing Carnival just in Victoria. In 2004 race-goers bought 47,960 hats, 39,578 pairs of shoes and 22,321 handbags (Australian Racing Museum 2005a) and by 2011 fashion enthusiasts purchased over 63,000 hats, 34,000 dresses, 12,000 suits and 52,000 pairs of shoes (IER Pty Ltd 2011). These figures indicate a major contribution to the millinery sector which is only generated due to the operating of this sporting event.

In 2013, 'Racing Style: 50 Years of Fashion on the Field', an exhibition at the National Sports Museum, celebrated 50 years of Australian racing fashion at the Flemington Racecourse (Figure 9.1). The Fashions on the Field competition was created by the Victoria Racing Club in 1962 in a bid to attract more women to the races. The inclusion of a fashion competition has been embraced by race clubs throughout Australia and internationally. Today it is one of the most iconic events in Australia's cultural, fashion and sporting calendar with Myer (the venerable Melbourne department store) becoming the official sponsor in 1983 (Australian Racing Museum 2005a; Williams 2012).

On Derby Day 1965, Fashions on the Field had its most publicised moment. There was a famous rebellion to dress convention when Jean Shrimpton, a

Figure 9.1 'Racing Style: 50 Years of Fashions on the Field', National Sports Museum, 2012–13.
Source: National Sports Museum and the Australian Racing Museum

22-year-old British model, attended Flemington Racecourse with no hat, no gloves nor stockings wearing a dress that was considered by many to be too short (Australian Racing Museum 2005a; Harrison 2005; Mitchell 2010). Shrimpton had been invited by the Victorian Racing Club to be a guest fashion judge. Her outfit seriously contravened the dress regulations of race-goers of the time. This fashion digression possibly opened the gates of a fashion revolution, allowing the growth of a general acceptance of casual dress at these racing occasions (see Chapter 1, Figure 1.1) (Australian Racing Museum 2005a; Harrison 2005).

In 2012, Myer Fashions on the Field recorded a prize pool worth more than AU$400,000, also including an invitation-only millinery award which focused purely on the hat or headpiece. Not only is there competition on the racetrack but on the fashion stage and also an adjunct competition to be seen and photographed at this sporting event. Paris Kyne suggested:

> There is competition between ladies, if you're in a major marquee or anywhere at the races you are trying to be photographed. You're trying to get attention and one way of drawing attention to yourself is by wearing a wonderful designer hat.
>
> (Kyne, December 2012)

The races are possibly the only time a woman in the modern Western world feels totally comfortable wearing a hat and perceives they are noticeably underdressed without one (Van Den Berg 2012). In fact there is a *subtle* or one might suggest an *extremely* competitive aspect for those who don a couture hat at one of these special race meetings (Edmiston 2012). Those involved with this sporting event may want to be noticed and possibly desire to be considered wealthier and more successful than they might otherwise be. A fabulous and expensive couture hat, therefore, may exhibit this to others.

Being noticed and gaining media publicity is very important to many who attend a racing carnival here in Australia and abroad. Horse racing events across the globe facilitate a women's opportunity for couture fashion, style and glamour. Serena Lindeman proposed that 'horse racing events allows individuals to dress in a way that is a little bit outside their ordinary lives, by wearing all the complementary fashion accessories: hats, gloves, bags, scarves and shoes, completing a fantastic ensemble' (Lindeman, December 2012). Competing in Fashions on the Field, via wearing designer fashions and milliners' hats provides a mechanism for women to take extended pleasure in a significant fashion occasion.

Richard Nylon pointed out 'there is an obvious connection between fashion and horse racing, stretching back to England and Royal Ascot which commenced in 1711 and the establishment of Flemington Racecourse in 1840' (Nylon, December 2012). He believes that:

> Ladies have always liked to show off their finery and in the past women were show pieces, a man could demonstrate how well he had done by having his lady friend, consort or wife dressed up in the finest clothes and the finest hats. Now, of course, women go and buy their own clothes and their own hats and everything else, so it's just a continuation of the tradition and what's more, it's fun.
>
> (Nylon, December 2012)

Paris Kyne suggested that hats are part of our costume when we go to the races. In the past, if not still in the present, the Victorian Racing Club (VRC) at Flemington was trying to attract more women to the races. Fashion and millinery became a quintessential part of racing events to encourage more women to attend (Williams 2012). Kyne explained that 'horse races are somewhere to go out and celebrate. Headwear is expected at these events as opposed to going to a barbeque or somebody's birthday party.' Recognising that headwear is not expected at other events, however, he could not explain exactly why, but suggested that may be it was 'attached to traditional societal norms associated with the races' (Kyne, December 2012).

The continued success of couture millinery in Australia is linked to a thriving horse racing industry. The commencement of spring racing is heralded by the new season's fashions. Serena Lindeman stated:

The racing industry succeeds because of glamour. If the women go, the men go. If the women are happy to go, then it just expands the audience massively for racing, racing events and social events connected to the races. The racing season is what keeps millinery alive in Melbourne. There is a synergy. I think the racing organisations are aware of how fashion contributes. I think Sue Lloyd-Williams, with her promotion of the Fashions on the Field and bringing women into Flemington has been instrumental in the millinery industry growing. If it wasn't for the racing industry, the millinery industry would be altogether less.

(Lindeman, December 2012)

Wearing a prominent and celebrated milliner's product can be the key to having a successful and enjoyable day at the racecourse for many ladies. Serena Lindeman explained:

There are certain types of women who walk around going, oh, there's a Philip Treacy, Phillip Rhodes, Stephen Jones; they are able to recognise the hand of the milliners. I know I've had clients bump into each other and say, oh, your hat's by Serena Lindeman. They'll start conversations that they wouldn't otherwise. So certainly, there's a bit of that goes on and that's kind of fun. A good hat will start a conversation where you can't just bounce up to someone and say, 'you look a bit of alright. I want to talk to you'. A fabulous couture hat is a good way to start a conversation.

(Lindeman, December 2012) (Figure 9.2)

In the year of the equine flu in Australia (August 2007), Richard Nylon indicated that 'the Sydney milliners were very hard hit' because Royal Randwick and Rosehill Gardens racecourses were locked down and there was a ban placed on horse movement and race meetings by the New South Wales Government. In the same year in Melbourne it was not so obvious since the spring racing carnival went ahead (Nylon, December 2012). Paris Kyne believes that the millinery industry in Australia would be very different without a robust horse racing events sector:

There would not be an industry as we know it today. There would be a few homeworkers and a couple of little hat shops bringing in mass produced junk. It wouldn't be the handmade couture items that we have at present. Remember, we're one of the only two places in the world that still has this, England being the other. There are little bits of it in Germany and elsewhere around the world, but it is England and Australia that are the most predominant in couture millinery.

(Kyne, December 2012)

June Edwards and Serena Lindeman believe the link between the horseracing industry and the millinery industry is enormous, however it is very seasonal

Figure 9.2 Ensemble worn by Classic Racewear Crown Oaks Day winner 2001. Barbara Wilson (designer), Serena Lindeman (milliner).

Source: K. Williams

which causes challenges for a milliner to make a living over the entire year. For most milliners in Australia it is their only outlet (Edwards, December 2012). Many milliners have to follow other racing fixtures across the globe to maximise their living. As mentioned previously, Paris Kyne produces hats for the spring racing in Melbourne, the Kentucky Derby in the USA and also the Hobart Cup (February). Other milliners also target the Dubai World Cup and others still endeavour to compete with milliners in Europe and the UK which can be very demanding.

Millinery events in Victoria, Australia

Hats and High Tea, *Hatsravagance*, the *Millinery Collection* and *Fashions on the Field* are some of the high-profile fashion events included in Melbourne's Spring Racing event calendar. These events exhibit couture hats to interested fashion-conscious racing attendees. The aspiration of those attending fashion events may be the desire to see, purchase or eventually wear an impressive hat at their chosen event during the racing carnival. The importance of style, glamour, elegance and the prestige of those associated with horse racing, the pursuit of kings, intensifies the desire to be able to afford a couture hat, rather than a mass-production item sold at a commercial department store.

The Millinery Collection started in 1999, and was held in a central Melbourne location and co-ordinated by Jacqueline Spruce for nine years (1999–2007) in collaboration with the Millinery Association of Australia. June Edwards believes that 'Jacqueline Spruce greatly assisted in improving the image of millinery during this time and was able to secure television and press coverage. The event was very extensive and successful in attracting milliners and potential customers' (Edwards, December 2012).

In 2008, the event moved to Flemington Racecourse and was renamed Hatsravagance. It was run by the VRC once again in collaboration with the Millinery Association of Australia. Thirty-five milliners took part in the event which attracted over 500 guests eager to view and purchase the latest couture millinery fashions (Nylon 2008). Hatstravagance ran for four years and it became the biggest annual showcase of millinery. By 2011, the event featured over 250 hats with 40 milliners on display (Collie 2011). Hatsravagance unfortunately didn't occur in 2012. Richard Nylon explained:

> The new deputy CEO at the VRC decided to refocus the business side of the club to make it more focused on horse racing because they are a racing club and hats and fashion are an adjunct to that. One of the prime reasons why Hatsravagance took place was because the previous deputy CEO was very much for millinery and for the milliners and also getting those big spaces at Flemington used.
>
> (Nylon, December 2012)

In 2012, Hat and High Tea was held at the Caulfield Racecourse. This event was a collaboration between the Millinery Association of Australia and *Ladies in Racing* magazine. Thirty milliners from across Australia displayed over a thousand hats and headpieces (Millinery Association of Australia 2012).

In 2012, the Millinery Association also introduced a new initiative – a *pop-up* shop at CBD shopping centre Melbourne Central, which provided a short term shop front for a range of milliners who were able to display their merchandise while volunteering their time to man the shop. Other than these racing connected events, there are very few avenues for a milliner to be able to showcase their products.

Millinery and matrimonial events

In certain parts of the globe covering your head before you enter a religious building is an expected requirement. Prior to the mid 1900s, in the western world, when entering a Christian church, one was expected to be wearing a hat. June Edwards believes that:

> The church attending populace used to be very familiar with wearing a hat to these religious occasions, however at a certain point in the twentieth century this stopped being the case. Thus not having to wear a hat to church could have been the impetus for the decline in headwear popularity, in addition to the casuality of dress in the current environment.
>
> (Edwards, December 2012)

Weddings however still engender the desire to wear a hat. If there was an occasion in a woman's life where a headpiece or hat could be considered as an essential part of her dress ensemble it is when she is getting married or attending a wedding as a guest. Bridal headwear symbolises the bride's purity and majesty with the use of veils dating back to Roman times. Bridal hats however are a fairly new phenomenon and only emerged in the twentieth century (Lacey 1969; McDowell 1992: 109).

In the United Kingdom, the protocol of donning a hat to attend a wedding celebration is still prevalent. Serena Lindeman remembers when she was working in England in the 1980s there was a specific wedding season (Spring to Summer). The fashion of wearing hats to weddings is always under debate, however it was rare to see a wedding without a number of people wearing hats. However when she came back to Australia in 1998 she found that very few people wore hats to weddings, which she found rather disappointing:

> I have been to weddings in Australia, where I have felt that it's encumbered upon me as a milliner to wear a hat and I am usually one of two people. I don't think I've ever really been the only person but certainly in the minority wearing a hat. One might say a little bit of an oddity.
>
> (Lindeman, December 2012)

Paris Kyne indicated that:

> The general populous still wear hats to weddings in the United Kingdom. They are an older and more traditional country than Australia. So certain customs have been there for longer than they have in Australia and I think it is just ingrained like so many other things are in the UK.
>
> (Kyne, December 2012)

Puente (2011) suggested there are numerous social occasions in Britain where one is required to wear a hat. The Royal Wedding of Prince William to Catherine Middleton in April 2011 was certainly one of these events: 'Every woman there will be wearing a hat but the rule, for such an occasion, is nothing too ostentatious' (Cowles 2011). The controversial hat worn by Princess Beatrice and made by Philip Treacy went viral immediately after the event with a Facebook page entitled *Princess Beatrice's Ridiculous Royal Wedding Hat* attracting at least 134,000 fans (Considine 2011). The hat, no matter what the verdict was of its suitability, eventually sold at a charity auction for the price of AU$123,325 a few weeks after the wedding. It could be suggested that any publicity is good publicity and this incident could motivate the general public to consider a hat to complement a special event outfit. Will the interest in millinery across the planet extend further than a few months from the royal event? Stephen Jones the British milliner believes so:

> I think fashion historians will one day look back on this current time as a brief period when people didn't wear a hat. That people stopped for the last 50 years or so, it is just a blip in the larger history of headwear.
>
> (Cowles 2011)

Richard Nylon's millinery work, apart from his contributions to race wear, is predominately produced for the bridal market. His studio is situated above a bridal designer shop which provides a synergy between the two businesses. Unfortunately, bridal wear can also be seasonal in Melbourne due to climatic conditions. It is not as though he is not involved with the racing sector but he also experiences great demand from brides, the wedding party and possibly the wedding guest: 'If the racing sector declined, I think bridal would still keep me afloat' (Nylon, December 2012).

Royalty, celebrities and couture millinery

Notable and high-profile women such as Princess Grace, Princess Diana, Coco Chanel, Jacqueline Kennedy and, more recently, Catherine, Duchess of Cambridge, have assisted in improving the profile of the millinery sector. In 1957, the Millinery Institute of America bestowed Princess Grace with a Golden Hat Award for her good taste in selecting millinery that coordinated with her complete outfit (Haugland 2010). Harris (2012a, 2012b) believes that there is still a strong presence of hats in the United Kingdom and other western nations because of the British Royal family, and also due to celebrities, who are bringing a variety of headpieces back into pop culture.

Many of the women from Royal Households have assisted the milli-nery industry enormously in the United Kingdom, and this is also true for

Australia. Royal hat wearers include Queen Elizabeth II, Princess Catherine and Crown Princess Mary of Denmark, and before that Princess Diana, Princess Margaret and the Queen Mother. All the milliners interviewed believed Royal Households have an influence on the general public. Richard Nylon indicated that:

> What I like about royalty at the moment is the popularity of Princess Kate. She wears hats and looks nice in them, so people for whatever reason think she is fantastic. If she promotes millinery by wearing it that is good for the industry everywhere.
>
> (Nylon, December 2012)

Bou's (2012) recent book entitled *Couture Hats* provides a discourse concerning the work of 22 milliners located across the globe. The overwhelming common link between these successful milliners is a strong connection to celebrity clients (e.g. Madonna, Kate Moss), as well as providing headwear to complement famous fashion houses and designers' creations on the catwalks of fashion shows (e.g. Givenchy, Ralph Lauren, Chanel). Serena Lindeman commented on the celebrity and millinery connection:

> I know that, when a milliner obtains a celebrity client, they tend to promote themselves by reference to that client. I guess they are seeking to have other people to emulate that particular famous person. Lady Gaga has probably done quite a lot for Philip Treacy's popularity and image.
>
> (Lindeman, December 2012)

The connection with royalty, world leaders, supermodels, television personalities, rock stars and an array of other celebrities attending the Spring Racing Carnival is very important to the Australian fashion sector (Brain 2012). Many of these guests are invited to a corporate marquee and in the tradition of the races wear a noteworthy couture millinery accessory. This display of millinery will be admired by others and possibly may inspire them to purchase a hat from a particular millinery designer in the future.

Potential new couture millinery markets

Polo and other equine sporting events such as show jumping were mentioned by some of the milliners interviewed as another event where hats are being worn. *Hat Life* (2013) discussed the opening of the International Polo season in Palm Beach Florida in 2013:

> Hats were everywhere this year, in the past vendors sold jewellery, swimsuits and watches, but this year, hats were the celebrity at hand. Last week was the perfect weather for the Opening Day and it was exciting and liberating to see so many women and men wearing hats.

Serena Lindeman re-enforced this by stating that:

> Outdoor events like the polo and show jumping are alternative events where hats can come into their own. The equine sector has synergised very nicely in that way. I think more people doing millinery and encouraging hat events is the way to go.
>
> (Lindeman, December 2012)

These events provide another market place for millinery but unfortunately they are also seasonal and limited in popularity but do have a strong connection to Royalty and the rich and famous.

Conclusion

This chapter has presented a discourse pertaining to the linkage between two industries – millinery and events – that possess a synergy of mutual benefit, especially for the millinery sector. Struggling industries in any sector are quite often dependent on very precarious circumstances that could easily alter due to social, economic and financial changes. Fashion has undergone major changes in the last century due to the introduction of mass production techniques and the changes of labour markets which have now transferred manufacture to off-shore locations such as the Asian region.

With a limited market place the contemporary milliner has to face the challenge of marketing their products effectively. In the twenty-first century, milliners produce pieces of *art* and these are displayed on the catwalks of fashion houses and on the heads of celebrities. This provides an avenue for the general populace to be influenced by what they see and to take direction on what might be desirable for a stylish, elegant and glamorous woman to wear.

Alterations in fashion including fads, trends and the relaxation of societal norms have had a devastating effect on millinery where the hat no longer has a place as a daily wardrobe staple (Van Den Berg 2012). Despite this, a hat still takes pride of place at prestigious racetracks. The horse racing sector has benefited from the inclusion of fashion as a major element at many racing events across the globe. Fashion attracts the ladies and as such it allows gentlemen to attend these events. Milliners have been able to capitalise and prosper due to the affluence and money made at a racing carnival. The racing and bridal arena has traditionally embraced the wearing of hats and is integral to the continuation and sustainability of a challenging sector of the fashion industry. It would be a great shame to imagine that as the world becomes more relaxed and casual the elegance and beauty of wearing a hat could eventually disappear.

References

Australian Racing Museum (2005a) 'Fashions on the Field: The Spring Racing Carnival', *Learning Resource* http://www.racingvictoria.net.au/asset/cms/Champions/fashions_on_theField_sn2_001.pdf (accessed 22 February 2013).

Australian Racing Museum (2005b) 'The race that stops a nation: The Melbourne Cup', *Learning Resource* http://www.racingvictoria.net.au/asset/cms/Champions/race_that_stops_a_nation_sn2_001.pdf (accessed 22 February 2013).

Barnard, M. (2002) *Fashion as Communication*, 2nd edn, London: Routledge.

Blum, D. E. (1993) 'Ahead of fashion: Hats of the 20th century', *Philadelphia Museum of Art Bulletin*, 89(377/378): 1–48.

Bou, L. (2012) *Couture Hats*, New York: Harper Design.

Brain, A. (2012) 'The greatest of them all', in E. Power, A. Brain, K. Cuthbertson, L. Van Den Berg and F. Williams (eds), *Fashion & Flemington: A Carnival of Creativity, Class and Celebrity*, Melbourne: Slattery Media Group.

Collie, E. (2011) 'Melbourne: Hatstravagance', 22 September, *Melbourne Girl*, http://www.melbgirl.com.au/2011/09/22/melbourne-hatstravagance (accessed 19 March 2012).

Considine, A. (2011) 'The perched, the frothy, the fascinator' [Style Desk], *The New York Times*, 8 May: ST.5.

Cowles, C. (2011) 'First look: "Hats: An Anthology by Stephen Jones" lands in New York', http://nymag.com/thecut/2011/09/hats-anthology-stephen-jones.html (accessed 26 September 2012).

Craik, J. (1994) *The Face of Fashion: Cultural Studies*, London: Routledge.

Cullen, O. (2008) 'Introduction', in S. Jones, *Hats: An Anthology*, London: V & A Publishing.

Dow, A. (2012) 'Dress code is promotor's bet to bring elegance back to Ascot', http://www.millinery.info/hats_articles_ascot.html (accessed 26 September 2012).

Edmiston, L. (2012) 'Introduction: A personal reflection', in E. Power, A. Brain, K. Cuthbertson, L. Van Den Berg and F. Williams (eds), *Fashion & Flemington: A Carnival of Creativity, Class and Celebrity*, Melbourne: Slattery Media Group.

Entwistle, J. (2000) *The Fashioned Body: Fashion, Dress and Modern Social Theory*, Cambridge: Polity Press.

Frost, W. and Laing, J. (2011) *Strategic Management of Festivals and Events*, Melbourne: Cengage.

Gamber, W. (1997) *The Female Economy: Millinery and Dressmaking Trades, 1860–1930*, Urbana and Chicago: University of Illinois Press.

Hat Life (2013) 'Polo Season is upon us', Volume 8, Newsletter 1, 16 January, http://www.hatlife.com/newsletters/2013/jan13_1/art1.htm (accessed March 2013).

Harris, J. (2012a) 'Hats are back on top', *Chicago Tribune*, 26 August: 6.19.

Harris, J. (2012b) 'Style: They're back on top', *Los Angeles Times*, 29 July: 2.

Harrison, S. (2005) 'Jean Shrimpton, the "four inch furore" and perceptions of Melbourne identity in the 1960s', in S. O'Hanlon and T. Luckins (eds), *Go! Melbourne in the Sixties*, Beaconsfield: Circa.

Haugland, H. K. (2010) *Grace Kelly Style*, London: V & A Publishing.

IER Pty Ltd (2011) *2011 Spring Racing Carnival Economic Impact Study*, IER Pty Ltd.

Kellock, J. (2010) 'The business of fashion', in B. English and L. Pomazan (eds), *Australian Fashion Unstitched: The Last 60 Years*, Melbourne: Cambridge University Press.

Lacey, P. (1969) *The Wedding*, New York: The Ridge Press, Inc.

Leong, R. and Somerville, K. (2010) 'Beyond the boundaries: Australian fashion from the 1960s to the 1980s', in B. English and L. Pomazan (eds), *Australian Fashion Unstitched: The Last 60 Years*, Melbourne: Cambridge University Press.

Martin, R. and Koda, H. (1995) *Haute Couture*, New York: The Metropolitan Museum of Art.

McDowell, C. (1992) *Hats: Status, Style and Glamour*, London: Thames & Hudson.

Millinery Association of Australia (2012) 'The Sparkling Ladies Spring Racing Hats & High Tea', http://millineryaustralia.org/event/the-sparkling-ladies-spring-racing-hats-high-tea (accessed 19 March 2012).

Mitchell, L. (2010) 'The Fabulous Fifties: Glamour and style', in B. English and L. Pomazan (eds), *Australian Fashion Unstitched: The Last 60 Years*, Melbourne: Cambridge University Press.

Nylon, R. (2008) 'Richard Nylon's hatstravagant night', http://www.iconpr.com.au/blog/detail/richard-nylons-hatstravagant-night (accessed 19 March 2012).

Puente, M. (2011) 'For Brits, fancy headpieces are old hat: Plenty will be worn at wedding, but none elaborate enough to outdo bride or queen', *US Today*, 27 April: D.3.

Reynolds, H. (2003) *A Fashionable History of Hats & Hairstyles*, Oxford: Heinemann Library.

Safa, H. I. (1981) 'Runaway shops and female employment: The search for cheap labour', *Development and Sexual Division of Labour*, 7(2): 418–433.

Sherwood, J. (2011) *Fashion at Royal Ascot: Three Centuries of Thoroughbred Style*, London: Thames & Hudson.

Troy, N. J. (2003) *Couture Culture: A Study in Modern Art and Fashion*, London: MIT Press.

Van Den Berg, L. (2012) 'Millinery – a style of its own', in E. Power, A. Brain, K. Cuthbertson, L. Van Den Berg and F. Williams (eds), *Fashion & Flemington: A Carnival of Creativity, Class and Celebrity*, Melbourne: Slattery Media Group.

Wark, M. (1991) 'Fashioning the future: Fashion, clothing, and the manufacturing of post-Fordist culture', *Cultural Studies*, 5(1): 61–76.

Williams, F. (2012) 'An evolving parade of style and flair', in E. Power, A. Brain, K. Cuthbertson, L. Van Den Berg and F. Williams (eds), *Fashion & Flemington: A Carnival of Creativity, Class and Celebrity*, Melbourne: Slattery Media Group.

10 Using fashion exhibitions to reimagine destination image

An interview with Karen Quinlan, Director, Bendigo Art Gallery

Jennifer Laing and Warwick Frost

The link between fashion and destination image is well recognised. Destinations such as Paris, Milan and New York are strongly associated with high-end glamour and haute couture, while Tokyo and London are more cutting-edge fashion centres. Some streets within these destinations are particularly evocative as fashion hubs, such as Fifth Avenue in New York, with its iconic Macy's and Tiffany stores, the Rue Cambon in Paris, headquarters to Chanel, and Carnaby Street in London, with its Swinging Sixties association with Mary Quant and mod/hippie clothing. An entire country can be branded in this way, with Italy and France inextricably linked with luxury fashion houses, top designers and a chic and elegant populace. These destinations are known for their high-profile fashion events. They have also often staged successful exhibitions based on fashion themes, sometimes at institutions known for their extensive fashion collections, such as the Victoria and Albert (V & A) Museum in London or the Musée Galliera in Paris.

While this association with high-profile fashion events has been a successful strategy for these large urban centres, it is now being used by some smaller destinations in order to brand themselves as stylish, creative and cultured. There is a growing recognition of the importance of marketing smaller cities, outside of the metropolitan hubs, with populations of between 20,000 and 200,000. For these regional cities, tourism offers a way to achieve sustainable growth, encourage a sense of place and identity and enhance their liveability. The difficult balancing act is to make them more sophisticated and cosmopolitan, while maintaining the lifestyle of a small regional city (Wheeler and Laing 2008).

This chapter provides a case study of the Australian regional city of Bendigo, in the state of Victoria. Originally established in the Gold Rushes of the 1850s, it has a population of approximately 100,000 and has adopted tourism strategies based on its heritage, culture and regional food and wine (Cornish 2012; Frost *et al.* 2012; Wheeler *et al.* 2009). Integral to this strategy is the Bendigo Art Gallery, which has been very successful in staging fashion exhibitions. These include the *Golden Age of Couture 1947–1957* (2009), the *White Wedding Dress* (2011) and most recently *Grace Kelly: Style Icon* (2012) (Figure 10.1).

Figure 10.1 View of street banners advertising the *Grace Kelly: Style Icon* exhibition.
Source: J. Laing

To explore how these fashion exhibitions have affected Bendigo, we conducted the following interview with Karen Quinlan, the Director of the
Gallery.

Q: Could you tell us a little bit about your background including your work
experience and qualifications?
A: I studied at the Melbourne State College as it was at the time. I had trained
to become a teacher, so my interest in art occurred at school. I wasn't
an artist but I knew that I wanted to do something further in the field. I
learned to sew when I was very young; I was always a dressmaker, right
from a very young age – just making clothes for myself with paper patterns
and that sort of thing. So that was one of my interests. But when I got to
college, it was a four year course, as a Bachelor of Education and a teaching course and I majored in Fine Art, so Art History and Printmaking and
there was a textiles component in there.
   I pursued textiles in the sense that rather than garment construction,
I did fabric printing and learned those processes which connected very
much with print making. I wrote a thesis I think at the time about an
Australian artist, so I was interested in women artists as well. I finished
the course and I started teaching and I taught for about five years in a
secondary school in Melbourne and I taught across year 7 to 12, Art

History again, practical studies as well. It was a girls' school and so I was teaching garment construction and textiles, which is what I loved doing. And really introducing those students to the fact that there could be a career beyond making aprons. One student actually entered the Gown of the Year competition, for example, by year 12 and she actually became a pattern maker and teaches at RMIT now.

So then I had a change of career. What happened was I was still sewing but I was really interested in collections; and in particular the conservation of textiles and costume. I started to work as a volunteer at the National Gallery of Victoria [NGV] and to work in the Department with Robyn Healy who was the curator at the time. I was successful when I applied for a position in there, so then I had my first curatorial position. I remember cataloguing the Thomas Harrison Hat Collection, which was a massive collection. There's more, but that's just briefly what happened there.

I then applied for the position at Bendigo for 12 months, which is what it was because I felt that I should try and expand my reach within the field and potentially start working with other sorts of collections. At the time, I couldn't see myself going any further in that department [at NGV]. There was one curator, one assistant curator. So, I moved to Bendigo for 12 months and I was exposed to the collection there, became the curator, stayed another three years, curated some exhibitions – not fashion – but painting and print making and all sorts of things. And my interest developed further in terms of Art History and my focus started to become more around late nineteenth, early twentieth century artists and in particular women artists. I was fascinated by the whole expatriate movement from Australia to Paris, Australia to London and what drove those women. I did a lot of study around that and over the years I have produced a number of exhibitions that relate to that and I've written quite a lot about that. So that's one side of me.

The other side said, 'One day I am going to do a fashion exhibition at Bendigo!' I became the director in 2000 and at the same time I had my children, so the first couple of years for me were slow for me – to really love the job but embrace the job and take it to the next stage, which is what I needed to do. I got international exhibitions in there and I wanted to expand upon that. So there was one show that we had in there from the National Portrait Gallery, which I delivered and that was a successful show – it was a photography exhibition. Then I went back to them, the curator there, and asked, 'What else have you got?' And two more shows came our way.

That was good and then I started to get a bit adventurous and thought, 'I'll approach the Victoria and Albert Museum [V&A], see whether we can get a fashion exhibition'. At that time, they were about to stage the *Golden Age of Couture*, so I went over and I had a look at it and I met with them. I explained what our gallery was like and what my background was, that I was confident in the display of fashion and my interest and that we were at the international standards that you needed.

At that time, the V&A was very interested in broadening its reach globally and they've got a massive touring programme, so it was just a case of whether or not they wanted to work with us. They worked with Melbourne [NGV] and they probably worked – only with Melbourne I think at that point – with the *Art Deco Exhibition*. They said yes. So a first exhibition with the V&A and the beginning of that relationship was the *Golden Age of Couture, 1947–1957*, which focused on Paris and London fashion trends at that time. A big success – 75,000 people came. It proved that you could bring people to a regional centre and that's what we needed to test.

My photography exhibition, *Sir Cecil Beaton Portraits – The World's Most Photographed* that we had brought out from the National Portrait Gallery brought in about 11,000 or 12,000 people. So that's what photography can do. But fashion seemed to do much more and it brought in many more women. And our demographic is so much about women; I'm not quite sure why.

Q: What do you think is the appeal of the fashion exhibition? Why do you think it captures so many more people than say a photography exhibition?

A: People, I think, relate to photography quite well. I think the nature of galleries has changed a little bit, particularly in a place like Bendigo. We are owned and operated by the Council, so it is the big cultural institution in town. Ratepayers are paying for it basically. So I've got to do more – I believe – than what traditionally a regional gallery would have done back at the turn of the century, which is paintings, sculpture, decorative arts. The way it was operating when I started there, it probably had about 17,000 people through annually. The last financial year we had over 300,000. It's a big change, but it did take about 16 years to do that. And fashion has driven that. I didn't write a strategy around this and say, 'I am going to turn this gallery into a fashion gallery'. It's not about that. It's part of what we do, but it's not all of what we do. In fact, in the last, say, decade, I've probably had more than a hundred shows – four have been fashion. It's just that fashion grabs the attention of the press. If it's an historic collection that's come out from London, it's obviously going to grab the attention of the press. We've had some great editorial around *The Golden Age of Couture*, the *White Wedding Dress* and most recently *Grace Kelly* [exhibitions]. But originally *The Golden Age of Couture* captured people's imagination. It's about being able to relate to something that we are doing all the time, which is wearing clothes and style ideas. We had a lot of fashion students that came up, sat there and sketched, I remember that. Celebrity, the notion of celebrity is in there. People wore that, Princess Margaret wore that dress. Fashion designers, how they work, looking at Christian Dior, looking at the *New Look*, looking at Coco Chanel. People could see – they knew about it – but you could actually see it in front of you and you could get up close to it. And it's the Victoria and Albert Museum and I think that helps.

People think we are now doing fashion [exhibitions] because we've done three. *Grace Kelly* wasn't all about fashion. But the *White Wedding Dress* exhibition, my nervousness around that was the notion of wedding dresses and you think of exhibition buildings and you think about big exhibits about contemporary wedding gowns, which I'm totally not into at all.

But the history was good. Two hundred years of wedding dresses to study. And so what we did – because it was very British in its curatorial rationale, of course it would be – we decided to curate an Australian exhibition that sat alongside it. With my knowledge of the collections here and some private collections, we were able to pull together a good overview of what actually happened in Australia at the same time. We went back, right through the decades, right back to colonial times. I'd hear people say, 'This is better than the V&A. We like this because it's even closer to us. This is what we know'. Also, it did finish very strongly – there was a John Galliano and some very strong examples of contemporary international fashion. So it worked and that brought in 76,000 people.

Then what happened in the same financial year, *Grace Kelly* was offered to me and I couldn't say no to that. That's a person's wardrobe. And she had such an exciting career and life, I had to say yes to that. So I did everything I could and I moved mountains to put that into the programme. Normally I wouldn't do that. They're probably going to be a year apart.

My curators are interested in contemporary art; we collect contemporary Australian art, photography, new media, painting, sculpture. So it's quite a diverse programme. It's not all about fashion, but as long as I'll be director there, I'll be doing them. And they are successful because of the way we market them, because we've built a clientele that wants them. So I can tell you now that the first show we did, *Golden Age of Couture*, crowds, queues, it was a nightmare. Second show and third show, we had online ticketing, people booked. That meant that they came and the experience was better for them. You don't want to be stressed. And so, in the future, that's how we'll do it. The marketing is really critical and there have to be the stories in there.

But it couldn't fail. If anything, I thought it might bring in 50,000. It brought in 152,000. I probably thought it would achieve a bit less than the other two. However, it's the life of a person and the life of an ordinary person who becomes a princess. And it was all about her film career, her life as a young wife and a mother and her later years, right up to her death. People were fascinated with the story, so we almost doubled the numbers there.

Q: Do you think that these kinds of exhibitions have brought in – and we mentioned that it's predominantly women – but do you think that they have attracted some people who perhaps would have been reluctant or perhaps haven't been to a gallery before?

A: Yes, I do. It's broadened our audience and I think with *Grace Kelly*, it went a little bit further, there were many more men who came to *Grace Kelly* because they were interested in the film history – Alfred Hitchcock – seeing dresses from *Rear Window*, her Academy Award was in there for *The Country Girl*. The romance inside – men are interested in romance just as much as women are. The Prince, the family, the children, their home videos, the images of them in public.

A gallery in the twenty-first century that's in a regional city like Bendigo can step outside the parameters that it was originally intended to be. In the nineteenth century, that was we are going to show the visual arts, we are going to show painting, sculpture, prints, drawings. Now we can do more, we can blur the boundaries and move into museum a little bit, because we don't have a museum in Bendigo. We have the conditions and the Gallery to do that. And design is just as important as the fine arts, you know, the painting and all of those, so I don't have a problem moving outside.

We've had Charles Rennie Mackintosh, the display of his work – furniture, decorative arts. Our collection spills over into all those areas. So those three shows, they've put it on the map, the Gallery, in a serious way … Bringing in large numbers of women is good. We've also, through that process, exposed our contemporary collection. Men come to town, they come to the show, they may not come in, they might go to the Bendigo Pottery or they go and do other things – ride on the tram, visit the Central Deborah Gold Mine, go to the bookshops, go and have lunch. You would see them, just roaming around while the women are all inside. It's quite fascinating.

Look, I think it would be great to bring in both genders, but for these shows it's predominantly female fashion. For *White Wedding Dress* we had some outfits that were grooms' outfits. For *Grace Kelly*, there weren't any.

Q: What about age demographics? Do you see a core group, outliers?

A: The online ticketing gave us postcodes so we knew where people came from, which was another advantage. But we also surveyed a sample … the age group was predominantly 30 and up. But especially 40s and then you've got this strength in the 50s, 60s, 70s – people who love the era of the 1950s and the 1960s. And people brought their grandmothers. There were families, women, children in prams, mothers, daughters, that sort of thing.

A lot of the anecdotal evidence suggests that people came up for daytrips, they brought grandma up, they brought great aunt up, had lunch, saw the show, had a great time. 'What's going to happen next? What are you doing next?' was what they want to know. *Grace Kelly* seemed to bring in some younger ones because I think it's the film star and the film career and princess. I think that appealed to that generation, girls in their twenties. And the notion of style. I think people are interested in what makes you stylish? How can you mimic it? It's like fashion magazines: how can we look this way? How did she do it?

Q: Do you think these exhibitions have changed the way that local people in Bendigo relate to the Gallery and also to themselves?

A: Yes. I think there is a great pride. The community owns that gallery and I think there is a great sense of that ... I think the community respects the Gallery. It's free and it's a sanctuary for that community. People have their favourite paintings that are always on display. And we are now, because of these exhibitions, expanding our building. We've got a building project happening right now – a big hole in the ground at the back – and I'm going to have another 650 square metres of exhibition space and a store ... I've had State Government support through Victorian Major Events Company [VMEC], the first regional gallery to receive support through that programme. And they funded – partially – *Grace Kelly* and *White Wedding Dress* – and it's called Bendigo International Collections and it's a bit like Melbourne Winter Masterpieces.

Q: And do you think too that there is a change in the way outsiders view Bendigo as a result of all this?

A: What's happened is that Bendigo is now in the subconscious of a lot of people and it wasn't before. I've got people who just come and say, 'I've just been meaning to come up because everybody is talking about it'. It's developed a name and it's put Bendigo on the map ... you can see international exhibitions and you can really situate yourself in Central Victoria. It's not the beach; it's a very different experience. It's goldmining country, it's surrounded by beautiful townships. Then you've got other places like Castlemaine and Daylesford and the wineries, the food, restaurants; there is a real appetite for all of this. It's a trail of people and weekenders, bed and breakfasts, hotels. We're not great on 4-star hotels, but we've got the bed and breakfast pretty much happening. And the Gallery is a big part of what these people do; it's part of the journey and so packages: we're doing short breaks and all that sort of stuff. I advertise at the airport, on the freeway. I had interstate marketing, working with VMEC meant that we could do interstate marketing, which is what they're about. We managed to get that up from 6 per cent to 10 per cent with *Grace Kelly*. And that is quite a big number really. A lot from NSW, Adelaide, Queensland. So when I do the breakdown of who comes, probably more than 60 per cent are from out of town, 20 per cent are from Bendigo and then 20 per cent are probably from the local region.

Q: And Melbourne would be a big market?

A: It's about 46 per cent. Yeah, it's huge and we're easy to get to and if you've been before. Like I said, these people are on our database, so we knew, *White Wedding Dress* they came; when they came back to book their tickets again, they were already on the database. There's lots of that happening. A very big percentage had been before. So we've developed an audience. So when I go out with my next show, they're the people I'll be targeting and we build upon it that way. The spend … $16.3 million into the local economy during *Grace Kelly*.

Q: The people that you are targeting, or that you envisage coming to your exhibitions, are they the sort of people that Bendigo is looking also to get, is it the same sort of market?

A: It's duplicating what we had on a much bigger scale I suppose. I would like to see younger people. I would like to see more men. It's just these exhibitions that bring the women because of the content. Having said that, other exhibitions bring in a good, even distribution of the two. So, I think you've got to grow your audience in whatever way you can. You've got to give people a reason to travel. Women tend to initiate this kind of travel from what I understand. They say, 'Let's go for a drive to the country for the day'. And it's a case of let's see what else is around. So these other venues benefit too. And men did come. There was a percentage – 8 per cent – and comments were really positive, they really enjoyed it.

Q: That sort of leads us to ask about feedback from say restaurants, cafes, wineries and so forth – how do they, as businesses and local people, relate to you?

A: Really well, really positive. They love us. It's all a case of – now it is – of what's next? Melbourne people are having a good experience or interstate people, visitors who have come a long way, are also having a culinary experience and they're sampling local wine and they're sampling local food and produce. And so they have risen to the occasion. And we've got many more restaurants that have just popped up around town. So it's very positive.

Q: We've had a few discussions with people from other regional centres and they sort of commented, well, how can we do this kind of thing? Do you think it is duplicable?

A: I feel for them because their Councils are saying to them, 'Why isn't our gallery doing this?' And I think you probably can. It's not a one size fits all. Bendigo is a bit different. I think if you look across all the relationships between Councils and galleries, they are different … If you are in our situation, we are owned and operated by the City and we are a big rate base, so they can afford a gallery. So you can only really do this in Geelong or Ballarat.

With us, my Board look after our bequests and they are quite healthy – probably got about six million dollars invested. The interest from those investments we purchase works of art for the collection. I'm purchasing contemporary art particularly at the moment. We've got a foundation as well and the foundation was set up in 2008 to do extra things such as publications.

Q: Are there any challenges or advantages in being in an historic building like that?

A: We're historic, though the wing that was built in the late 1990s is contemporary. Karl Fender did that and Fender Katsalidis, they're doing the next stage. We're probably more contemporary than we are historic. The nineteenth century galleries, I don't change them. It's gold, gilt frames and all that. And it's a beautiful contrast, I think it works really well. Our streetscape is beautiful. It's a site that has enormous potential in the future as well, beyond what's happening now ... Expanding the building, probably the question to ask is where do you stop? How big do you become? How can you justify the growth? ... And the exhibition space, the idea in expanding exhibition space is so we can run a programme alongside the permanent collection. So I'm not taking down post war to contemporary so that I can put in the *Golden Age of Couture* runway or something, which is what I had to do. This gives us additional space and it gives us rooms for projecting images – two little spaces to do that, which we've never had before.

Q: You talked about your love of fashion. What is it about fashion that you love?

A: I think it's a form of expression, fashion, the way you dress. It's about how you present yourself to the world. I think it's important. And to some people it's fluffy and superficial and fairly meaningless ... But the thing about fashion, probably when you get inside the construction of clothing, it's kind of interesting, because there are some amazing ways to put fabric together to create shape. And the way a costume is decorated, and texture. There is something that you can connect with and for me it is an art form. And I love displaying it. I like the challenge of a costume exhibition because they really are challenging. You can hang a wall and you can space them and you can group them and there is only so much you can do. But when you have garments and mannequins and that challenge about the drape, the lighting, is it a chronology, it's also just getting them to sit right when they've been on a human. They've got a memory; there is a memory in textiles. They are very fragile as well if they're not looked after properly. And I think that's what people find challenging when they go into the display. The light levels are low, you can't touch it, it's behind glass; and they don't like that. Because in a shop, you just run your hand along the rack and feel the textiles. You go into a fashion boutique or whatever, you feel it, you want to feel it; and I think that's a natural reaction to costume. But you can't do that in a museum, so people find that challenging.

...If I take that dress, how am I going to repair it? If I take that flag and it's an eighteenth century flag and it's been moth eaten here or whatever, how do I fix it? And this is meticulous, scientific work. So there is that side to it and I love that as well. And I think that's the side that students don't know about. For the care of wedding gowns. People often have a wedding gown in their cupboard that they've worn once, thrown it in the wardrobe, six years later or whatever, they come out, it's all yellow, it's been eaten. And it's about how you look after these garments. And what I found with *White Wedding Dress*, it's very much about the individual story of the garment.

It had been passed down; it had been changed by the next generation. It had been made especially. And the story, the human story is in there.

Q: Social media, do you see that as a tool?

A: That's just something in the last couple of years that we've been able to tap into. So Facebook, absolutely yes, definitely. Facebook and Twitter, one particular staff member does that work and tweets a lot and tweets about our programming and that brings in a younger audience I have to say, and audience that understands technology. So that is the challenge. Our audience that come in through the door, that like to receive the paper newsletter, they are not so focused on this. So if I set up a survey in the Gallery and try and understand the demographic of *White Wedding Dress*, only the young people are going to fill it out, which is what happened and we are only going to get their perspective. But the bigger clientele don't know how to do it and don't want to know about it. So it's very hard. So again, you are back to doing a sample of 500 people and you have to go up to someone and talk to them and ask them to fill it out and then you get your broad cross-section of ages. But yes, look, Twitter, Facebook, those things, we are definitely online with that and I would like to do a lot more but technology is the way to go.

Q: You also had a traditional print media campaign. Lots of ads in *The Age* and things and billboards?

A: It's not all coming out of the Gallery. The city has a tourism department and they have their own budget. They are marketing cultural tourism for the City, and so they are a strong support for us. I have my marketing budget as well. We determine the look of the shows. So the *Grace Kelly* image – that came from us – and the look and then they market it – interstate it went into all the campaign, it was quite a big campaign and we can share the cost that way ...

The Capitol Theatre is next door to the Gallery and they do our online ticketing. They book online, it's all managed by that box office; I don't have to do it. And that makes my life a lot easier too. Pick up your tickets there and come into the Gallery. My desk staff just have to meet and greet, they don't have to do anything and you go through to the door and you go into the space and you hand over your ticket. And they are timed tickets. So all of that works ...

However, I don't have the staff to service big crowds. So that's why we went down the path of ticketing. And because we are regional, and people have to plan their trip and stay and work out where they are going to have lunch, online ticketing says I've got to see the show between 11 and 1 or whatever and then I'll have lunch after that. So I'll book a restaurant. And they get it all in that website – you can work out where lunch is, and train times, we put it all in there. So it made their job a lot easier and it's all about the visitor experience and it being a positive ... we had 36,000 people in three weeks. For a little regional gallery, it was a massive undertaking.

Q: With these exhibitions, do you have a sense of a certain time period that an average person will go through and maintain their interest?
A: If we allow 1,000 square metres for a show that size, an hour. I was so fascinated by the film archive that I added extra footage into the *Grace Kelly* and it meant that you couldn't actually stay for too long. But I hate it when there's only ten minutes of film so I made it half an hour. So we did have some bottlenecks that occurred because of that. But not everybody sat through both little films. But you could do a show like that in an hour. I expect people to get through in an hour – the reading and the taking in the film if there is any – an hour. And so we could have 10–11, 11–12, etc. And we'd stop at about 3.30. And then what we did in the end is we extended and we opened late and we put it online so they could get in because we sold out two weeks before. And so I extended the hours into night and I went to midnight and that worked. I think there was one day we had 3,500 people through.

Night openings work well, especially in cities. A lot of people are working during the day. The crowd that were coming were the people that were retired and had a lot of time and might have been on holidays. So the time of year that's best for us is March to July – that's the best time in Bendigo. Summer is quite hard, I've discovered. We had the bushfires one year, but it's often, people are going to the beach – they're not so fixated with Central Victoria. So I try to fit around *Winter Masterpieces* [in Melbourne] too a little bit. I'm not in competition with them, but people can only do a few things each year. Even with our schools, one show a year, the schools will choose one exhibition a year and that will be the excursion. I've got to make sure there is something in it for school as well and that the time of year is right. So I wouldn't typically put a show over summer because I miss out on the education market. It's fascinating working it all out.

This interview demonstrates some of the thinking around staging fashion exhibitions in Bendigo, including how they were marketed and how they have shaped the image of Bendigo as a tourist destination, as well as playing a role in developing community pride and a sense of identity. The next exhibition to be staged at the Gallery will also be themed around fashion. *Modern Love* will look at the work of contemporary designers from the collection of the FIDM Museum in Los Angeles.

References

Cornish, R. (2012) 'Boomtown Bendigo finds country cool', *The Age*, 24 August.

Frost, W., Reeves, K., Laing, J. and Wheeler, F. (2012) 'A golden connection: exploring the challenges of developing interpretation strategies for a Chinese Heritage Precinct on the Central Victorian Goldfields', *Historic Environment*, 24 (1): 35–40.

Wheeler, F. and Laing, J. (2008) 'Tourism as a vehicle for liveable communities: case studies from regional Victoria, Australia', *Annals of Leisure Research*, 11 (1/2): 242–263.

Wheeler, F., Reeves, K., Laing, J. and Frost, W. (2009) 'Niche strategies for small regional cities: the case of the Bendigo Chinese Heritage Precinct', *Tourism Recreation Research*, 34 (3): 295–306.

Part III

Emerging trends and a view of the future

11 Emerging fashion

Berlin Fashion Week

Kristen K. Swanson and Judith C. Everett

By nature, special events are produced to generate excitement, enhance corporate image, sell product, and in general create buzz and serve as an important motivator of tourism and destination competitiveness (Getz 2008). They are one-off or reoccurring events of limited duration, with the primary focus of enhancing awareness, appeal, and profitability of a tourist destination (Richie 1984). Many places seek to host special events because of the increased economic activity and new job creation that the event is assumed to generate through increased demand for goods and services (Dwyer *et al.* 2005). Governments too are often willing to offer funding incentives, and upgrade infrastructure to attract events.

In the fashion industry, *fashion weeks* are a particular special event produced to generate excitement and buzz for the upcoming fashion season. Fashion weeks are organized times in which designers launch their collections en masse to retail buyers, celebrities, and tourists. Fashion weeks have traditionally been staged in the four major fashion capitals of the world – London, Milan, Paris, and New York. As fashion has become more globalized, other cities have begun to realize the benefit of hosting a fashion week to create excitement for designers from these lesser known, but fashion forward destinations. In 2003, Berlin became a player on the world fashion stage by hosting its first contemporary fashion trade fair. In 2012, Berlin Fashion Week has grown to stage over 60 large-scale events and contributed to an 11.4 percent growth in visitor numbers and room nights (Berlin Tourismus 2012). The purpose of this chapter is to explore the formation of and excitement surrounding Berlin Fashion Week.

Fashion weeks

Fashion weeks are organized times, usually 4–10 days, in which designers launch their collections to retail buyers, international media, private clients, celebrities, and tourists. Broadly defined, fashion weeks cover a range of fashion industry events including collection fashion shows, fashion trade fairs, show room visits, consumer buying events, and after-show parties. These bring together individuals and businesses engaged in fashion production and event marketing. The key personnel involved in fashion weeks include designers and manufacturers, models, buyers, traditional and new media journalists, fashion and beauty industry stylists, and clients and celebrities. Additionally, fashion consumers, tourists, and fashion students are part of fashion week audiences. As indicated by the *Women's Wear Daily* International Trade Show biannual calendar, fashion weeks, or fashion trade shows happen nearly every week somewhere around the world (WWD International Trade Shows 2012).

More narrowly defined, fashion week specifically refers to collection-opening fashion shows. Fashion shows are the biggest inspiration for the fashion industry (Bhardwaj and Fairhurst 2009). Designers, stylists, media personalities, and celebrities continually discover innovative fabrics, styling details, and silhouettes during the nonstop action of runway shows along with fashion forward street fashion on display during these semiannual events. Photographs, video, and sketchbooks are used to capture ideas that will, in turn, be used as inspiration for the next season's new looks. Fashion watching and trend-spotting are continual processes and fashion weeks give viewers the best exposure to new stimuli within the shortest amount of time. During fashion weeks, fashion shows are the primary promotion tool to communicate the latest fashion trends to fashion audiences (Everett and Swanson 2013). A fashion show is more than a trade event; it is also a cultural event (Entwistle and Rocamora 2006). As cultural events, fashion weeks serve as conduits that increase attendees' knowledge and enjoyment of the host communities' cultural, social, intellectual, and artistic heritage, as well as helping them to appreciate the nuance of taste and style that each place provides. In some cases, the collection-opening fashion shows are presented in temporary tents with many different designers using the same stage. The shows are scheduled so buyers and other guests might attend as many as six or eight shows each day. Often, shows are scheduled at the same time requiring retailers and journalists to make decisions as to which shows they will attend (Everett and Swanson 2013).

Historically, fashion distribution has been organized around two seasons: Spring/Summer and Fall/Winter (Hines and Bruce 2007). The term *season* refers to a period of time during which fashion products are sold to the public. Typically, seasonal merchandise has been presented to the retail buyers six months prior to when consumers will wear the merchandise. In the Northern Hemisphere, Fall/Winter trade shows and fashion weeks take place in January through March and Spring/Summer fashion weeks are hosted in August through October. This convention dates back to the nineteenth century when environmental conditions dictated that clothing matched seasons, and social conventions of the upper class required more formal, social, city dress for the winter season, and more informal, secluded, countryside dress for the summer season (de Marly 1980). Fall/Winter fashions were and still are characterized as more tailored silhouettes, outerwear, and holiday wear, while Spring/Summer fashions were and are characterized as sportswear, more casual silhouettes in lighter weight fabrics and brighter and lighter colors.

Fashion capitals

Fashion weeks have been hosted as planned events in global fashion capitals such as London, Milan, Paris, and New York. The first fashion shows were started by the French as a way to promote their high fashion industry. The Chambre Syndicale de la Haute Couture, founded in 1868, organized the Paris fashion shows by the top French designers (Everett and Swanson 2013). Nearly a hundred years later, in 1958, The Camera Nazionale della Moda Italiana [The National Chamber for Italian Fashion] was established to promote the development of Italian fashion. London Fashion Week was created in the West End in 1984 (Gregory 2010). American fashion weeks can be traced to Fashion Press Week, initiated by fashion publicist Eleanor Lambert in 1943 (Tiffany 2011). Miss Lambert, working for the New York Dress Institute, organized fashion presentations aimed at getting information in the hands of the national press, six months before the garments would be in the stores. The first Fashion Press Week was held at the elegant Plaza Hotel, where an onsite pressroom made press releases and photographs from each collection available to the American fashion or lifestyle newspaper editors. In addition to the shows, parties and theatrical entertainment produced a festive atmosphere.

Paris, Milan, London, and New York have been designated as fashion capitals because they have the manufacturing capability and image to promote fashion. Global fashion cities have proven industrial innovation and efficiency in product development and production, and offer fashion insiders – designers and buyers – attractive places in which to show fashion, as well as providing the necessary channels for negotiation and communication of fashion branding processes (Jansson and Power 2010). Fashion weeks provide the venue for communication of the fashion capital's ability to be a fashion leader. This supports the upper-class leadership fashion theory that suggests that fashion is an elitist phenomenon initiated by the highest socioeconomic classes and copied later by lower classes (Sproles and Burns 1994). In the case of fashion weeks, the major fashion capitals have always been considered the fashion elite, while smaller, albeit fashion forward cities have been the later adopters. Fashion weeks in fashion capitals present couture designer brands for an exclusive clientele of retail buyers from worldwide boutiques and department stores, the international press, and private customers and celebrities. Fashion capital fashion weeks are widely reported by the worldwide media to an audience who have a great interest in high fashion but neither the taste-level nor the budget to afford the fashions shown. Therefore, these shows serve an image-creating function, rather than an economic stimulator function (Skov 2006).

As fashion has become more globalized, other destinations, besides the four fashion capitals, have begun to realize the benefit of hosting a fashion week (both as collection openings and larger fashion industry events) to create a buzz for designers from these lesser known, but fashion forward places.

Australia, New Zealand, Brazil, and Russia, among other countries, have embraced the fashion week concept. Even some Muslim countries have experimented with fashion weeks. Jansson and Power (2010) point out that globalization has caused much manufacturing of fashion clothing and accessories to be outsourced to lower-cost regions, causing fashion centers to transition from manufacturing-based centers to fashion image industry centers. Because many countries are using the same lower-cost regions to manufacture, many emerging countries are also beginning to brand themselves as fashion image industry centers. The advent of regional fashion weeks within the fashion week cycle parallels the mass-market fashion theory that proposes that the emergence of mass production and mass communication has allowed the simultaneous diffusion of fashion across all socioeconomic classes (in this case countries) at once (Sproles and Burns 1994). Regional fashion weeks provide a better economic stimulus for the host community because they present brands for the regional markets as well as long-distance buyers who visit the markets to also investigate the manufacturing capacity of these areas (Skov 2006).

Purposes of fashion weeks

From a fashion perspective, fashion weeks serve three purposes: to create and validate structures of fashion knowledge, to transfer fashion knowledge and innovation, and to stabilise market strategies for an inherently unpredictable commodity (Weller 2008). According to Entwistle and Rocamora, another function of fashion week is to 'produce, reproduce, and legitimate the field of fashion and the positions of those players within it' (2006: 736). Historically, fashion weeks were restricted to industry insiders – designers, buyers, and fashion managers, excluding the general public and tourists. In 1999, fashion week collection-opening fashion shows became a public phenomenon (Bhardwaj and Fairhurst 2009) in part due to the spread of photographs via the Internet. In the late twentieth century, fashion became a cultural form – like cinema, photography, and music – that gained substantial editorial prominence in the serious press (Janssen 2006).

Fashion weeks and tourism

Fashion weeks are an example of events that as Getz (1989) described were first developed for nontourist reasons, but have subsequently been exploited for tourism purposes. Fashion weeks serve as events that have the potential to intersect fashion and tourism. From a tourism perspective, hosting a fashion week serves as place marketing, linking the mental image of a destination to fashion, and using that association for commercial purposes. Fashion week's incorporation into a *global* fashion network raises the value of its host city by reinforcing its claim to cosmopolitan *World City* status (Weller 2008: 116).

Weller (2008) has described the interdependence and complementary flows of value at work during a fashion week. Fashion weeks are produced by transnational entertainment corporations that use the events to maintain support for demand of its management, media, and hospitability services. IMG Worldwide produces 11 global fashion weeks (collection-opening fashion shows) including *Mercedes-Benz Fashion Week Berlin* (IMG World 2010). The fashion media play a significant role in fashion weeks by producing interesting content and attracting audiences and advertising dollars (Weller 2008). Luxury sponsors from the fashion, cosmetics, haircare, beverages, and hospitality industries use fashion weeks to showcase their luxury products to high profile participants. Fashion week sponsors such as Mercedes-Benz provide the capital for the next event on the fashion week cycle. Lastly, according to Weller, the city in which the fashion week is held needs a constant stream of activity to support its cosmopolitan image and service-based economy. For Berlin, 'It's not just the money that the fashion fairs bring to Berlin … they also generate a priceless boost to the city's image' (Berlin Tourismus 2010: 3).

Berlin

The city of Berlin was first documented in the thirteenth century. It was the capital of the Kingdom of Prussia, German Republic, Weimar Republic, and the Third Reich. Berlin's history has been repeatedly marked with political and social upheaval, the specifics of which are beyond the scope of this chapter. Several times during its history, most recently after reunification, Berlin has been the trend-setter for German avant-garde and counterculture groups, often to the irritation of the rest of Germany which is more conservative (Becker-Cantarino 1996).

During its history, Berlin has faced repeated abrupt political and social transformations and as a cultural site has been repeatedly renegotiated (Becker-Cantarino 1996). Compared to other capital cities such as Paris, London, and Madrid, Berlin was a late arrival on the European scene with regard to culture – literature, philosophy, painting and sculpture, the theater, music, and decorative arts. As Taylor notes:

> In the early centuries of its existence, through the Middle Ages and Renaissance, it had only token manifestations of culture to offer. With the advent of the Enlightenment, however – surely no accident – begins the surge of activity which sweeps like an ever-swelling flood down to modern times.
>
> (Taylor 1997: xi)

One example of abrupt social, political, and cultural change came in 1871 when Berlin became the capital of Prussia and the new German Reich. As a result, the city began to grow rapidly and optimistically through industrialization up to the beginning of World War I. Berlin's economic opportunities attracted businessmen, bankers, industrialists, intellectuals, writers, artists, as well as

Eastern European immigrants who found work in small businesses, shops, construction, restaurants, and entertainment. As the capital, Berlin became a magnet for the young avant-garde. It quickly gained fame for its innovative and cultural scene, for its theaters, musical events, art studios and galleries (Becker-Cantarino 1996).

At the beginning of World War I, Berlin was the world's third largest city after London and New York (Jelavich 1993). Berlin was an urban city with an active artistic and cultural community that included cabaret. This was an entertainment form, set on small stages in small halls, where audiences sat around tables and spectators and performers had direct eye-to-eye contact. The show consisted of short musical numbers, comic monologues, skits, dances, puppet shows, and short films. One of the primary topics presented in the cabaret was fashion, current styles and trends: 'Cabaret zeroed in on faddishness as well ... [in] high culture, popular entertainment, habits of speaking, styles of clothing, new commercial goods and the advertisements that touted them' (Jelavich 1993: 6).

Another example of abrupt social, political, and cultural change came in 1961 when the Berlin Wall was erected. During World War II, Germany and Berlin were invaded by both the Western Allies and the Soviets, each of which took a part of Germany and Berlin. After the war, this division continued with the development and rivalry of 'the two Berlins' (Becker-Cantarino 1996: 11). Finally, the rivalry came to a crisis and the wall was built to seal West Berlin from East Berlin. West Berlin was completely surrounded by the wall. During the three decades of the wall's existence West Berlin and East Berlin grew apart from each other socially and culturally. Once again, West Berlin became a magnet for unconventional youth and the development of the alternative lifestyles of the counterculture attracted young West Germans.

When Germany was reunified in 1990, Berlin once again became the capital. When the wall came down, so did the social systems that had sustained East and West Berlin since 1961. The removal left Berliners with the need to find new defining parameters in its place (Taylor 1997). Berlin became a microcosm of opportunities and pressures, joys and responsibilities as a new nation.

Berlin fashion history

With a population of over 3.5 million people, Berlin is the largest city in Germany and is quickly becoming Germany's *Capital of Fashion* in the twenty-first century (Fashion United 2012). The first documentation of Berlin fashion can also be traced to the thirteenth century. In 1288, a tailors' guild foundation document (*Stiftungsurkunde*) was acknowledged by the government (Ingram and Sark 2011). However, it was not until the nineteenth century that a ready-to-wear industry was identified in Berlin. The Manheimer brothers began making men's coats in 1837, Rudolph Hertzog started a ready-to-wear shop in the Breitegasse in 1839, and a women's coat manufacturing firm was started by David Leib Levin in 1840 (Ingram and Sark 2011). The first fashion week (industry fashion event), organized by the Association of Women's Fashion and Its Industry (*Verband der Dumenmode und ihrer Industrie*), took place in 1917. Fashion week continued on a semiannual basis under increasingly difficult conditions, until 1925, when it was replaced with a clothing fair (*Bekleidungsmesse*).When Adolf Hitler came to power in Germany in 1933, he announced that he wanted Berlin women (*Berlinerinnen*) to become the best-dressed women in Europe. The Berlin-based German Fashion Institute was established.

Berlin Fashion Weeks between 1958 and 1962 were presented as 'achievement shows' to demonstrate the commitment by the German Democratic Republic (GDR) to revitalize the East German state-owned garment industry. Post WWII fashion weeks featured educational lectures and booths staffed by 'fashion designers from the state-owned women's garment factories, from the fashion magazine *Sibylle*, and from the German Fashion Institute' (Stitziel 2005: 74). One of the purposes was to explain the process of fashion production to participants. However, the government-sanctioned fashion weeks were not the only source for clothing and design inspiration in this era. East German designers, such as Sabine von Oettingen, made clothes for underground fashion shows from shower curtains or agricultural plastics during the GDR age (Ingram and Sark 2011).

How did this once divided city become one of Europe's trendiest cities, with a unique vibrant and creative spirit? Berlin did what it had always done. After the Wall came down, Berlin again became a magnet for the young avant-garde. Similar to the growth of Berlin in the late nineteenth century, at the beginning of the twenty-first century the counterculture once again emerged to oppose the conservative mindset in place after reunification. The city determined that essential elements, such as affluent, style-conscious residents and the requisite infrastructure of a real fashion city were important and the city went about creating a fashion image. In 2008, Berlin, branding itself as selling freedom and creativity, launched a marketing campaign *Be Berlin* to attract capital investors, small entrepreneurs, and artists and designers (Ingram and Sark 2011). From the campaign, an idea for a young designers' fashion show was launched. Young designers who did not have the notoriety to be part of Mercedes-Benz Fashion Week Berlin were invited to participate in the fashion show which helped them establish their labels and become part of the Berlin community of creative entrepreneurs: 'City branding campaigns function as communication platforms and media vehicles for collective identity and image projection and formation and act as multipliers for events such as fashion week' (Ingram and Sark 2011: 192). Linking fashion with a cosmopolitan lifestyle allows fashion weeks to deliver direct and indirect economic benefits. Berlin visitor statistics indicate that more than 200,000 additional visitors attended Berlin Fashion Week, generating almost €100 million of additional income to the city (Berlin Tourismus 2010).

The push to be a creative mecca was also spurred on by the media. Agenda-setting theory suggests that there is a strong correlation between the emphasis that mass media places on certain issues and the importance attributed to these issues by mass audiences (McCombs and Shaw 1972). When the wall came down, Berlin, more than any other city in German, became the news-maker. Berlin was on the minds of people around the world. At the turn of the twenty-first century, overseas fashion retailers began to look at Berlin as a promising fashion market. For too long the German fashion and retail industry had not been innovative. 'It was boring' (Drier 2013a: 9). German consumers were not satisfied with purchasing German fashion. While a few retailers had misfires, H&M, Zara, Mango, and D'Orsay were some of the first retailers to succeed in the Berlin market.

Fashion trade shows

Fashion influentials witnessing the creative spirit within Berlin encouraged the development of a fashion trade show as a first step on to the global fashion stage. In 2003, the fashion trade show Premium held its first fashion event in Berlin (Fashion United 2012). Similar to the cabaret of the twentieth century, the first fashion trade fair allowed contemporary, up-to-date fads and fashions to be seen by an interested public. Premium continued to grow in popularity, attracting other small fashion exhibits. Ideal Showroom, which promoted young designers from Berlin and Scandinavia, increased Berlin's charisma. Premium's success also encouraged Karl-Heinz Muller to move Bread & Butter, his denim and streetwear exhibition, to the capital in 2003. Muller and others were attracted to Berlin due to its growing creative reputation as well as its ability to attract more international visitors. In an effort to expand, Bread & Butter decided to hold back-to-back trade shows in Barcelona and Berlin two weeks apart (Ingram and Sark 2011). However, the coordination of both events was too difficult and Muller relocated Bread & Butter to Barcelona until 2009, when, using the slogan *Bread & Butter is coming home*, the trade show relocated back to Berlin (Ingram and Sark 2011: 189).

Mercedes-Benz Fashion Week Berlin

Berlin was still missing a key element to become a fashion center. It still needed an iconic fashion event to attract attention in order to become a major regional center on the fashion world's stage. That pivotal event began in 2007 when the first Mercedes-Benz Fashion Week Berlin was held. According to Maia Guarnaccia, Vice President, IMG Fashion, Europe, 'we were determined to establish one of the most glamorous fashion events in Germany' (quoted in Holzmann 2010: 3). This became the platform for emerging brands and designer companies that were expanding, and IMG decided that Berlin was the creative city in the heart of Europe where the right target audience would be attracted. The prestigious German brand Mercedes-Benz became the title

Figure 11.1 The Brandenburg Gate, previous home of the tent for Mercedes-Benz Fashion Week Berlin.
Source: C. C. Everett

sponsor for the event that has continued to attract the attention of the media, buyers, and opinion leaders from all around the world, making Berlin one of the increasingly important cities for its semiannual exhibitions of fashion.

Berlin Fashion Week is a regional fashion week promoting Berlin as a fashion image industry center as well as a center for manufacturing in Germany: 'Berlin is literally "ready to wear" ... its identity has been predicated on its ability to make things [including] clothes' (Ingram and Sark 2011: 16). Berlin Fashion Week draws industry professionals to the leading trade shows, including Mercedes-Benz Fashion Week (tent shows), Bread & Butter (leading global trade fair for street and urban wear), Premium (international fashion trade show), and other fashion and trade fairs which present extreme avant-gardism fashion, sustainability fashions, and fashions that are focused on an ecologically fair lifestyle. Berlin has become the international center for jeans and casual wear. According to Fabio Mancone of the Giorgio Armani Group, 'what Milan is to *prêt-à-porter*, Berlin is to sportswear' (Drier 2011: 4).

Classic catwalk fashion shows at Mercedes-Benz Fashion Week Berlin have been presented in a tent across from the Brandenburg Gate (Figure 11.1), once the site of the wall dividing East Berlin and West Berlin. In 2012, the shows moved further down the Strasse des 17 Juni (17th of June Street) in Tiergarten, in central Berlin, nestling up against the *Golden Else*, as the Siegessäule, or Victory Column (Figure 11.2) is known to Berliners (Drier

Figure 11.2 The 'Golden Else' atop the Victory Column, the current home of the tent for Mercedes-Benz Fashion Week Berlin.

Source: C. C. Everett

2012). Both locations are significant tourist sites. New designers have shown their creations at a nontraditional presentation space called the *Studio*. Here, designers were given the freedom to express their creativity by building their own unique scenery, which allowed the professional audience to roam freely in the presentation space. It gave them the opportunity to view the collections up close. With alternative presentation methods, such as the Studio, it is hoped the number of designers participating in Berlin Fashion Week will increase as this emerging fashion center grows.

With close to 2,500 brands converging on Berlin during Fashion Week, the city's retail stores, hotels, restaurants, museums, and tourist attractions host a

Figure 11.3 Berlin's divided history now serves as stimulus for creative fashion entrepreneurship and tourism opportunities.
Source: C. C. Everett

large number of fashion professionals visiting the city. Trade visitors to Berlin are able to see various corners of the city (Figure 11.3), as well as historical landmarks, while visiting the various show venues. Today, Berlin is not only the capital of Germany, it is Germany's most noted City of Fashion.

Tenth anniversary of Berlin Fashion Week

Ten years after Berlin Fashion Week staged its inaugural event underground in a disused subway tunnel on Potsdamer Platz (Drier 2013a), the fair has grown from an unexpectedly successful experiment into a major international presentation. With over a dozen trade events, representing almost all conceivable fashion market segments, the German capital, with its cool vibe, has become the undisputed capital of contemporary and street fashion.

According to Melissa Drier (2013a), as the city grows, changes, and becomes more international, there is also a noticeably more sophisticated designer look emerging at trade show booths as well as on the runways. Berlin, known for its leadership with ecological friendly fashion design, introduces new trends and discusses questions about eco-design during Fashion Week. Among the events promoting ecological fashion are: GREENShowroom, Ethical Fashion Show, Lavera Showfloor, and Showfloor Berlin. Sustainable fashion catwalk shows, such as the one featured at Showfloor Berlin, are presented to the general public and tourists, as well as the traditional trade participants.

Showroom Days are special events that feature more than 150 national and international designers and artists, from emerging to established. Berlin Fashion Week will present their collections, installations, retrospectives, and photographs at over 50 locations across Berlin (Showroom Days 2013). These events are open to tourists and anyone interested in fashion, along with the trade show oriented fashion crowd.

Although Berlin Fashion Week was not expected to be very successful during its first season, partially because it was such a poor city in 2003, the event and the city of Berlin have flourished. President of Bread & Butter, Karl-Heinz Müller, acknowledged the growing influence of Berlin Fashion Week over ten years:

> The success of Berlin is that it's a good breeding ground for everything to do with young culture ... Apple decided to build its largest European flagship in Berlin. In the meantime, there's shopping tourism in Berlin, which I think the fashion fairs together have helped to create. The city has found its place in contemporary fashion.
>
> (Drier 2013b: 11)

Conclusion

While global fashion capitals have long-established histories of using fashion weeks to promote their city's fashion leadership, global competition among emerging countries is creating opportunities for many other countries to also become fashion image-makers. Hosting a fashion week allows emerging countries to demonstrate their country's ability to be a world fashion player and become a fashion tourist destination. Berlin with its focus on creativity and freedom is an example of an emerging city that has used the development of a fashion week to launch its participation as a world fashion leader and, more importantly, used Fashion Week as an important motivator of Berlin's tourism competitiveness among other European countries. The growth in the number of distinctive venues presented and development of German designers, as well as the increased number of visitor nights recorded during the four-day event are indicators of the continued success of Berlin Fashion Week and Mercedes-Benz Fashion Week Berlin.

References

Becker-Cantarino, B. (1996) *Berlin in Focus: Cultural Transformations in Germany*, London: Praeger.

Berlin Tourismus (2010) 'Economic stimulus programme – fashion fairs', http://www.visitBerlin.de (accessed January 22, 2010).

Berlin Tourismus (2012) 'More guests: Berlin with a good start into the New Year', http://www.visitBerlin.de (accessed March 15, 2012).

Bhardwaj, V. and Fairhurst, A. (2009) 'Fast fashion: Response to changes in the fashion industry', *The International Review of Retail, Distribution and Consumer Research*, 20: 165–173.

de Marly, D. (1980) *The History of Haute Couture, 1850–1950*, New York: Holmes and Meier.

Drier, M. (2011, June 6) 'Bustle and flow: Berlin prepares for a rousing show season', *Women's Wear Daily: Berlin Preview*: 4.

Drier, M. (2012, June 19) 'Change in the air', *Women's Wear Daily*: 10.

Drier, M. (2013a, January 2) 'Overseas retailers making way to Germany', *Women's Wear Daily*: 9.

Drier, M. (2013b, January 9) 'January ten years after: Following are the runway and trade show schedules for Berlin Fashion Week, Jan. 14 to 19', *Women's Wear Daily: Berlin Preview*: 10–11.

Dwyer, L., Forsyth, P., and Spurr, R. (2005) 'Estimating the impacts of special events on an economy', *Journal of Travel Research*, 43: 351–359.

Entwistle, J. and Rocamora, A. (2006) 'The field of fashion materialized: A study of London Fashion Week', *Sociology*, 40: 735–751.

Everett, J. C. and Swanson, K. K. (2013) *Guide to Producing a Fashion Show* (3rd edn.), New York: Fairchild Books.

Fashion United (2012) 'Germany's fashion capital in the improbable rise of Berlin', http://www.fashionunited.co.uk (accessed January 17, 2012).

Getz, D. (1989) 'Special events: Defining the product', *Tourism Management*, 10: 125–137.

Getz, D. (2008) 'Event tourism: Definition, evolution, and research', *Tourism Management*, 29: 403–428.

Gregory, A. (2010) 'A brief history of London Fashion Week', *The Independent*, http://www.independant.co.uk (accessed August 31, 2012).

Hines, T. and Bruce, M. (2007) *Fashion Marketing Contemporary Issues* (2nd edn.), Oxford: Butterworth-Heinemann.

Holzmann, C. (2010) *Backstage Mercedes-Benz Fashion Week Berlin*, Kempen, Germany: teNeues.

IMG World (2010) *Event Management – Fashion*, http://www.imgworld.com (accessed August 31, 2012).

Ingram, S. and Sark, K. (2011) *Berliner Chic: A Locational History of Berlin Fashion*, Chicago: Intellect, The University of Chicago Press.

Janssen, S. (2006) 'Fashion reporting in cross-national perspective 1955–2005', *Poetics*, 34: 383–406.

Jansson, J. and Power, D. (2010) 'Fashioning a global city: Global city brand channels in the fashion and design industries', *Regional Studies*, 44: 889–904.

Jelavich, P. (1993) *Berlin Cabaret*, Cambridge: Harvard University Press.

McCombs, M. E. and Shaw, D. L. (1972) 'The agenda-setting function of mass media', *Public Opinion Quarterly*, 36: 176–187.

Ritchie, J. R. B. (1984) 'Assessing the impact of hallmark events: Conceptual and research issues', *Journal of Travel Research*, 23: 2–11.

Showroom Days (2013, January 15–20) *Berlin Fashion Week*, http://www.fashion-week-berlin.com/en/service/imprint (accessed January 2013).

Skov, L. (2006) 'The role of trade fairs in the global fashion business', *Current Sociology*, 54: 764–783.

Sproles, G. and Burns, L. (1994) *Changing Appearances: Understanding Dress in Contemporary Society*, New York: Fairchild.

Stitziel, J. (2005) *Fashioning Socialism: Clothing, Politics, and Consumer Culture in Germany*, Oxford: Berg.

Taylor, R. (1997) *Berlin and its Culture*, New Haven: Yale University Press.

Tiffany, J. A. (2011) *Eleanor Lambert: Still Here*, New York: Pointed Leaf Press.

Weller, S. (2008) 'Beyond "global production networks": Australian Fashion Week's trans-sectoral synergies', *Growth and Change*, 39: 104–122.

WWD International Trade Shows (2012) *Women's Wear Daily*: 14–19 (accessed May 16, 2012).

12 The role of fashion in sub-culture events

Exploring steampunk events

Warwick Frost and Jennifer Laing

Imagine a world where history proceeded differently, where Victorian technology still holds sway. It is a world where plastics, electronics and polyester were never invented, where machinery is still made of wood and brass and is powered by clockwork or steam. Where there are airships instead of jet aircraft; steam vehicles instead of petrol or diesel. Where the fictions of Jules Verne and H. G. Wells came true. This is the imaginary world of *steampunk* (Laing and Frost 2012; VanderMeer and Chambers 2011).

The term was coined by writer K. W. Jeter in 1987 to half-jokingly describe a growing literary sub-genre. Its antecedents go far back beyond that. It has been argued that 'the steampunk aesthetic has been woven throughout our media and consciousness for more than a century in books, film, music, fashion and art' (Grymm 2011: 6). In the late nineteenth century, early science fiction flourished, particularly in the works of Verne and Wells, though it extended far beyond them. Popular magazines, such as *The Illustrated London News*, *The Strand* and *Pall Mall Magazine* regularly featured fictional accounts of gentlemen inventors and apocalyptic disasters (Evans and Evans 1977). In such literature, future developments were imagined in the light of existing steam and metal technology. In the 1960s, film rediscovered these classics and brought their imagery to life. George Pal's film of *The Time Machine* (1960) was particularly influential. Previously with *War of the Worlds* (1953), Pal had placed the action in contemporary California, but for this film he retained the setting of fin-de-siècle London. Rod Taylor was the inventor hero, strutting through the future in tweed trousers and a dandified waistcoat. However, it was the design of the machine that held one's attention. In the novel it had been described simply as 'parts were of nickel, parts of ivory, parts had certainly been filed or sawn out of rock crystal' (Wells 1895: 11). For the film, Pal's opulent creation combines plush leather with brass fittings, concocting something that looks like it could believably be invented in 1900.

Other influential films were *20,000 Leagues Under the Sea* (1954), *The First Men in the Moon* (1964) and *The Great Race* (1965). Television series included *The Wild Wild West* (1965–1969) and *Doctor Who* (1963–1989, 2005 onwards), with more recent series of the latter having an even stronger steampunk imagery, particularly in the design of the TARDIS and the archaic clothing of the Doctor. Michael Moorcock's trilogy *The Nomad of Time* (1971–1981) was set in an alternative universe dominated by airships, as was Philip Pullman's *His Dark Materials* (1995–2000). K. W. Jeter's novel *Morlock Night* (1979) was an imaginative sequel to *The Time Machine*. Steampunk has also become a standard of graphic novels (and their film versions), including *The League of Extraordinary Gentlemen*, *V for Vendetta* and *Adèle Blanc-Sec.*

Apart from its widespread use in fiction, steampunk gains historical verisimilitude through the extraordinary story of the *analytical engine*. Plans and some parts for this early computer were developed in 1837 by Charles Babbage and Ada Lovelace (who added further to the story by being the daughter of Lord Byron). For steampunk aficionados, this not only demonstrates that steam-powered computers and other technology were possible, but that we could have gone down that path except for a series of historical accidents.

While steampunk is rooted in a rich body of literature, its physical manifestation is in fashion and design. Like many sub-cultures, its adherents use fashion both as a defining marker of otherness and as a means of demonstrating *communitas* for those in the know. These sub-cultures may organise events such as festivals or parties, which act as a backdrop for their fashion. Steampunk fashion is best described as Victoriana with an edge, and is self-mockingly referred to as *corsets and goggles*. Accessories are often the key to an outfit. Women's corsets are studded with brass and chains, and teamed with little top hats placed on an angle in a Mad Hatter style, veils, laced-up boots and bustled skirts with petticoats. Their hair is piled up on their head in a crazy version of the Victorian Gibson Girl look. Men wear waistcoats, bowler or top hats, and aviator goggles. They often sport a fob watch on a chain and mutton chop whiskers. Generally dark colours, particularly brown, are preferred by steampunk enthusiasts. A greatcoat is often worn by both sexes. This style has now crossed over from its sub-culture roots to the high street, with stores like Asos and Topshop offering items of steampunk influenced clothing, and IBM in one of its social surveys noting that steampunk will be the next big trend in retail (Murphy 2013; Skarda 2013). Couture hasn't been far behind, with designers like Prada in its 2012 Fall–Winter collection presenting tailored double-breasted men's suits, some in pin-stripes, while Sarah Burton of Alexander McQueen's 2013 Spring–Summer collection featured corsets and crinolines (Murphy 2013; Skarda 2013).

Much of this steampunk fashion pays homage to a character in literature or film, guided by detailed exposition of their garb. In Jeter's *Morlock Night* (1979), the soldier heroine, Tafe, is dressed in 'a man's rough trousers and jacket, with a belted leather harness crossing her shoulders and waist', while Dr Ambrose is 'swathed in an overcoat so black it seemed a hole into which the dim street light poured and was swallowed up … with the glossy points of his patent boots the only stars'. In Michael Moorcock's *Nomad of Time* trilogy, Una Persson is a militaristic fantasy. She wears a 'long black leather topcoat with a narrow waist and a flaring skirt' (Moorcock 1974: 41), and later 'a long black military topcoat which had evidently been tailored for her. She had a black divided skirt and black riding boots' (p. 74). In *The Steel Tsar* (1981), the fantasy is given a Russian twist, with her 'Smith and Wesson revolver on her hip, a fur hat pulled to one side of her face' (Moorcock 1981: 126). Men wear 'a miscellaneous selection of clothing which included a black bowler hat, a deerstalker and a panama, a woman's fur cape, golfing trousers, a leather shooting-coat, a tailcoat and an opera cloak' (Moorcock 1974: 74). The evocative detail about clothing found in many steampunk novels thus helps the fidelity of reenactments.

In this chapter, our interest is in examining how events are used to promote steampunk fashion and design and the role these elements play in these public events. Our chapter is divided into three parts. The first considers steampunk events within the theoretical frameworks of serious leisure and social worlds. The second and third parts explore case studies of steampunk events, these being respectively the Steampunk Exhibition at the Kew Bridge Steam Museum (London, UK) and the Oamaru Steampunk Festival (New Zealand).

Serious leisure and social worlds

Steampunk can be conceptualised as a *sub-culture*; that is, a distinct cultural group operating below (perhaps even hidden) from the mainstream. Modern society is distinguished by the existence of a wide variety of sub-cultures, many of whom use fashion as a marker to distinguish themselves from the rest of society. Thornton (1996) describes this as a form of *sub-cultural capital*, after Bourdieu (1984, 1991). Whereas cultural capital focuses on knowledge which confers status (*what* you know) and social capital is based on the status of one's connections (*who* you know), sub-cultural capital is founded on the prestige conferred by *hipness* or being *in the know* (Thornton 1996: 11), with sub-cultures forming 'hierarchies within popular culture' (p. 7). As inner-city residents, we regularly see many examples of such loose groupings. These commonly include those proudly displaying hippy-chic, grunge, retro look, gamer and the urban cowboy. The goth and emo looks seem more confined to the outer suburbs and the Hello Kitty cutsie image is apparent among some of our students. Mixed in with this are rarer fashion statements, such as the occasional female in Native American costume. Steampunk fashion takes its place among this panoply of distinctive looks. Like most sub-cultures, its main visible manifestation takes place at events.

The coming together of steampunk fans at events can best be understood through the use of two theoretical frameworks – *serious leisure* and *social worlds*. Both of these are being increasingly applied to the analysis of events, particularly for the meanings of events within society (Frost and Laing 2012, 2013).

Serious leisure

The concept of serious leisure was developed by Stebbins to describe the growing phenomena of people in 'systematic pursuit of an amateur, hobbyist, or volunteer activity that is sufficiently substantial and interesting for the participant to find a career there in the acquisition and expression of its special skills and knowledge' (1992: 3). While those involved in serious leisure develop their interest in the same way as one would develop a career, the rewards are not in money, but in personal fulfilment and status through achieving excellence in a field which fascinates them. Developing that expertise may take years of painstaking study and practice and that commitment is important to the ensuing satisfaction.

Belk and Costa (1998) examined the pursuit of serious leisure in their study of Mountain Men reenactment events in the USA. These focus on recreating the lifestyles of Mountain Men – trappers travelling well beyond the frontier in the period 1825–1840. These events involved the establishment of short-term camping communities, where participants dressed in period costume and engaged in traditional activities. As Belk and Costa analysed these:

> participants socially construct and jointly fabricate a consumption enclave, where a fantasy time and place are created and experienced ... The modern mountain man rendezvous as a fantastic consumption enclave is found to involve several key elements: participants' use of objects and actions to generate feelings of community involving a semimythical past, a concern for 'authenticity' in recreating the past, and construction of a liminoid time and place in which carnivalesque adult play and rites of intensification and transformation can freely take place.
>
> (1998: 219)

This transformation takes serious time and effort. Newcomers, known as *pilgrims*, are expected to participate in quite a number of events before being fully accepted into this fantasy social world. Developing Mountain Men costumes and accoutrements is a slow and cumulative process. While gear can be purchased, part of the fantasy is engaging in ceremonial bartering as the Mountain Men did nearly two hundred years ago. Great respect and status is gained by those who are adept at making their own authentically styled costumes. Others are valued for expertise in archaic crafts such as flint-making, tanning hides, horsemanship and bead-work. A third vehicle for excellence is in exercising appropriate *braggadocio* during the carnivalesque evenings, outshining others in prodigious displays of swearing, vernacular language, tale-telling and drinking (Belk and Costa 1998).

Empirical research by Hunt (2004) into costumed reenactors in the UK concluded that their primary motivations could best be understood in terms of serious leisure. Similarly, studies of battle reenactors reveal that they place great value on painstakingly researching and recreating their character's costumes and weaponry (Frost and Laing 2013). This, however, raises an interesting question of authenticity. Steampunks are not duplicating a real historical period, rather it is an imagined world they are immersing themselves in. In this sense, their pursuit can more accurately be compared to *Star Trek* enthusiasts (Kozinets 2001), though these fans are constrained to a certain extent by the parameters of that television show. Another group worth making comparisons with are females at Wild West events. In these, history provides a certain context, but many women feel free to invent a wide range of imaginative characters to play, such as the saloon girl or the prostitute, that allow them to take on roles which diverge from and in some cases invert those displayed within their everyday lives (Frost and Laing forthcoming).

Social worlds

Steampunk adherents could also be argued to move within the same *social world*. Unruh (1979) describes this as a flexible unit of social organisation, which lacks formal boundaries, a defined list of members and centralised structure. This amorphous quality can make them difficult to identify, unlike say a club or an association. Unruh (1979) identifies some of the key *qualities of interaction*, which are pertinent to a discussion on steampunk fashion events. First, social worlds create layers of relevance around themselves, as a way of communicating 'what their world is about' to others. This might be done through *appearance* (Argyle 1988; Unruh 1979), including clothing, hair, makeup, jewellery or body art. For example, Punk in the 1970s was recognisable by mohawk hairstyles, torn clothing and piercings. Sloane Rangers in the 1980s dressed like Princess Diana, when she was still Lady Diana Spencer and wore twinsets and pearls. This does not mean that social worlds necessarily welcome all newcomers, but simply that they provide outsiders with enough information 'for strangers to decide that it is not relevant for their purposes' (Unruh 1979: 123) or vice versa.

Second, some social worlds are more *accessible* than others, and thus likely to attract more potential participants. Unruh (1979) cites examples of social worlds like drug cultures, which are recognisable but not necessarily easy to access, unless one is *in the know*. The social world might only appeal to a small minority, perhaps because of its anti-social behaviours or the response of wider society to their activities or hallmarks. One might argue that manga and anime are more socially acceptable social worlds than punk ever was, and thus potentially likely to attract more people. Other social worlds are more fluid and their boundaries may overlap with other social worlds, making it easier for people to hop from one social world to another. Long distance cyclists might for example move freely to the world of long distance marathons, if there are commonalities between these social worlds, including the type and personality of *regulars* or *insiders*. Regulars are those individuals who have made a particular social world a habitual part of their lives, while insiders are more entrenched within and committed to the social world and generally take a prominent role, helping to organise activities and get-togethers. They 'know the intimate details and workings of a social world' (Unruh 1979: 120), due to their steadfast involvement over many years.

Third, some social worlds are more open to receive newcomers. There might be lower barriers to entry (cost, location) and more acceptance/less suspicion of those interested in joining the social world. For some social worlds, gaining regulars is a matter of survival. This might be the case, for example, for collectors, where the item of interest is not entrenched in popular culture or is somewhat rarefied. It might also apply to music or fashion movements which have had their day. Revivals of movements are always possible, and some social worlds are perennially popular, even when connected to the past.

The steampunk exhibition at Kew Bridge Steam Museum, UK

The *Steampunk Exhibition*, held in London over the summer of 2011, was our introduction to steampunk and its associated fashion events. Apart from the ongoing display of items such as a brass studded Dalek from *Doctor Who*, there were dedicated fashion shows on certain weekends, showcasing the creations of various individuals. Most of the general activities, however, involved or highlighted clothing, and thus the exhibition as a whole could be characterized as a *fashion event*. The weekend we attended, insiders dressed up in steampunk regalia (Figure 12.1) demonstrated activities such as *tea duelling*, and presided over trestle tables and racks with clothing and accessories for sale such as pith helmets, corsets and our favourite – the fez (Figure 12.2).

We found some of the rituals associated with steampunk unexpected and fascinating. Tea duelling comes with its own set of rules, which were explained with gusto to the crowd who gathered, accompanied by a practical demonstration. Clearly it is a witty spoof on Victorian duels with swords or pistols, but taken no less seriously. It involves two individuals, each with a cup of tea in which a digestive biscuit is dunked. The protagonists or dunkers must then eat at least 94 per cent of their biscuit, without it falling back into the cup or elsewhere. The person who achieves this over the longest period of time is the winner. Most of the people who watched these matches were not dressed in steampunk garb, and appeared to be akin to Unruh's (1979) *tourists*, in that they were curious to find out more but were not necessarily planning to commit to this social world. The participants, dressed in steampunk finery, were playing to the crowd and hamming it up, but still careful to emphasise 'the rules' behind the proceedings. They were happy to pose for photographs, which served to highlight their status as being *different* from those outside the steampunk world, and thus bestowed upon them a form of prestige. These photographs, presumably, were later shared with others, helping to make steampunk a better-known concept in the broader community.

Figure 12.1 Couple wearing steampunk fashion at the 2011 *Steampunk* exhibition at the Kew Bridge Steam Museum, London.
Source: J. Laing

Steampunk is thus a social world in which the insiders or regulars are interested in making their activities accessible to others, while still pre-occupied with authenticity, both of dress and of activities. Wearing the right clothes, such as the corset or aviator goggles for steampunk devotees, might reflect a concern for acceptance, with clothing required to meet certain standards or levels of authenticity in order to afford the participant *insider* status. While the artists involved in steampunk are described as 'a tightly knit community [where] artists help other artists by inspiring, motivating, and challenging each other to create' (Grymm 2011: 7), their works are still required to meet certain parameters to allow them to go on display. They must represent 'a reimagined [Victorian] past ... recycled into an unbelievable future' (p. 7).

Figure 12.2 Steampunk clothing and artefacts for sale, 2011 *Steampunk* exhibition at the Kew Bridge Steam Museum, London.

Source: J. Laing

Oamaru Steampunk Festival

Our visit to Oamaru in New Zealand's South Island began with taking photographs of the sign on its outskirts labelling the town the 'Steampunk Capital of NZ' (Figure 12.3). We then moved on to Steampunk Headquarters, an attraction located in a converted nineteenth century industrial building. The man taking our admission fee promised us sights 'that will blow your mind', a phrase he repeated a number of times, including at the end of our visit. While this hyperbole was not borne out by the reality of the various exhibits we saw, we were intrigued by the evangelism inherent in this statement, which marked him as an insider with respect to the steampunk sub-culture. A few steampunk fashions were on sale in the foyer, including a corset, but when we asked about the Steampunk Festival and the associated fashion shows, he directed us down the road to the *Steampunk: Tomorrow As It Used to Be* exhibition at the Custom House Gallery – 'that's what *they* do'. Clearly there were two camps involved in steampunk activities, and they kept a courteous distance.

The Gallery's exhibition was much more clothing-focused, and showcased the fashion show which formed part of the Festival programme. Those who enter the fashion show are required to provide a character name, a story for

Figure 12.3 Car advertising Oamaru as the 'Steampunk Capital of NZ'.
Source: J. Laing

the audience and a concept drawing, which frames what Belk and Costa (1998: 219) label 'carnivalesque adult play'. Like the Mountain Men Belk and Costa studied, steampunk enthusiasts have the 'liberating opportunity to play a wildly different character whose behaviour bears faint resemblance to quotidian life' (p. 234). Fashion becomes a form of self-expression, with clothing used, with accompanying role play, to transport members of the subculture to a different era or another world, or allow them to express their *secret self* (Eicher 1981). While Miller (1997: 224) suggests that 'adult fantastic socialization [unlike children's] often occurs in private (such as at home)', the steampunk insiders and regulars utilise a public setting in the form of a fashion event. Clothing and makeup might provide the mask that the individual needs to keep their play effectively under wraps. The selected characters can be slotted into various categories helpfully supplied by the organisers – children's clothing, adventurer/explorer, inventor/scientist, evening wear and working wear – which are *tropes* or 'scripts and motifs' (Belk and Costa 1998: 220) underpinning the steampunk fantasy.

The 2013 Festival will continue the tradition of a fashion show. The entry form states that:

The purpose of this Fashion Show is to take the fashion of Steampunk beyond ornamentation and accessorising. As well as the drawing designs,

Figure 12.4 Mannequin displaying costume, including prosthetic limb, from Steampunk Festival fashion show, Oamaru, NZ.

Source: W. Frost

the character wearing the garment must be developed. The garments will be based on the Victorian genre: they will have a functional science fiction component. The characters wearing them must have a story behind them and wear their clothes for good reason. This is about developing Victorian Science Fiction and deepening the Steampunk genre.

(SteampunkNZ 2013)

Examples of award-winners from previous Festivals were on display to the Gallery visitors. A potted history of the relevant character was found beside each costume, bringing it to life. All had a name, and an invented history. A mannequin with a feather in her hair, darkened John Lennon sunglasses, a studded corset, frilled skirt and lace-up boots looked like a dance-hall good-time girl, except for the purple hair and artificial arm (Figure 12.4). The latter is

Figure 12.5 Mannequin displaying steampunk nurse costume from Steampunk Festival fashion show, Oamaru, NZ.
Source: W. Frost

a recurrent theme in steampunk, which is associated with apocalyptic narratives that leave the hero or heroine sporting a prosthetic limb (Brass Goggles 2013). Another mannequin wore a studded khaki nurse's uniform, with her ray gun in a holster (Figure 12.5); another quasi-military heroine in a post-apocalyptic world. Thus, the clothing worn might have a symbolic meaning for adherents, perhaps making an ironic statement about an era characterized by optimism in the future, before the invention of the nuclear bomb and growing fears about climate change and environmental destruction reared their head. It might also be conceptualised as a reaction against the sterility of modern technology, as illustrated by the *steampunk computer*, with its wooden keyboard and mouse, brass rimmed monitor and attached typewriter (Figure 12.6). This fashion show and associated exhibition thus had ideological points to make, as well as providing a liminal space for the imagination to run riot.

Figure 12.6 Steampunk computer at the 2013 *Steampunk: Tomorrow As It Used to Be* exhibition, Oamaru, NZ.
Source: W. Frost

Like the UK steampunk event, there were attempts to broaden the base of enthusiasts. School groups had been approached to create drawings and paintings based on steampunk themes like airships. These decorated the staircase as we headed up to the various rooms of exhibits. The entrants in the fashion show also seemed to cover a spectrum of ages and both genders were represented. This is not a sub-culture that appeals only to a minority, perhaps because it is relatively socially acceptable and taps into nostalgia for the Victorian era, as exemplified by the popularity of magazines like *Victoria* and Christmas decorations and theming which mimic scenes from a Dickens novel (Havlena and Holak 1991; Stern 1992).

Conclusion

This chapter explores the role played by fashion in sub-culture events and considers their influence and wider meanings from a societal perspective, particularly as these fashions become more pervasive within popular culture. Steampunk fashions can be argued to be relatively accessible, perhaps because this social world shares a boundary with those groups interested in the Victorian era more generally, as well as science-fiction enthusiasts, given its genesis within this genre of fiction. It is not mainstream fashion, but we can see how the High Street is borrowing from this look. Thus there is a blurring at the edges of this social world, providing entry to those who might be interested in experimenting with Victorian style with a quirky edge. The fashion events we have looked at in this chapter facilitate this process, by introducing the broader public to steampunk and its hallmarks in a fun and non-threatening way. The insiders and regulars who frequent this social world appear to be happy to welcome newcomers, which will help to ensure that steampunk (and its associated events) continues to flourish.

References

Argyle, M. (1988) *Bodily Communication*, 2nd edn, London; New York: Methuen.

Belk, R. and Costa, J. A. (1998) 'The mountain man myth: a contemporary consuming fantasy', *The Journal of Consumer Research*, 25(3): 218–240.

Bourdieu, P. (1984) *Distinction: a social critique of the judgement of taste*, Cambridge, MA: Harvard University Press.

Bourdieu, P. (1991) *Language and Symbolic Power*, London: Polity.

Brass Goggles (2013) *The Steampunk Forum at Brass Goggles*, 2 December 2011, http://brassgoggles.co.uk/forum/index.php?topic=33948.0 (accessed 13 March 2013).

Eicher, J. B. (1981) 'Influences of changing resources on clothing, textiles, and the quality of life: Dressing for reality, fun, and fantasy', *Combined Proceedings, Eastern, Central, and Western Regional Meetings of Association of College Professors of Textiles and Clothing*, 36–41.

Evans, H. and Evans, D. (1977) *Beyond the Gaslight: science in popular fiction 1895–1905*, New York: Vanguard.

Frost, W. and Laing, J. (2012) *Strategic Management of Festivals and Events*, Melbourne: Cengage.

Frost, W. and Laing, J. (2013) *Commemorative Events: memory, identities, conflict*, London and New York: Routledge.

Frost, W. and Laing, J. (forthcoming) 'Gender, rituals and Wild West re-enactments: Helldorado Days, Tombstone, Arizona', in J. Laing and W. Frost (eds) *Rituals and Traditional Events in the Modern World*, London and New York: Routledge.

Grymm, D. with Saint John, B. (2011) *1000 Steampunk Creations*, Beverly, MA: Quarry Books.

Havlena, W. J. and Holak, S. L. (1991) ' "The good old days": observations on nostalgia and its role in consumer behavior', in R. H. Holman and M. R. Soloman (eds) *Advances in Consumer Research*, 18, Provo, UT: Association for Consumer Research.

Hunt, S. (2004) 'Acting the part: living history as a serious leisure pursuit', *Leisure Studies*, 23(4): 387–403.

Kozinets, R. V. (2001) 'Utopian Enterprise: articulating the meanings of *Star Trek*'s culture of consumption', *Journal of Consumer Research*, 28(1): 67–88.

Laing, J. and Frost, W. (2012) *Books and Travel: inspiration, quests and transformation*, Bristol: Channel View.

Miller, K. A. (1997) 'Dress: private and secret self-expression', *Clothing and Textiles Research Journal*, 15(4): 223–234.

Moorcock, M. (1974) *The Land Leviathan*, 1984 omnibus, London: Panther.

Moorcock, M. (1981) *The Steel Tsar*, 1984 omnibus, London: Panther.

Murphy, M. (2013) 'Steampunk! Introducing Britain's latest fashion craze', *The Independent*, 20 January, http://www.independent.co.uk/life-style/fashion/news/steampunk-introducing-britains-latest-fashion-craze-8458861.html (accessed 20 February 2013).

Skarda, E. (2013) 'Will steampunk really be the next big fashion trend?' *Time*, 17 January, http://style.time.com/2013/01/17/will-steampunk-really-be-the-next-big-fashion-trend (accessed 20 February 2013).

SteampunkNZ (2013) *SteampunkNZ*, Steampunk Fashion Show Registration Form, http://www.steampunknz.co.nz/index.php/component/jforms/1/67 (accessed 24 April 2013).

Stebbins, R. A. (1992) *Amateurs, Professionals and Serious Leisure*, Montreal and Kingston: McGill-Queen's University Press.

Stern, B. B. (1992) 'Historical and personal nostalgia in advertising text: the *fin de siècle* effect', *Journal of Advertising*, 21(4): 11–22.

Thornton, S. (1996) *Club Cultures: music, media and subculture capital*, Hanover; London: University Press of New England.

Unruh, D. R. (1979) 'Characteristics and types of participation in social worlds', *Symbolic Interaction*, 2(2): 115–130.

VanderMeer, J. and Chambers, S. J. (2011) *The Steampunk Bible: an illustrated guide to the world of imaginary airships, corsets and goggles, mad scientists, and strange literature*, New York: Abrams.

Wells, H. G. (1895) *The Time Machine*, 2011 reprint, London: Penguin.

13 Très chic

Setting a research agenda for fashion and design events

Jennifer Laing, Kim M. Williams and Warwick Frost

Fashion and design events, wide-ranging phenomena with a long history, have paradoxically not been widely researched from an academic standpoint, despite their ubiquity and global significance from a societal and economic perspective. We have attempted to address this shortcoming in this text. It is the first research book to consider this topic in depth, and as such, contains an eclectic array of contributions covering different theoretical approaches, international contexts and types of events. Future research should adopt a multi-disciplinary perspective, as a focus on fashion events may involve fields of study as varied as economics, sociology, fashion, art and design, marketing, tourism, events, history and cultural studies, as this book highlights.

In this final chapter, we consider some of the gaps in the existing literature and discuss the potential for cross-disciplinary research to fill some of these gaps. In doing so, we set out a research agenda for the future, underpinned by the issues and findings discussed in the other chapters in this book.

The radical edge of fashion events

The unsettling nature of some fashion events sets them apart from the mainstream. Exhibitions featuring fashion by designers such as Valentino and Armani or historical retrospectives like the *Golden Age of Couture* exhibition staged by the Bendigo Art Gallery or *Ballgowns: British Glamour Since 1950* at the Victoria and Albert Museum attract high interest, but so do those exhibitions featuring more contemporary and edgy styles. The recent exhibition *XTRAVAGANZA. Staging Leigh Bowery*, at the Kunsthalle in Vienna, focused on the late Australian performance artist, Leigh Bowery, who was a contemporary of Boy George, Marilyn and Divine, and 'used his body as a canvas' (Bunyan 2013). The clothing he designed was on display and showcased his ability to shock and confront audiences: 'Bowery sabotaged glamorous, ornamental and transparent materials with steel helmets, toilet seats and skulls. He fastened artificial lips in his cheeks with safety pins and wore flesh-colored velvet suits that transformed his body into a vagina' (Bunyan 2013). In an example of how the *shock of the new* influences more mainstream fashion offerings, his work has inspired couture fashion designers such as John Galliano and the late Alexander McQueen (Bunyan 2013), although it should be acknowledged that they were regarded as trend setters in their own right and were always somewhat avant-garde.

Other examples abound throughout history of fashion's ability to shock and surprise. In Chapter 1, we highlighted several examples, including the introduction of the New Look in 1947 and the mini-skirt in the 1960s. The fashion show or catwalk has often been the setting for the debut of revolutionary styles, which eventually trickle their way down to the mainstream. Yves Saint Laurent's 1971 collection, showed off in his couture salon in Paris, caused outrage for its 'huge great Carmen Miranda velvet turbans, foxy boas, lipstick-stained mouths and a marked absence of underwear … [which contributed to] the slutty feel to the collection' (Drake 2006: 114). Despite criticism that 'these are clothes to be worn sitting on the bidet!' his reinterpretation of 1940s Paris fashion and square shoulders in particular led to the birth of the *Saint Laurent Shoulder* in his jackets, which became his trademark and a fashion staple. As Drake (2006: 115–116) notes: 'These were clothes that changed the tide of fashion, taking it retro, camp, anecdotal, letting risqué thoughts of a tarty sexiness race all through its imagination'.

Some would seek to argue that the reign of the catwalk is now over. Argyle (1988: 244) observes that these days, the trickle effect is really horizontal rather than vertical, with new fashions introduced at all levels simultaneously and many designers having diffusion lines (Fernie *et al.* 1997) which offer styles at different price points and to different market segments, for example, Prada and its Miu Miu line. Stores like Zara take the latest fashions and get them to the high street as quickly as possible, with an almost monthly turnover of clothes. Yet even this strategy relies on the cutting-edge style first being seen on the catwalk (Barnes and Lea-Greenwood 2010; Nokatli 2008). More research needs to be carried out on the changing influence of fashion shows, and how this is affected by so-called *fast fashion* (Barnes and Lea-Greenwood 2010) – cheap clothing designed to be worn only when it's *hot* and discarded when it's not.

Another view on fashion trends is that they may diffuse upwards from the high street, 'when the styles of youth, even of rebellious and radical youth, become popular' (Argyle 1988: 244). This grass-roots development of style might occur within a subculture, where fashion is used as a mark of identity and denotes membership to those outside the group. Chapter 12 by Frost and Laing contains a case study of steampunk events in the UK and New Zealand and demonstrates the contribution of fashion to subculture events, as well as the potential for the group to influence fashion trends. This is a potentially rich area of future research, which could be expanded to include other subcultures such as manga, gothic and anime.

Celebrity and fashion events

The connection between celebrity and fashion has always been strong and is an increasingly popular theme for events. Church Gibson (2012) observes that the *art-celebrity-fashion* nexus is an important area to be explored, given the extraordinary and rising influence of celebrity culture and its manifestation as new patterns of consumption. Fashion leaders of the past were mostly royalty (Marie Antoinette, Charles II, the Prince Regent, Empress Elisabeth (Sisi) of Austria) or the aristocracy (The Duchess of Devonshire). Napoleon's consort Josephine made the diaphanous Empire line popular in post-revolutionary France. As Argyle (1988: 244) notes: 'Changes in fashion were started by the upper classes; other people imitate them to gain status and attractiveness themselves; the elite then change their appearance to distinguish themselves from imitators.' In Chapter 2, Goodrum considers the influence of aristocratic equestrienne participants and spectators on sportswear and how racing fashion displayed at hunts and horse races reflected broader social issues, including the changing role of women. It is part of an emerging discourse on the use of fashion to reflect and drive female emancipation.

In the 1950s, post-war, the fashion elite changed to movie stars, models and rock gods. Women wanted to look like Grace Kelly or Audrey Hepburn, and still do. The swinging Sixties saw the youth culture exemplified by short hemlines and bell-bottoms, worn by models like Twiggy, Jean Shrimpton and Veruschka. The Beatles made the short-back-and-sides haircut seem ludicrously outdated and boys were sent home from school for imitating their famous bowl cut and, later, their long locks and beards. In more recent times, there has been a swing back to royal fashion influence, with Princess Diana in the 1980s and 1990s and now Catherine, Duchess of Cambridge, and Denmark's Princess Mary regularly heading the best-dressed lists (Wackerl 2012).

In Chapter 4, Strickland considers Royal trend-setting in the form of national dress worn by the King and his new wife for their wedding in Bhutan, and how this helps to instil national pride and a sense of identity for the local community, as well as attracting tourists to the Kingdom. Future research could look at the wearing of national costume at other events, including the social and cultural impacts that this might have. Chapter 7 looks at Royal style at the wedding of Prince William and Kate Middleton in 2011, notably the outrageous hat worn by Princess Beatrice of York, and how this has led to intellectual property concerns connected to the copying of the hat and its use in merchandise like fridge magnets and party hats. This research by Sugden makes a distinctive contribution to the events literature, which is arguably deficient thus far on considering the legal aspects of event management, design and staging. This is particularly so in a fashion event context, where the opportunities for infringing registered designs, copyright and trademarks, as well as creating the grounds for actions under trade practices legislation, are manifest.

A growing number of exhibitions display clothes and accessories belonging to a famous person, such as *Jacqueline Kennedy: the White House Years*, which might be seen as revealing more about these individuals than a simple retrospective on their lives or achievements. Princess Diana's fashion sense was extolled as much as her philanthropy in the *Diana: A Celebration* exhibition, which followed a high-profile auction of her clothes for charity. The catalogue for the auction is now a collector's item.

A new exhibition opening in Melbourne at the Australian Centre for the Moving Image (ACMI 2013), *Hollywood Costume*, 'explores the central role costume design plays in cinema storytelling' but is accompanied by photographs showing the original star wearing each costume, such as Audrey Hepburn wearing the iconic black dress as Holly Golightly in *Breakfast at Tiffany's* (1961). The costume is worth viewing as much because of *who* wore it as in which film it was worn. The influence of these costumes on fashion design more broadly, yet the failure to acknowledge the source in the form of the *costume designer*, perhaps because of an over-emphasis on the celebrity model, was pointed out by the exhibition's curator, Deborah Nadoolman Landis (Westwood 2013: 4):

> When fashion designers are asked to talk about their inspiration, nine out of 10 will talk about the movies, most will talk about the movie star, and 99.9 per cent will never know, or certainly never mention, or it may not occur to them to mention, the costume designer who created the look in the movie.

Several chapters in this book examine the use of fashion or design associated with celebrities as a theme for an event. Chapter 3 by Best considers a display of classic cars owned by fashion designer Ralph Lauren, while Laing and Frost in Chapter 10 look at a celebrity-themed fashion event, the *Grace Kelly: Style Icon* exhibition, which has been used to brand the destination of Bendigo as a stylish and elegant place to visit. More research however is needed on these types of events, including links with nostalgia, heritage and identity.

As mentioned in Chapter 1 by Williams, Laing and Frost, gender issues might be relevant in this context, with less emphasis arguably placed on fashion associated with famous men. The Academy Awards or Oscars are often portrayed as a glorified fashion show, with approval for one's dress on the red carpet seen almost as important as winning a statuette (Church Gibson 2012). The media focus is largely on the female appearance and conforming to popular ideals of beauty and elegance. Those women who aim for a unique or quirky look are largely panned by commentators and fashion experts. Approval is largely only bestowed on young, beautiful, thin, fashion icons who don't take risks with what they wear at movie premieres or awards evenings. Future studies might consider the different ways that celebrities involved with fashion events are treated, based on gender (and arguably age and body shape), but extend this to consider gender issues with respect to other fashion events such as fashion weeks or shows (see the discussion on ethics later in this chapter).

The economic dimension of fashion events

Some fashion-themed events are more industry focused, such as trade shows, launches and fashion weeks. They are used to present new collections (Entwistle and Rocamora 2006; Quinn 2002; Reinach 2005) or new brands (Skov 2006) to buyers. Fashion weeks such as Paris, London, Milan and New York might play a part in shaping the image of a destination (Skov 2006), and emerging destinations like Shanghai (Reinach 2005) are now trying to link themselves with high fashion. Several chapters in this book explore the concept of a fashion week in different geographic contexts, highlighting different issues. Successful fashion weeks are currently run in Melbourne (Chapter 8) and Berlin (Chapter 11). According to Webster, the Melbourne Fashion Festival is eclectic and inclusive, open to the public to attend as well as the fashion industry, and forms an integral part of Melbourne's events portfolio, with the destination now arguably regarded as one of the world's leading events cities (Richards and Palmer 2010). The work by Swanson and Everett on Berlin suggests that it has leveraged off its cultural heritage associated with cabaret and existing creative industries, to develop a fashion week which is a strong strategic fit for the new capital of Germany. In Chapter 6, Shand, however, argues that fashion weeks are not necessarily a foolproof strategy for industry development, and examines the perceived failure of New Zealand Fashion Week, which has become insular and needs to innovate in line with changing industry and market conditions. He suggests a model for the future based on the way the Melbourne Fashion Festival is staged. Further research could involve a comparative case study of the two fashion weeks, or the original study could be broadened to cover fashion weeks in other geographic locations.

Another emerging area of research with an economic dimension relates to the Internet and its application to events like fashion weeks or fashion shows. Lock (2013: 8) argues that this is a 'paradigm shift' for the entire industry:

> Once, fashion weeks were trade buying events for retailers and magazine editors to review collections. Orders were taken, collections arrived in store three months later, coinciding with magazine coverage. As such, they were industry-only events. Now the industry has to face the fact we just live-streamed every show on the internet to anyone around the world who wanted to take a front-row seat … Production lead times have not kept pace with this new consumer demand.

Social media is another area of rapid change. Australian designers Sass and Bide recently claimed that they were the first designers in the world to upload photos of their fashion show live on Instagram: 'We wanted to allow our followers to have a bit of a front-row seat so they feel like they're at the show' (Sunday Herald Sun 2013: 32). Buyers now have less power, as:

fashion weeks around the world prefer to pack their collection show-rooms with the likes of Tommy Ton, Susie Bubble and Bryanboy who through their social media feeds can reach millions. During New York Fashion Week Tommy Ton's coverage on Style.com received about 14 million page views.

(Lock 2013: 8)

This leads to a 'convergence ... where fashion weeks will get closer to purchasing availability dates and production lead times will become shorter, driven by demand'.

The downside for the industry is that copying of designs is easier than ever, but paradoxically simpler to detect at fashion shows. Lock (2013: 8) observes that his journalist fiancée, while attending 2013 Mercedes-Benz Fashion Week Australia: 'Googled images from previous international collections to show me what had just walked down the catwalk was an exact copy'. The discussion of intellectual property rights with respect to hats worn at weddings in Chapter 7 is instructive here, and future studies could extend this analysis to fashion shows and fashion weeks.

Unlike fashion weeks, with their international focus, some industry fashion events are aimed purely at a domestic market. The launch of a new fashion line or label or opening of a new store might be accompanied by an event that aims to maximise media exposure and create a buzz around a new brand. There has been little research to date on product launches (Frost and Laing 2012, 2013; Theaker 2008). Future research could examine the economic impacts of these fashion events, as well as their role in brand awareness and building market share.

Another economic outcome of fashion events is to prop up or support industries that might otherwise suffer financially in a global market where cheap imports predominate. An example is the millinery industry, which largely survives in Australia due to the wearing of hats at horsing racing events like the Melbourne Spring Racing Carnival. In Chapter 9, Williams examines the way that professional milliners supplement their income through teaching, but largely rely on horse racing to keep their businesses afloat.

Another industry which is largely dependent on fashion events for survival is the *haute couture* industry in France. It 'caters to no more than 200 of the world's richest women' (Weekend Australian 2013: 10) but keeps alive techniques and craftsmanship (Zazzo and Saillard 2013) and safeguards employment. The role of haute couture within the French economy was considered so vital that during the Second World War, great efforts were made to avoid the industry moving to Germany in the wake of the occupation of France. This led to rumours of collaboration and accusations of an emphasis on frippery at a time of great hardship, but at stake were 70,000 businesses and 300,000 individuals (Palmer 2009). The couture industry continued to function throughout the war, and began showing their new

Figure 13.1 Fashion exhibit (giant jewelled shoe) on display in 2012 at the Palace of Versailles, Paris.
Source: J. Laing

collections just months after Paris was liberated (Palmer 2009). In modern times, haute couture is the prestigious and aspirational hook which is used to sell lower-price items such as makeup and perfume (Wark 1991), and influences the creation of fashion garments right across the industry, notably in the highly successful ensembles of global stores like Zara, Mango and Topshop. It is also an integral part of the destination image of Paris – a city which thrives on its reputation for chic, elegance and luxury (DeJean 2005) – and arguably contributes to its appeal to tourists the world over. Figure 13.1 depicts a giant jewelled high heeled shoe, part of a 2012 fashion exhibition in the Palace of Versailles, illustrating the close connection between heritage, fashion and tourism in the French capital. Further research might usefully examine the economic role of haute couture, as well as its social impacts more broadly.

The importance and role of fashion within events

Fashion and design are also integral elements of events in general, yet few studies to date acknowledge their role in the event experience. The clothes attendees wear, and the fashion worn by those participating in an event are all worthy of study as social phenomena. For example, traditional or national costume worn during events such as religious festivals or weddings can influence fashion trends, as Chapter 4 on Bhutan suggests. They might also have other important socio-cultural impacts. Fernandes (2013: 197) refers to the wearing of traditional costume during the Festa de Nossa Senhora in Viana do Castelo in northern Portugal: 'Nearly all merchants, residents and visitors dress in the traditional local embroidery shirt'. He discusses this as an example of how the event facilitates the building of social capital, by engaging and empowering local people and helping to create a community of place. This link between costume, events and social capital warrants further studies in various contexts.

The differences between costume and fashion more generally might be a worthwhile area of research, as well as studies focusing specifically on the making and wearing of costumes at events, by both spectators and performers. Clothing, along with its synonym *costume*, has been defined as 'the generic raw materials of what a person wears' (Kawamura 2005: 3), although the term costume is often used in connection with 'attire or dress belonging to a nation, class or period' (p. 4). *Fashion*, on the other hand, refers to the mode of dress or style which is in current or conventional usage and ever-changing (Kawamura 2005), although this definition should be extended to cover dress or style that *transcends* or *leads* current modes or trends, like cutting-edge creations on a catwalk or subculture styles. Arguably, costume is about reproduction, which may or may not be authentic.

Figure 13.2 depicts participants at a commemorative event at the Tomb of the Unknown Revolutionary Soldier in Alexandria, Virginia. It is one of a series of events for George Washington's Birthday – an anniversary of special significance as Washington surveyed the town. It is notable that both audience and participants are in costume. As the photo shows, boy scouts are deliberately placed at the front to watch the ceremony. The reenactors wear uniforms from the period, including powdered wigs, tricorn (three-cornered) hats, and breeches. All are bound by strict conventions and it is about fitting in and looking the part.

There is a growing literature on recreations of historical clothing, such as the work of Belk and Costa (1998) on the clothing worn by participants in a mountain men rendezvous, and Chhabra *et al.* (2003) on the tartan tradition and the use of the kilt within Highland games. Chapter 5 by Miller-Spillman and Lee looks at the role of dress in Civil War reenactments and considers how this creates *magic moments* for participants. There is scope for extending this research to other forms of reenactments, including those involving armour, battle gear or uniforms, like the recreated Battle of Hastings (Frost and Laing 2013).

Figure 13.2 Participants wearing historic clothing at the George Washington Birthday Parade 2013.

Source: W. Frost

Clothing worn for an event might reflect issues of authenticity, identity, self-expression, or fantasy. This might be associated with the idea of an event as a liminal or *ludic* space, where people may feel free to adopt different personas or instead be their true selves (Ravenscroft and Matteucci 2003; Sharpe 2008). This is particularly pertinent for historic reenactments (see Chapter 5) or clothes that act as markers of membership of a group, fan club or subculture (Kozinets 2001), such as the garb worn at the steampunk events discussed in Chapter 12. Other clothing might be worn out of a desire for conformity or peer pressure, such as the casual but trendy gear worn by young people at outdoor music festivals. Even though these are seemingly laid-back events, there are now *best dressed lists* for celebrities attending the Coachella Festival in California (E! 2013) and coverage by the fashion supplements of newspapers and fashion magazines like *In Style* and *Vogue*. Research would be valuable to explore the reasons why event-goers wear certain clothes or adopt various fashions or styles and how this clothing, or the lack of it, might contribute to the ambience or atmosphere at an event or help to create a more memorable experience.

Ethical considerations with respect to fashion events

There are a variety of ethical matters that could be explored within the context of fashion events. However it is important to define a key term associated with this area. Joergens (2006: 361) defines *ethical fashion* as 'fashionable clothes that incorporate fair trade principles with sweatshop-free labour conditions while not harming the environment or workers by using biodegradable and organic cotton'. The growing acceptance of the need for ethical fashion is a concept which requires future research attention to identify both beneficial and problematic issues.

Fair trade and sweatshop labour are a huge concern with respect to the fashion sector. Much of the production and manufacture of the garment industry is currently sourced off-shore from countries in South-East Asia (Kellock 2010), as mentioned by Williams in Chapter 9. In many of these countries, there are issues with regard to fair prices and fair working conditions for producers and suppliers, and the need for the development of equitable trade agreements (Shaw *et al.* 2006). Utilisation of sweatshop labour has been exposed in recent years as a practice of the exploitation of workers via low wages, excessive hours or engagement of under-age or child workers. This generally occurs in developing counties due to economic circumstances and the lack of labour laws and workers' rights (Weadick 2002). The discerning consumer may wish to avoid products produced in this context but limited labelling available on clothing can make appropriate choices about ethically manufactured products difficult, if not impossible.

In the twenty-first century, there is an increasing trend towards encouraging recycling of any kind. This could also include the rediscovery of *vintage* clothing and the use of sustainable or recycled materials and fibres in fashion. There is a lack of research to date in the area of sustainable or *green* events (Laing and Frost 2010) and issues of sustainability which pertain particularly to fashion events.

Winge (2008) observes that fashion designers, such as Giorgio Armani, Oscar de la Renta and Stella McCartney are creating *ecofashion* for their runway shows and boutiques. McCartney is also known for promoting vegetarian fashion in line with her dietary beliefs, including making shoes without leather or skins. Her Website includes information about sustainability, including questions and answers about her beliefs and her company ethos (Stella McCartney 2013). This ecofashion is aimed at the mass market but also focused on celebrity clients who have the capacity to influence others by their apparel choices. Celebrities or their partners, as in the case of Livia Firth, the wife of actor Colin Firth, are also entering the eco fashion arena. Livia Firth opened a shop in Chiswick stocking predominately high-priced eco products (Jones 2009) and is photographed wearing eco fashions at events like the Academy Awards.

In addition, international fashion shows are starting to incorporate the concept of sustainability and the use of recyclable materials in the construction of garments (East 2007). Delong *et al.* (2005: 39) indicate that consumers may have started purchasing vintage items due to their economic or personal history but this has evolved into recognition and revaluing of the self. It is about a switch from being a person wearing used clothes to a person expressing their individuality through wearing a vintage item. Frost and Laing discuss the subculture of steampunk in Chapter 12, where aficionados adorn Victoriana fashions with an edge. These costumes may be a combination of new and vintage. This contrasts with the ethos of a Zara or Topshop, which is about encouraging on-trend, cheap fashion which is to be discarded when the latest fashion hits their stores, usually within a month of being displayed. The ethics of fast fashion (Barnes and Lea-Greenwood 2010) requires further research, particularly its juxtaposition with a renewed interest in retro or vintage creations.

In a world of growing environmental consciousness, it is essential for all industries to consider what their carbon footprint is and how can this be managed and reduced. International fashion weeks and designer fashion shows attract large audiences from all over the globe. However, is there any consideration taken into account for the air miles consumed by those travelling to these shows, exhibitions and trade events, given that: 'aviation is a growing contributor to greenhouse gas emissions' (Mair 2011: 215)? This air travel also involves international designers and models with an entourage of support personnel. In the future, we might see a switch towards virtual fashion events, and this could be a worthy avenue of research, to explore whether this is being contemplated, or rejected due to the visceral nature of the fashion show experience and the importance of creating a spectacle using live models (Evans 2011).

Other important societal issues can also be linked to fashion events. Unfortunate and uncomfortable ethical issues can emerge from the choice of models who appear on the fashion catwalk and in fashion advertising materials. The use of ultra-thin models and their influence on women's and teenagers' body image, body dysmorphia, eating disorders and self-esteem has been continually under debate. However this dilemma does not only apply to the female model. Grazia (2013) exposes the practice of male models exhibiting characteristics of being *manorexic*, described as being underweight and very gaunt. There are now steps to discourage the employment of an ultra-slim female model in the industry but this seems not to have been transferred to their male counterparts. A study by Shaw (1995) suggests that adolescent girls tend to respond to fashion images by displaying greater body dissatisfaction than adults. A further study by Groesz *et al.* (2002) observes that exposure to ultra-thin media images can lead to increased body image concerns among females. However, another study conducted in this area by Halliwell *et al.* (2005) found the opposite but they had included the use of images of average-size models, which did not have this negative effect on observers. At the same time, there is also the debate of utilising 'real' size women as in the Campaign for Real Beauty launched by Unilever in 2004 for Dove beauty products (Anonymous 2011). Image, self-esteem and body-related anxiety is an area which will continually require further research, especially in connection to appropriate models for advertising images, in addition to models employed at catwalk events.

The utilisation of children in fashion events and the wearing of sexualised clothing and makeup is another serious area of concern for the fashion industry, but also for wider society. In recent years, there has been a growing propensity for designers to use pubescent girls to display their clothes on the catwalk of international fashion shows. Example of this are Rachel Kirby, who started her career in 1996 at 12 years of age, Elizabeth Jagger, who debuted at 14 at London Fashion Week and Ivanka Trump, who appeared at the New York Fashion Week at 16 (Graafland 1998). Advertising images also employ children in what might be considered ill-advised situations. Calvin Klein was slammed in the 1980s for its advertisements featuring the then 15-year-old Brooke Shields, already infamous for her nude role at the age of 12 in the movie *Pretty Baby* (1978). The controversy centred on the sexualised byline, accompanying a shot of a denim-clad Shields: 'You wanna know what comes between me and my Calvins? Nothing.' Arthurs (2011) reveals that Prada, a fashion giant, had one of its advertisements censored because of the use of a 'dangerous' image featuring a 14-year-old girl (Hailee Steinfeld, a child actress who came to fame in the 2010 remake of *True Grit*) alone and crying on a railway track. The danger of the image was the association with possible youth suicide.

The expanding influence of fashion events in encouraging a *cult of consumption* and the desirability of luxury brands is another area to be explored. In recent years there has been rapid growth in the consumption of luxury goods (Fionda and Moore 2009; Lloyd and Luk 2010). Shopping centres and malls have included high-end designer shops in the mix of retail choices and advertising of luxury items has become more prevalent. Luxury products are often purchased simply because they cost more and not due to any superior functionality (Dubois and Duquesne 1993; Mandel *et al.* 2006). There is a powerful connection between luxury and status, which attracts and seduces the consumer into believing that these items display success to others. Fashion events can portray luxury items as though they were the norm rather than the extraordinary. Increasing exposure of the public to these events has arguably increased the desire for purchase and ownership. The relationship between fashion events and consumption of luxury goods is arguably nothing new. However, it might be interesting to explore the ethics of this in a world which is increasingly looking to downsize and re-use its limited resources, in an effort to save the planet, yet paradoxically cannot resist the siren call of the latest styles and the desire to be *in fashion*.

References

ACMI (2013) *Hollywood Costume*, http://www.acmi.net.au/hollywood-costume.aspx (accessed 28 April 2013).
Anonymous (2011) 'On the wings of Dove', *Marketing*, 116(5): 22.
Argyle, M. (1988) *Bodily Communication*, 2nd edn, London; New York: Methuen.

Arthurs, D. (2011) 'Prada advert starring Oscar-nominated child actress Hailee Steinfeld BANNED for use of "dangerous images"', *Mail Online*, 23 November, http://www.dailymail.co.uk/femail/article-2065285/Prada-advert-starring-Oscar-nominated-child-actress-Hailee-Steinfeld-BANNED-use-dangerous-images.html (accessed 29 April 2013).

Barnes, L. and Lea-Greenwood, G. (2010) 'Fast fashion in the retail store environment', *International Journal of Retail & Distribution Management*, 38(10): 760–772.

Belk, R. W. and Costa, J. A. (1998) 'The mountain man myth: A contemporary consuming fantasy', *Journal of Consumer Research*, 25(3): 218–240.

Bunyan, M. (2013) *Art Blart*, 27 January, http://artblart.com/2013/01/27/exhibition-xtravaganza-staging-leigh-bowery-at-kunsthalle-wien-vienna (accessed 23 April 2013).

Chhabra, D., Healy, R. and Sills, E. (2003) 'Staged authenticity and heritage tourism', *Annals of Tourism Research*, 30(3): 702–719.

Church Gibson, P. (2012) *Fashion and Celebrity Culture*, London; New York: Berg.

DeJean, J. (2005) *The Essence of Style: How the French invented high fashion, fine food, chic cafés, style, sophistication and glamour*, New York: Free Press.

Delong, M., Heinemann, B. and Reiley, K. (2005) 'Hooked on vintage', *Fashion Theory*, 9(1): 23–42.

Drake, A. (2006) *The Beautiful Fall: Fashion, genius and glorious excess in 1970s Paris*, New York: Bay Back Books.

Dubois, B. and Duquesne, P. (1993) 'The market for luxury goods: Income versus culture', *European Journal of Marketing*, 27: 35–44.

E! (2013) 'P'trique weighs in on Coachella's best and worst dressed celebs', *E!Online*, http://au.eonline.com/news/412356/p-trique-weighs-in-on-coachella-s-best-and-worst-dressed-celebs-mdash-watch-now?cmpid=rss-000000-rssfeed-365-topstories&utm_source=eonline&utm_medium=rssfeeds&utm_campaign=rss_topstories (accessed 27 April 2013).

East, G. (2007) 'Davie fashion show features designs made of recycled materials', McClatchy – Tribune Business News, 28 July, 1.

Entwistle, J. and Rocamora, A. (2006) 'The field of fashion materialized: A study of London Fashion Week', *Sociology*, 40(4): 735–751.

Evans, C. (2011) 'The walkies: Early French fashion shows as a cinema of attractions', in A. Munich (ed.), *Fashion in Film*, Bloomington: Indiana University Press.

Fernandes, C. (2013) 'The role of cultural events in building social capital and the implications for tourism development', in G. Richards, M. de Brito and L. Wilks (eds), *Exploring the Social Impacts of Events*, London; New York: Routledge.

Fernie, J., Moore, C., Lawrie, A. and Hallsworth, A. (1997) 'The internationalization of the high fashion brand: The case of central London', *Journal of Product & Brand Management*, 6(3): 151–162.

Fionda, A. M. and Moore, C. M. (2009) 'The anatomy of the luxury fashion brand', *The Journal of Brand Management*, 16(5–6): 347–363.

Frost, W. and Laing, J. (2012) *Strategic Management of Festivals and Events*, South Melbourne: Cengage.

Frost, W. and Laing, J. (2013) *Commemorative Events: Memory, identities, conflict*, London and New York: Routledge.

Graafland, A. (1998) 'Child of the catwalk: So chic ... but should she model at just 13', *The Mirror*, 5 October, 3.

Grazia (2013) '"Manorexic" model shock Paris', 26 February.

Groesz, L. M., Levine, M. P. and Murnen, S. K. (2002) 'The effect of experimental presentation of thin media images on body dissatisfaction: A meta-analytic review', *International Journal of Eating Disorders*, 31: 1–16.

Halliwell, E., Dittmar, H. and Howe, J. (2005) 'The impact of advertisements featuring ultra-thin or average-size models on women with a history of eating disorders', *Journal of Community & Applied Social Psychology*, 15: 406–413.

Joergens, C. (2006) 'Ethical fashion: Myth or future trend?', *Journal of Fashion Marketing and Management*, 10(3): 360–371.

Jones, L. (2009) 'Colin Firth's wife is flogging eco fashion – but is it just middle-class guilt trip?' *Mail Online*, 18 May. http://www.dailymail.co.uk/femail/article-1183806/LIZ-JONES-Colin-Firths-wife-flogging-eco-fashion – just-middle-class-guilt-trip.html (accessed 29 April 2013)

Kawamura, Y. (2005) *Fashion-ology: An introduction to fashion studies*, Oxford; New York: Berg.

Kellock, J. (2010) 'The business of fashion', in B. English and L. Pomazan (eds), *Australian Fashion Unstitched: The last 60 years*, Melbourne: Cambridge University Press.

Kozinets, R. V. (2001) 'Utopian enterprise: Articulating the meanings of Star Trek's culture of consumption', *Journal of Consumer Research*, 28: 67–88.

Laing, J. and Frost, W. (2010) ' "How green was my festival": Exploring challenges and opportunities associated with staging green events', *International Journal of Hospitality Management*, 29(2): 261–267.

Lock, S. (2013) 'Copycatwalk has to stop', *Weekend Australian*, Weekend A Plus, Style, 20–21 April, 8.

Lloyd, A. E. and Luk, S. T. K. (2010) 'The Devil wears Prada or Zara: a revelation into customer perceived value of luxury and mass fashion brands', *Journal of Global Fashion Marketing*, 1(3): 129–141.

Mair, J. (2011) 'Exploring air travellers' voluntary carbon-offsetting behaviour', *Journal of Sustainable Tourism*, 19(2): 215–230.

Mandel, N., Petrova, P. K. and Cialdini, R. B. (2006) 'Images of success and the preference for luxury brands', *Journal of Consumer Psychology*, 16(1): 57–69.

Nokatli, N. (2008) 'Global sourcing: Insights from the global clothing industry – the case of Zara, a fast fashion retailer', *Journal of Economic Geography*, 8(1): 21–38.

Palmer, A. (2009) *Dior*, London: V & A Publishing.

Quinn, B. (2002) 'Exhibition review: "Radical" fashion? A critique of the radical fashion exhibition, Victoria and Albert Museum, London', *Fashion Theory*, 6(4): 441–446.

Ravenscroft, N. and Matteucci, X. (2003) 'The festival as carnivalesque: Social governance and control at Pamplona's San Fermin Fiesta', *Tourism, Culture and Communication*, 4: 1–15.

Reinach, S. S. (2005) 'China and Italy: Fast fashion versus prêt à porter, towards a new culture of fashion', *Fashion Theory*, 9(1): 43–56.

Richards, G. and Palmer, R. (2010) *Eventful Cities: Cultural management and urban revitalization*, London; New York: Routledge.

Sharpe, E. K. (2008) 'Festivals and social change: Intersections of pleasure and politics at a community music festival', *Leisure Sciences*, 30: 217–234.

Shaw, D., Hogg, G., Wilson, E., Shiu, E. and Hassan, L. (2006) 'Fashion victim: Impact of fair trade concerns on clothing choice', *Journal of Strategic Marketing*, 14(4): 427–440.

Shaw, J. (1995) 'Effects of fashion magazines on body dissatisfaction and eating psychopathology in adolescent and adult females', *European Eating Disorder Review*, 3(1): 15–23.

Skov, L. (2006) 'The role of trade fairs in the global fashion business', *Current Sociology*, 54(5): 764–783.

Sunday Herald Sun (2013) 'Sass and Bide rap up a first', *Sunday Herald Sun*, News, 17 February: 32.

Stella McCartney (2013) 'Sustainability', http://www.stellamccartney.com/experience/en/stellas-world/sustainability (accessed 30 April 2013).

Theaker, A. (2008) *The Public Relations Handbook* (3rd edn), Abingdon, OX; New York: Routledge.

Wackerl, L. (2012) *Royal Style: A history of aristocratic fashion icons*, New York; London: Prestel.

Wark, M. (1991) 'Fashioning the future: Fashion, clothing, and the manufacturing of post-Fordist culture', *Cultural Studies*, 5(1): 61–76.

Weadick, L. (2002) 'Sweating it out', *Ethical Consumer Magazine*, 76 (April/May), 12–15.

Weekend Australian (2013) 'Dresses fit for the world's wealthy', *The Weekend Australian*, 26–27 January, 10.

Westwood, M. (2013) 'Frock 'n' role', *The Weekend Australian*, Review, 13–14 April: 04.

Winge, T. M. (2008) ' "Green is the new black": celebrity chic and the "green" commodity fetish', *Fashion Theory*, 12(4): 511–524.

Zazzo, A. and Saillard, O. (2013) *Paris Haute Couture*, Paris: Flammarion.

Index